OUT OF MONTANA

A MEMOIR

GORDON L. NOEL

Second Edition Published in the United States
by University of Montana Press Copyright © 2018 by Gordon Noel
First Edition Published in the United States
by Quimby House Press Copyright © 2017 by Gordon Noel

All rights reserved, including the right to reproduce this book
or portions thereof in any form.

For information, please contact the University of Montana Press,
147 Corbin Hall, Missoula, MT 59812

Interior Design by The Book Makers
Cover Design by The Book Makers

Library of Congress Cataloging-in-Publication Data

Names: Noel, Gordon, Author
Title: Out of Montana—a Memoir/Gordon Noel
Description: Second Edition. Portland Oregon, 2018
Identifiers: ISBN: 978-0-9992169-2-7 Print Edition (paperback)

Out of Montana—a Memoir is a work of non-fiction. However, the names of several characters have been changed and the circumstances and their descriptions modified to protect their anonymity. Any resemblance to persons living or dead that has resulted is purely unintentional.

*For the four strong women in my life
—my daughters Katharine, Margaret Lea and
Jennifer, and my wife Margaret—
And in memory of my mother Leah Noel and my
grandparents Sam and Lotte Orvis*

PART ONE

CHAPTER ONE

BEGINNING

THE FIRST SETTLERS who crossed over the Rocky Mountains searching for land to farm and game to hunt founded Missoula at the confluence of the three great rivers that flow out of the vast forested wildernesses of a half-dozen mountain ranges. The river that flows through the heart of Missoula is the Clark Fork, which originates in the mountains around Butte that separate western Montana's forests from the eastern slopes of the Rockies that give rise to the Missouri River that flows east and south to the Mississippi. From Missoula the Clark Fork runs west and then north to the Idaho border, and from there into the Columbia River, which runs north into Canada before looping south on its way to the Pacific Ocean.

Just upstream of Missoula, the Blackfoot River empties the springs and snowfields of the Continental divide north of Butte and surges through narrow, twisting canyons, entering the Clark Fork at the upper end of Hell Gate Canyon.

PART ONE

The Bitterroot River flows along the eastern slopes of the Bitterroot Mountains from Lost Trail and Lolo passes and joins the Clark Fork just a few miles to the west of the earliest village, which was named Hell Gate Town.

During three ice ages, a vast inland sea stretched from the mountains east of Missoula far to the north and west where Montana abuts Idaho and Canada. What is now the valley was the bed of the ancient Lake Missoula. When the ice dams near the Canadian border were breached, the massive floods left behind deep rich soil and millions of fossils of small marine plants and creatures. Missoula's very flat valley is the old lake bottom, and Missoula's flat neighborhood roads and streets made walking and biking easy for the kids with whom I grew up.

At the edges of Missoula the flat land yields to the hills and mountains that still show the shores of Lake Missoula. As we grew older and stronger and more adventurous, we began biking the endless canyon roads that ascended the narrow valleys where hundreds of small streams ran down into the great rivers. Later we would drive there to hike, to gather Christmas trees, to learn the crafts of living in the woods with our Boy Scout troops. We were never out of sight of the mountains and navigation was easy.

The industries that drew families to Missoula for work and to raise families depended on the seemingly unlimited lumber milled from trees hauled out of the mountains, much of it from still virgin forests. The headquarters for the US Forest Service's Northwestern region was in Missoula, the famous smoke jumpers and the hotshot fire fighting crews were born there, and fishermen came from around the world to test themselves against the Montana trout. Montana's liberal arts university was founded in Missoula, its schools of music and forestry were world-famous.

I grew up in the mountains and valleys of western Montana, and except for a few brief trips to the West Coast when I was in grade school, I knew nothing about life anyplace else until I was 17. When I was 18 I couldn't wait to leave. *Out of Montana* is the story of the years stretching from just before the entry of the United States into World War II to my headlong departure in 1959.

For years I tried to put Montana as far behind me as I could. Although I never did fully return, I also never completely left. Most of the difficulties and the wonders of my childhood are as potent to me now as they were at the time.

CHAPTER

TWO

MCLEOD AVENUE

OUR HOUSE ON the 300 block of McLeod Avenue was small even by the standards of the 1930's when it was built. It was the kind of house that a young couple with a family could rent on the salary of a bank clerk. I haven't seen the inside of the McLeod house since 1947, but from the street it still looks as it did when I lived there. It says something about Missoula that there are still families that want—or can only afford—a simple, one-floor, two-bedroom, one-bath house, and that the block and the street on which it stands still has every house I remember from my earliest childhood; in 70 years not one of them has been enlarged or even painted a different color. Down the street the multi-car garage of the former mansion next to Rollie Trenouth's house has been turned into bungalows, but that happened decades ago, when Rollie and I were in high school and no longer regularly broke the garages' windows with my wild pitches on our two-man ball field squeezed in between Dr. Trenouth's rose garden in left field and the mansion's tall stand of spiny spruces in right field.

McLeod was a good street in the University section of Missoula, walking distance both to the University of Montana campus and the business district across the Clark Fork River. Like most of Missoula just after the war, the neighborhood housed families with a broad range of ages, professions, and incomes.

If you stood in the quiet street looking at our house, the two-tone green-shingled house that Professor Clark and his wife lived in was next door on the left; Professor Clark had taught Mom journalism at the university and he and his wife were benign assistant grandparents for my big brother Sammie and me.

Our neighbors on the right were Bill and Jean Campbell who had moved in when the old Goforths left to retire someplace where the winters were less harsh. The Campbells started a family in that house; it was not much bigger than ours and a few years later they outgrew it and moved away. Bill was a vet just back from the war who owned the laundromat two blocks from where the Milwaukee depot sat next to the river. Jean, who was half Bill's size, gave dance classes in a big room next to the washing machines where I could smell the wet clothes as I walked in and the flowery smell of the driers when I walked back to the dance floor. Years later Rollie and I learned how to foxtrot and waltz there with Mary Kraabel and Maryanne Zimmerman, to worn-out recordings by Glen Miller, Jimmy and Tommy Dorsey, and Guy Lombardo.

Next to Bill and Jean Campbell, Mrs. Whitney lived alone. She was the oldest woman I knew for many years, and the first person I knew who smelled old, perhaps because of the talcum powder she dusted herself with. Her skin was pale and thin and as insubstantial as the dry, brittle outer peels of the white onions Mom stored under the sink. Her white hair was fine and wispy, like spider web silk. She always dressed in black, with a collar that she fastened with a white broach with the stark silhouette of an old woman with a hooked nose. Mrs. Whitney's only family was a faraway son whose toys she had saved. If she had baked cookies she would come looking for me and then watch me play with his toys while she talked about him when he was a little boy. I liked Mrs. Whitney.

In the biggest house, on the corner, made of red brick where all of the rest of the houses on our side of the street were built of less-expensive wood, lived the McCreas, who we thought of as rich and snooty because they paid someone to shovel their sidewalks and mow their lawn; we rarely saw them outside.

If you turned your back to our house, the home across the street was not even a house. During my nearly six years on McLeod, on the whole street from Higgins to the University, only that lot was vacant. Rollie and Sammie and Rollie's sister Cecily and I captured grasshoppers and looked for treasures in the trash discarded in the vacant lot's weeds during the summer; in the winter we built snow forts there. We once discovered open buckets of thick, barely liquid tar dumped in the weeds and we all showed up at home, as happy as golden retrievers that had just rolled in mud, with our hair and skin and clothes smeared with the black, nearly unremovable stuff. Our moms spent hours scrubbing it off of us with turpentine, heaping imprecations variously on whoever had left the buckets, and on us for tarring ourselves and then adding a feathery coat of dead leaves, scraps of paper, dried seed pods, and bugs as we happily romped in the weed patch. We tried to chew the tar because we had been told that it would whiten our teeth. That information turned out to be incorrect.

Within months of the end of the war, a basement was excavated in the vacant lot and the concrete foundations of a house were poured, but no walls were put up. A sub-floor was put down on the foundation and covered with tarpaper to make it a waterproof temporary roof so that the basement could be lived in. A little slope-roofed hut

PART ONE

the size of an outhouse was put up over the basement stairwell as the entry porch. That and about two feet of foundation wall pierced with a few windows were all that you could see from my front yard. Soon a family moved into the basement and lived there for years until they had enough money to build the rest of the house. There were basements being lived in all over Missoula for years after the war, mostly owned by vets for whom the "GI Bill" provided cheap mortgages with low down payments while they attended the University or started jobs. A few years after I moved away the house had been completed, but it never looked right on McLeod—it was too modern, a flat, fifties ranch-style house with light-yellow-colored brick walls on a street where the other houses were 1920's prairie-style bungalows or Dutch colonials with clapboard walls.

On the other side of the street, on the far left, was my favorite house with my favorite people, Mr. and Mrs. Higgins and their beautiful daughter Colleen and their equally beautiful Irish setter Val. Colleen was a year older than Sammie, five years older than I. Colleen seemed to live in a world apart from the rest of us, one of those people comfortably at home in Missoula growing up but destined from the beginning to move away. Colleen and her mother rode in horse shows, both western saddle horses and English show horses. Years later she went away to the East to Wellesley College and later she married one of the Nicholson boys and lived in Washington D.C. and overseas where the State Department posted them.

When I was very young, what had happened before I became a direct observer of the lives of our neighbors was a fabric of loosely woven and often unrelated strands that never have become coherent. One of my earliest memories is hearing several times from an adult or Sammie that there had been some kind of tragedy in the Higgins family that I never understood and that was spoken of in brevity and a tone that signaled that I was to ask no questions. There had been another child after Colleen, a boy I think, who had died.

One of the strands in my memory that I believed for decades was that he died in an accident, that he ran out into the street and was hit by a car. I often thought of the boy; I imagined an awful scene outside their house where there would have been the squeal of brakes and the sound of house doors slamming and neighbors running, and frightened voices. He was my introduction to the idea of dying, of the transience of life. I imagined being him, and him being me. But I later heard that none of that ever happened, that the story of an accident was wrong, that the boy died shortly after birth.

Mrs. Higgins and I were pals. I adopted her and I hung around in her house a lot, especially after Mom had to go to work. I sometimes played in Colleen's sand box and I thought of it as mine, and of Val as my dog. Sammie said that Mrs. Higgins and I became pals because she lost her own boy. I don't know, but I still think about that house, remember its rooms, remember the sandbox, and went into adulthood wanting my children to have a sandbox like the Higgins' and a dog like Val.

Mr. Higgins—George Higgins—was a lawyer, pleasant-faced and nearly always silent around me. For years I assumed that his father must have been a lawyer too, or a successful merchant, because his family name and the name of the main street in Missoula—Higgins Street—were the same, and there was a Higgins Bridge and a Higgins block downtown and a Higgins building. But decades later I discovered the Higgins that founded Missoula was from a different family.

I was more or less in love with Colleen even after she went east to go to college in Boston. When I was fourteen and between grade school and high school I had a summer job busing tables at the University. It was my first real job: I got a paycheck and I needed a social security number. Colleen was back from Wellesley, taking summer school courses. She often came into the student center cafeteria and sat by herself to have coffee and read. I would do anything possible while she was there to catch her attention so that she would look up and

PART ONE

smile at me, the scrawny former neighbor kid in ill-fitting, white bus-boy pants and coat splotched with catsup and coffee: I swept the floor near her table, filled sugar-shakers, rewashed clean tables. Five years later when I finished high school I vaguely considered Colleen to have been the first beacon that guided me out of Montana.

So there we were, all together in one block in 1946: a professor at the university; a bank cashier—my father—with a wife and two small children; a veteran who ran a laundromat and his wife who taught dancing; a widow who invited me in to play with her grown son's toys; and the Higgins, a family that was about as refined as any I ever knew growing up.

My view of the neighborhood was limited, but it did extend one block to the west and across McLeod to 235, where my best friend Rollie Trenouth, Dr. Trenouth and his wife, and his sister Cecily lived. Rollie's name was really Roland, but I didn't call him that until we went away to college and he became Roland and I became Gordon. Mrs. Trenouth's first name was Ruth, but in those days I usually knew only the fathers' whole names, because their whole names were on the mail and in the telephone directories and their wives' names were not: Dr. and Mrs. Stanley Stewart Trenouth; Mr. and Mrs. Pat Wilcox; Mr. and Mrs. Stuart Brown. By the time I was old enough to read the mail that came to our house it was just Mrs. Leah Noel; I can't remember seeing my Mom and Dad's name connected in the usual way, Mr. and Mrs. Robert E. Noel. Mail with that address went to a different house and was meant for a new Mrs. Noel. To other houses Christmas cards were addressed "Dr. and Mrs. Clem Svore and Family," but ours came to Leah Noel and Gordie.

I was a teenager before I learned to say hello to Rollie's father correctly. I always called him "Mr. Trenouth" even though I knew he was a doctor. But all of my other friends' fathers were "Mr. Something" and I had to be paying attention more than I usually did to remember to say "hello, Dr. Trenouth." I rarely saw Dr. Trenouth when Rollie and I were not either running through his house or talking, usually both, and Dr. Trenouth never seemed to mind that I did not get his name quite right. He was a slender man of ordinary height with a small mustache; at some point he became partially bald and that is how I remember him, always in a suit, usually with a fedora, usually serious, sometimes quietly bemused.

Years later when Rollie and I were feeling the first stirrings of puberty we would hide ourselves away with Dr. Trenouth's well-thumbed dermatology textbook in a basement room that Rollie used for his hobbies and that for a few years housed a large collection of breeding parakeets. Tucked on an old couch, surrounded by chirping birds and the sprawling parts and wires of Rollie's latest short-wave radio kit, one eye on the door and our ears cocked for footsteps on the stairs, we gagged and shuddered as we sped through the gross photos of decaying skin looking for pictures of what appeared to be normal breasts (although, if they were in a dermatology text, they probably weren't normal); we would point out the best of them to each other "here, you gotta see these!" We never looked for pictures of those other female parts, the existence and precise nature of which were still too veiled in taboo for us to acknowledge. Photos of men were of no interest. Such were the limitations of our experience and curiosity.

The geographic and emotional center of my childhood, the launch pad for all that followed when I left Montana, was Paxson Grade School, a few blocks from our house on McLeod. The children from the entire southeast section of Missoula, wrapped around the sprawling University of Montana, went to Paxson. In 1947 Sammie and Colleen and Cecily were already in the third and fourth grades at Paxson. Most of the University faculty lived in the Paxson area and so did many of the doctors and bankers and successful businessmen. Decades later, at high school reunions, I heard gentle complaints that our high school's academic and social lives were dominated by kids who started school in the Paxson district. If it was true, I hadn't noticed that growing up.

When the neighbors looked at our house they saw a creamy-yellow clapboard Cape-Cod with a red shingle roof. Now the shingles are asphalt, but when we lived there they were dried-out cedar stained red. The shingles baked hot enough in the summer that if we walked on them without shoes the soles of our feet would be burned red; in winter the shingles froze brittle in temperatures as cold as twenty or thirty below and they shattered like thin sheets of ice if stepped on.

The house was two rooms across from front to back. Like almost all of the houses on the street there was a small front porch—not the sitting-down-and-neighbor-watching kind of front porch, but more of an outdoor mudroom useful for storing boots in the winter and tricycles and baseball bats and an afternoon's collection of rocks and worms and birds' nests with bits of abandoned egg shell in the summer and horse chestnuts in the fall. From the porch on the south side, the front door entered directly into the living room, which ran along the right on the east side of the house. The back of the living room was the dining room, separated from the living room only by columns along the walls at both sides. At the back of this room a door entered into a narrow kitchen that ran almost the entire width of the house east to west, with a door leading to the basement on the west side and a back door in the north wall.

From the living room—just in front of the column that created the illusion that the dining room was separated from the living room—a doorway led into a hall running a short distance south to Mom and Dad's room and a short distance north to the room I shared with Sammie. The bathroom was straight across from the door to the living room, between the two bedrooms, just big enough to hold a sink, toilet, and tub; showers were a luxury. Mom and Dad's room had windows on two sides, but our room had windows just on the west, looking toward the sunset, which in the summer flooded the room with light long after our bedtime.

The house had wood floors: wall-to-wall carpeting also was a luxury in 1947 and wood was cheap in Montana. Dad must have taken the dining room table when he moved out because Mom and I did not have one—or a space large enough to hold even a small dining table—for another six years.

I remember parties around this dining room table when the men they knew drifted back from the war and Mom made her specialties—barbecued spareribs or cabbage balls or Swiss steak with scalloped potatoes. When I awoke from my nap I was brought in from my crib in their bedroom into the dining room that was filled with cigarette smoke and the excited, laughing voices of people who had been drinking, punctuated with the clinking of ice in highball glasses. These were Mom's childhood friends from Glasgow and Mom and Dad's college friends, people who 18 years later would send me modest, practical wedding presents—sheets in rainbow stripes and bathroom towels in brown and black that failed every test of attractiveness; food warming trays and ice buckets and copper ash trays. I would uncomfortably try to explain to my wife's family who these people were, most practically strangers to me, and distanced further by my embarrassment at how inelegant their gifts looked on the small table for the groom's gifts amidst three large tables for gifts from the bride's relatives and friends, laden with sterling silver and porcelain and crystal.

The basement of our house was mostly Dad's domain, too dirty and too dangerous for children. The main thing I remember about the basement was an enormous coal furnace with an octopus plenum

PART ONE

of cold and hot air ducts. During blizzards and cold snaps the firebox filled up with clinkers and the fire reliably died, a source of enormous exasperation for my father. I knew even at five that every father behaved like Dad when the coal furnace couldn't put out enough heat to create the updraft needed to keep the fire burning. At 2 AM—when the temperature outside was twenty below and the temperature inside was forty and falling rapidly—sleepy, scowling, angry, cranky, they had to pad in slippers and pajamas to the basement to spend an hour or two coaxing a coal fire back to life with newspaper and kindling, the open door of the burn box intermittently belching clouds of black smoke in their faces.

The "dangers" of the dimly lit, musty basement are less specific in my memory: Dad's tools for sure, knives, I suppose guns—because he always owned guns—and sharp things like nails and saws, and jars and bottles full of poisonous liquids and powders. And there were steep stairs that Mom was afraid I would fall down—I was told that I had tumbled down them a few times, although I don't remember. In the best of times my Mom or brother would accompany me down the stairs so I could play with a hand-turned grinding wheel, or endlessly crank a wood vise open and closed. I was fascinated by anything mechanical.

The event that most shaped the direction my life has taken and separated me from all of the other kids I grew up with happened in the McLeod house, but for years when I told someone about where I grew up, I told them about Missoula but not about the McLeod house where we had once been a family. And I didn't talk about my family. After I was five, by the standards of Montana in the forties and fifties, I didn't have a family.

I once heard Sammie say that Dad never got along well with Mom's mother and father and that they were never impressed with him. Part of Dad's discomfort may have been that they paid for a part-time maid to help Mom with the laundry and the cleaning and the cooking. A maid was well beyond Dad's reach on his small bank salary and Sammie guessed that the fact that Dad's immigrant father-in-law paid for a standard of living for his daughter that Dad could not provide may have galled him. It may also have been beyond Dad's reach to rent a house on McLeod, even our little house.

Probably there were other problems bigger than those. As a five-year-old boy I didn't know anything about why our family came apart; decades passed before I began to figure it out.

CHAPTER

THREE

DAD

BEING ONLY FIVE when Dad left, it is hard to separate what I actually remember from what I was later told about him. He is one of those people in my life about whom other people's experiences count for more than my own. I learned very little from Mom—for the most part she never mentioned him. When I had been away from Montana for years I asked my half-sisters about what they had experienced growing up in his house: in their telling, the fragmented, unhappy stories I had heard about him from my brother Sammie became even darker.

For years after I left Missoula my story about growing up never mentioned Dad. When asked where my father was, I would say that my Mom and Dad were divorced when I was five; that Dad lived in the same town, just a few blocks away on Central Avenue; and that my brother lived with him and I lived with my Mom. Usually I would say that he was the Vice-president of the First National Bank. More curious people wanted to know if I ever saw him, and I would say that I only saw him a few times a year. And with that the conversation moved on to my well-worn stories of childhood adventures, in most of which I almost died, but usually didn't.

Dad had a hot, fast temper and exerted strong discipline. When we still lived together he was often angry about something I had done, and even more often furious and harsh with Sammie, who was constantly in trouble with him. Once we had collected dozens of horse chestnuts from a huge tree near the University and when he came home I had scattered them around the living room floor and was happily organizing them into a little village. I whined when he told me to throw them away. He became red-faced mad and made me stand in the corner with my finger on the wall, his next-to-most severe punishment, spanking being the most severe. I had to stand facing the wall with my right arm extended as high above my head as possible with my index finger on a spot that Dad marked on the wall below a higher one for Sammie, and that finger could not move down the wall no matter how long I was standing. I was told to stand for an hour, but I could never make it that long. I remember this mild but faintly medieval torture well, as I was very wiggly and standing doing nothing for any length of time would have been enough punishment without having to keep my arm raised.

Dad expected children to do chores and I mostly failed at my tasks; waves of his exasperation flowed over me every day. My worst failure I still remember as clearly as if it just had happened. Most weeks I was dragged to Sunday school at the Congregational Church just a block away on University Avenue. When I was four I was supposed to be in the children's service on Christmas Eve, but I couldn't learn my part—I didn't yet read, so the dozen or so words had to be memorized. Dad rehearsed me with growing impatience right up to the time we were supposed to leave. Finally he angrily grabbed my hand and towed me to the church. We sat in the stuffy sanctuary until the children were to recite. When we were asked to stand, Dad read my part, his voice thick among the tiny, piping voices of the little children. I was confused, standing jammed between the adults next to us, ashamed but not sure what I had done wrong.

Dad told me a few stories about the Noel family. I am sure some were true. The rest seem to have been partially or completely fabricated.

Dad claimed that the Noel family came to America from Britain, near Nottingham, and that we were descended from the famous English romantic poet, George Noel Gordon, Lord Byron, for whom Dad had named me. Some years later when I was studying English literature and came across Byron in my romantic poets course, I looked up Byron's history. We could not have been descended from Byron himself. Titled but poor, Lord Byron needed money to keep up his family estate in Nottingham. In 1815 he agreed to marry the wealthy daughter of Judith Noel and take her family name so that she could claim nobility and become Lady Milbanke. In exchange Byron was named heir to half of his mother-in-law's estate upon her death, against which he could borrow money to support his profligate life. Byron abandoned his wife after the birth of their only child, a girl. During their brief marriage he had affairs with a number of married and single noble women, actresses, and his own sister, by whom he had another daughter. Lord Byron is reputed to have had three hundred illegitimate children in Europe. Being descended from Lord Byron, had it been true, would hardly have been something that a Noel could be proud of.

In another story Dad said that the Noels came to the United States at the time of the earliest Jamestown settlement at the beginning of the colonization of North American by the English in 1607. I later discovered that the original settlers at Jamestown either died or returned to England, but it is possible that at some point the first

PART ONE

American Noels lived in coastal Virginia in the colonial era. This also would have been well before Lord Byron's marriage to the Noel family. A family tree researched by my Uncle Clint's wife Freddie late in her life showed Noels living in Virginia and the Carolinas in the early 1800's with later generations gradually moving west to Kentucky, and finally Missouri.

Dad had a lot of Noel relatives around Clarence, St. Joseph, and Hannibal, Missouri. His father, Elbert Noel, was an accountant and left Missouri when Dad was a child to take a position with the Montana state government in the capitol, Helena. I knew Dad's mother, who we called "Nana," just a little, but when I attended her funeral in Helena—I was about nine—the stiff, heavily powdered face I stared down at in the open casket was a stranger to me. I had no feelings for her other than the horror of being forced in spite of my frantic protestations to look at a corpse.

Dad grew up in Helena and he told everyone that Gary Cooper attended the same high school. He said that in a way that implied that he and Cooper were classmates, but Cooper was there fifteen years earlier and the accounts I read later suggested that Cooper probably spent little time in Helena. After high school Dad enrolled in the University of Montana and moved to Missoula, where he spent the rest of his life. He had two older brothers, Lloyd and Clinton. Lloyd also lived in Missoula. Clinton, a geologist, lived in Colorado; I only saw him once or twice that I remember, but Uncle Lloyd was the man next to my grandfather whom I saw most growing up.

Dad liked to hunt and fish. He and Mom and Sammie and I sometimes went off with friends and their children for a day of fishing and picnicking on one of the dozen or so beautiful, fast-flowing trout streams close to Missoula. Their two or three cars would park near a fire pit along the riverbank. The men assembled their rods, stuffed grass in their creels, and headed upstream to fish the big holes and the riffles below while the moms set up a picnic. The children—I only remember the boys—would race to the water to wade, find salamanders and tiny crawfish skeletons and rock worm cases in the shallow water at the edge. Always we would build a dam from stones to make a pond, and always we would fall in, staggering out yowling in shock in the early weeks of summer when the water was still chilly and fast, basking in the low, warm water in August. The mothers would strip us and spread our clothes on big rocks to bake dry in the sun, and we would go right back to the stream, naked now, to fall in again. We made chains of snake grass and tried to catch the orange and black butterflies where they hovered over hot gravel. In the late afternoon, we ate hot dogs doused with relish and ketchup and drank orange soda and Cokes. Played out to exhaustion, we fell asleep in the back seat in a minute and never remembered getting home or being put to bed. In the morning we woke up sandy and groggy, asking when we could go fishing again.

Once we ate a duck that Dad had shot and dipped in molten paraffin to strip its feathers and that Mom had roasted. Mom warned Sammie and me to be careful not to break a tooth on any birdshot that she might have missed. She told us about friends who had cracked teeth on birdshot, and after that I refused to eat any of the ducks that Dad brought home.

Every Christmas they invited friends over to set up our tree after Sammie and I were in our beds, a fresh aromatic spruce that they had harvested in the woods that surrounded Missoula. They drank Tom and Jerrys and opened presents from each other and decorated the tree, increasingly giddy, throwing tinsel up to the top branches where the strands hung crooked until the tree was thrown out after New Year's day; Mom, who liked order and jobs well done, complained every time she walked by the tree. Later, when she and I were decorating our own small trees that stood on tables, she told me about Dick Snider who, just back from the war, broke out in an itchy rash from finishing off our tree with angel hair that was made

PART ONE

of spun glass. Every Christmas Mom forbade me to touch the angel hair, although she never threw away the cardboard box of it that was unpacked and then put away again with the Christmas ornaments for fifty years.

Dad drank a lot, frequently excessively, sometimes at parties, but often by himself. In the few times he took me fishing he carted along a couple of beers in his fishing creel and stopped at bars as we drove to the stream. My half-sisters Arlene and Judy told me he drank every night, sometimes to the point where he couldn't go to work the next day. He seemed to have the "flu" and be at home more than anyone I had ever known.

Around 1974 I got a call from Dad's physician saying that Dad was very sick and probably would die soon. He suggested that I fly from the East Coast immediately if I wanted to see him again. When I got to Missoula Dad was in a hospital bed receiving oxygen through a loosely fitting mask, taking short, shallow breaths, sweating with the labor of breathing. We talked off and on over the rest of the afternoon—small talk, mostly my answers to his questions about my family and recent work, two awkward men who had never exchanged words of affection. For a while before I left I held his hand, and with difficulty, just as I was about to break away, I said I loved him, although I didn't.

In a few weeks he recovered enough to leave the hospital, but his years of smoking and drinking and high blood pressure had left him with a barely functioning heart and a failing liver. In July, my half-sister Arlene called me in the middle of the night and said that Dad's body had been found at Flathead Lake floating in the water next to his dock by a neighbor who saw that Ruffles, his Golden Retriever, had not left the dock for a day and would not come when called. We never knew if Dad had a fatal heart attack or stroke that caused him to fall in the water, or if he jumped in deliberately knowing that he was at the end of the road and wanting to get it over with. Dad hadn't gone swimming for years, and at that point his heart failure was so severe that he wouldn't have been able to rescue himself in either case.

Dad's religion was foggy to me even when he died. I think whatever church he belonged to was mostly a matter of convenience. After I had gone off to the East Dad gave me his confirmation Bible for a reason known only to him, inscribed, "The Holy Bible, containing the old and new testaments, presented to Robert Noel, September 11th, 1927 for regular attendance at Christian Church Bible School."

When we lived together on McLeod he attended the Congregational Church close by. After he remarried, he belonged to the Episcopalian Church of the Holy Spirit to which his new wife Marjorie belonged. I don't know if Dad actually attended the Church of the Holy Spirit on Sunday morning or if he stayed at home with shades drawn like other non-attenders in those years when what you did and did not do was noticed, commented on and held against you by your neighbors. As a divorced man who had left his family for another woman, he might have felt unwelcome, but I never thought about it until long after I moved away. His funeral was at the Episcopal Church of the Holy Spirit, so in some sense he still belonged. After Marjorie died of cancer he married again, and his wife, who was a devout Catholic, wanted him buried in a Catholic Cemetery, but the Catholic Church was not flexible enough to figure out whether Dad belonged in Hell or Heaven and he ended up alone in unconsecrated ground in a Missoula cemetery, buried with none of his three wives.

I came back for his funeral. Mom was furious and said: "Why did you come back? I thought you didn't like your Dad." She didn't attend.

PART ONE

I have a picture of Dad as a young man that I found in one of my mother's photo albums. He is standing with his right foot up on the running board of a pre-war roadster, spiffily dressed in a light-colored vested suit, tightly cut, leaning forward with his right elbow propped on his right thigh, his left hand on his hip, white shoes on tiny feet, wavy blonde hair precisely parted on the left. He looks like a college rake, marriage bait, too attractive for his own good. In the days after Mom died and we were free to talk about their brief marriage without violating Mom's unspoken prohibition on mentioning her marriage to Dad, Sammie and I speculated about when he was conceived. I don't know if Sammie ever discovered whether Mom was pregnant when they got married; the stories we heard were silent on this delicate point. In those days, when a single girl became pregnant the end result was marriage, voluntary or compelled. We only knew that Mom was a year or two older than Dad, that she graduated from the University with a degree in journalism, and that Dad did not graduate but was working as a clerk in the First National Bank when Sammie was little and that he stayed with the bank all his life. When I was much older I heard Dad described as a "womanizer," and it is easy to imagine that Mom was one of those women drawn to him and that they married only because of Sammie's existence. I could have checked their marriage certificate and Sammie's birth certificate and it would have been clear, but by the time I became curious about why Dad left Mom for another woman the marriage was long-since over and it wasn't important enough to me to make the effort: whatever their reasons for marrying, Dad's reasons for leaving were stronger.

CHAPTER

FOUR

GRANDPA AND GRANDMA

MOST OF WHAT I know about Mom's father I learned after he died. When I was ten or eleven, Grandpa told me that when he was a boy in Lithuania he wanted to be a poet—in fact, I think he said that he was a poet. He said that, like me, he had spent a lot of time as a child in an orchard reading, but whether his family was poor or rich, whether his life was urban or rural, I don't know.

He left Lithuania around 1906 after several decades of Russian oppression or killing of revolutionaries and Jews in Russia, Lithuania, Ukraine, and Poland. He never talked about why he came to the United States. It is my presumption that he came to have a better life, perhaps at first simply to survive, because thousands were emigrating from the Baltic States for those reasons, most of them to England or the United States.

I have never known anyone who was more devoted to his adopted country than Grandpa Orvis, or anyone more passionately grateful for all of the good things that happened for him and his family because he became an American. He practically worshipped Franklin D. Roosevelt, whose name he pronounced "Rooooosevelt."

When he retired from the day-to-day running of his dry-goods store in the late 1950's, the Glasgow newspaper interviewed him about his years as a pioneer merchant in Eastern Montana. After arriving in New York City he went directly to Glasgow, Montana where a cousin had a clothing business. Grandpa was 23 and by his own words he knew nothing about clothing or business, but the offer of $35 dollars a month and a room in the back of the store to sleep in was enough to pay for 21 meals a week, leaving $7.50 for his other needs and another $7.50 that he sent back to his "poor parents" in Lithuania.

For decades the railroads and federal government heavily promoted the availability of farmland in the Dakotas and eastern Montana; a lot of immigrants from Sweden and Norway, Germany, Finland, Scotland, Latvia and Lithuania—all used to harsh weather and stubbornly unyielding earth—were tempted by the promise of free land to try their luck at dry farming. As an additional incentive for building rail lines tying the Midwest to the West Coast, the federal government had granted the railroads alternate sections of land along the tracks to help them recover their investment in steel and railroad ties and labor and rolling stock. The railroads could cut down the forests or quarry or mine that land, sell it for farms or build towns, or use it for anything else they thought might turn a profit. Look at a map of Montana that shows land ownership and you can still see the pattern of alternating mile-square blocks of railroad and state government land along the routes of the Great Northern, Northern Pacific, and Milwaukee railroads, given by the federal government in conjunction with the homesteading plan to expand the nation's prosperity and strength by filling the land with prosperous ranches and farms.

What the railroads wanted was settlers whose household furnishings and supplies and fuel and relatives they could move west, and whose produce of grain and flax and cattle and sheep and sugar beets they could move to the east to feed the big cities or to the west to export to Asia. About every twenty miles along their right-of-ways they built a siding and a station and laid out a primitive town. Some of these towns still survive today, but many more were abandoned when their settlers could not make a crop during drought years or better prospects elsewhere tempted them to move on.

Grandpa joined thousands of others in the northern European westward migration. When he got off the train in Glasgow, Montana, near where the Milk River—snaking down from the east slopes of the far-northern Rockies—joins the Missouri, what he found was a rough prairie town with a few wooden buildings set out along the railroad tracks, half of them bars or hotels or restaurants. Around the beginning of the new year his cousin left for Chicago, leaving Grandpa in charge because there was wasn't much business. Grandpa hardly spoke English, but people were kind to him because he was earnest and honest and most also had just recently arrived and put a life together in an empty country.

Grandpa and a lot of others nearly died during their first few winters, barely holding on through temperatures that were often between minus twenty and minus thirty, with constant winds. Few of the early settlers had the money to buy his goods: they had barely enough to buy groceries to supplement what they had grown the previous summer.

Firewood was scarce on the eastern plains of Montana. The railway crews kept Grandpa and many others alive by "accidentally" dropping coal off the tenders while they were loading and unloading freight or passengers and baggage at the Glasgow station. When the trains left, the new settlers, living on the edge of survival, scavenged the tracks. Grandpa hesitated to take the coal because he thought he

PART ONE

would be stealing, but a friend said it was dropped on purpose; still, he brought just enough coal back to his room to keep a tiny fire burning through the night. If the drifting snows of a big blizzard kept the trains from getting through and there was no coal, he would burn any scraps of wood or cardboard he could find. There were nights when he was not sure that he would wake up the next morning.

When his cousin came back from Chicago in the spring, he sent Grandpa west to a town further down the tracks to set up a second store, and over several years Grandpa moved back and forth between Glasgow and two other little towns along the high-line to try to expand the business.

His cousin proved to be an irascible and unreliable employer and after the third summer, with $200 in his wallet, Grandpa quit and took the train back to look for a better opportunity in Chicago. He had little luck and soon was down to 35 cents. He had relatives in Waukegan and used his last pennies to buy a boat ticket and then walked miles to their house, arriving penniless and hungry. He had missed dinner, but not wanting to put them to further trouble, he declined their offer of food and went the night without eating. He was offered work with another cousin and the cousin's cousin, who was the father of the vaudeville comedian Jack Benny.

After several years in a barely profitable clothing and furniture store he knew he would never be more than a sales clerk in the business and when his Montana cousin wrote asking him to come back, promising better behavior, he returned to Montana. During the next few years there were good rain and good crops and the business boomed, but his boss was still hard to work for and in 1911 Grandpa returned to Chicago. As written in the interview, "I had my plans formulated. The girl I loved back home in Europe was in Chicago then living with her sister. Mrs. Orvis and I were married in March 1912."

That winter he wrote to a wholesale warehouse in St. Paul, Minnesota asking for their spring catalogue. In April he went to St.

Paul with a list of merchandise he wanted to order with the $500 he had saved. The owner was impressed with Grandpa's plan and industriousness and gave him full support in credit and the cost of shipping the merchandise to him. Grandpa put $200 down and with the remaining $300 returned to Glasgow, rented the space his cousin had formerly occupied, and opened his own store, which he called the Fair Store. He partitioned off half the space and he and Grandma lived there for the first year. The best year the farmers had had for flax and wheat was 1912, and new customers and residents kept coming in. Gradually Grandpa's business expanded; a year and a half later Grandpa moved his store to larger quarters.

The settlement of eastern Montana in the early decades of the 20th century was slow. Eastern Montana and much of the western Dakotas were settled on a misconception—a misconception fostered by the railroads and dry-land farming theorists since the 1880's—that farming in the high plains would be easy and crops would be abundant based on beliefs that the climate was changing and that the plains would become less arid. Some academics claimed that farming actually created more rainfall—"rain follows the plow." There was adequate rainfall for good grain and flax crops in the wet years of 1906 to 1916—above the average of eleven inches a year. But the truth is that Montana is a dry state. Hundreds of miles to the west, the Rockies wring the last of the moisture out of the Pacific airflows, and everything east of the continental divide is arid, lush with wild grasses as the winter snow melts, but sear and sparse once the skimpy spring rains stop. Although large amounts of water surged down the Missouri and Milk from headwaters in the Rockies, irrigation beyond the floodplains near the river was primitive: farmers depended on crops like fall-planted winter wheat that could soak up the thin, melting snow and the spring rains and mature before the hot, rainless summers set in. Other crops gave a decent yield in years of average or better than average rainfall but failed in the drier years. Drive in any direction from US Highway 2 around Malta, Saco, Wolf Point, Poplar, Havre—the little towns lined out along the Great Northern tracks in the late 1800's—and beyond the broken down barbwire fences you will find the old wheel ruts, the ancient solitary lilacs and apple trees, the collapsing sheds and cabins, the crumbled foundations of homesteads settled in optimism and abandoned by the hundreds when a cycle of wet years gave way to a longer cycle of dry years beginning in 1917, when little would grow and grasshoppers ate whatever survived.

During Grandpa's first years on his own, the farmers who had the luck and skills made a go of it. For ranchers, they could never count on making enough to pay back their expenses: raising cattle to ship east to the Chicago stockyards was possible if a rancher could buy or lease enough rangeland from the government to support a herd. To feed a single steer required several acres of the thin summer grasses, and even more land was needed to grow enough hay to feed a herd through the long harsh winter when open range grazing was close to impossible even for the hardiest breeds. Given average rainfall or better they could survive. Two dry years back-to-back could wipe them out.

In 1916 Grandpa bought a new building in which the Fair Store remained for the rest of his life. By the 1920's Glasgow had developed the character of a settled town. Frame houses replaced the cabins and shacks, a few businesses invested in brick buildings, the commercial base became broader than just subsistence farming and ranching. People needed insurance and banks and schools. Schoolteachers and bank clerks and secretaries needed staple groceries and dry goods and coal and oil and gasoline to heat their homes and power their cars. Before and during the First World War his business steadily grew and he opened a store in Malta which did almost as much business as the Glasgow store; in 1920 he started a third store in Havre.

The loss of men during the First World War and from the Spanish flu epidemic had left hundreds of thousands of widows and children in poverty. The country had only begun to recover when the Great Depression hit in 1929. Two years later a second catastrophe struck the country: years of extreme drought in the West and Midwest led to the Dust Bowl, which lasted for eight years. Thousands of farms and hundreds of farm towns failed, and for years cars stuffed with children and with a family's few possessions tied to the roof and fenders could be seen on the roads in every season, heading for what the family was hoping would be some better place.

When Mom and her friends from Glasgow were together they talked about the locust plagues during the Dust Bowl, hot, dry years when the grasshoppers would devour all the crops in a few hours, when the noise of grasshoppers eating and flying kept people awake at night, when the sun was obscured by billowing, dingy clouds of grasshoppers moving from one field to the next, the grasshoppers multiplying rapidly until finally the early frosts killed them, leaving wrecked fields and shattered hopes as the residue of their pillaging.

When loans and mortgages were due and there was not enough money to make payments, the banks foreclosed. There was almost no one who wanted or could afford what the banks reclaimed in land and, although used cars and trucks and livestock had some value, thousands of banks failed, wiping out their customers' life savings. I imagine Grandpa recovered some of what his customers could not pay in cash with their vegetables and pies and chickens and help with chores, the same way that doctors and teachers and mechanics were often paid when cash was short. If someone could not make a crop

PART ONE

and needed a loan to get through the winter until the next planting season, there were few prospects.

Then, in 1933, there was an enormous lucky break for eastern Montanans and it made Grandpa prosperous enough that he could keep his business and house, send his daughters to college, and build a summer home near Glacier Park, at Flathead Lake. One of the Roosevelt administration's economic recovery projects was to build an enormous earth dam—the 'biggest landfill dam in the world"—across the Missouri River just above where the Milk River joins it, at a rundown Sioux and Assiniboine Indian reservation trading post that was first stockaded in 1867, called Fort Peck.

The dam was the top-most of four dams built by the Army Corps of Engineers to control the spring runoffs of the Missouri and Mississippi Rivers that every few years inflicted enormous damages on the towns and farms laid out in the floodplains all the way to the Gulf of Mexico. The enormous lake that grew behind the dam sank hundreds of farms in 250 feet of water, but it also provided steady work for eleven thousand unemployed men and women whose jobs had disappeared in the Dust Bowl and Depression years. Eleven thousand destitute farmers, blacksmiths, power-shovel, dredge, and caterpillar tractor operators, pick and shovel men, steel workers, cooks, surveyors, out of work teachers and bankers poured into the mad new town of Wheeler that was created to house the workers. Glasgow, just sixteen miles from the construction site, grew in a few months from a quiet, unexceptional farm town into the main staging and supply area for one of the biggest construction projects of the government-fueled recovery. Grandpa's Fair Store suddenly had customers—lots of them—with a regular paycheck in their back pockets. His store went from the small cash transactions of farm wives and townspeople, many of whom he had to provide with credit that he carried on his books for years, until the seven-year-long boom of a town with an industry.

In the mid-1930's, when Mom and her sister Nonie were off in college, Grandpa began to build a summer cabin on a piece of land they had bought to camp on at Flathead Lake. The cabin got improved as it was built and turned out to be more of a house than a cabin, with knotty pine walls, larch and fir floors, a large stone fireplace, an orchard of apples and cherries and plums up the hill behind the house, and a rock garden down in front next to the road. By the time I was born in 1941 Grandpa and Grandma were spending their summers there. Grandpa turned over the day-to-day management of the store to his assistant, Gene Benson, who ultimately took over completely. Gene ended up with his hand in the till and the store went downhill, but not before Grandpa and Grandma had saved enough to live in comfort for the rest of their lives and pass a little bit on to Mom and Aunt Nonie.

Every summer when I was in grade school I spent long hours in Grandpa and Grandma's attic in the Flathead Lake house pouring through old copies of *Life Magazine* and *National Geographic*. They had kept every issue of both in an attic under the aromatic, dusty, windowless eaves. By the dim light of a single unfrosted light bulb tacked to a rafter, over several summers I worked my way back through *Life Magazine* to the Korean War issues, then the two hundred or so Second-World War issues, and finally, when I was about eight, I read the stories and looked at the pictures of the Depression years. At the bottom of the earliest stack, I found the very first issue: the cover story was about the building of the Fort Peck Dam. Hidden away during a long sultry August afternoon when I was supposed to be napping in my room under framed prints of sleepy cherubs and seraphim, I read the story that explained Grandpa's eventual success as a business man, looked at the pictures of happy, half-drunk workers dancing with women who had found their ways there to provide lonely men in a desolate place with some company. In a country stricken with poverty, the government projects were providing

PART ONE

enough money for carousing in saloons, paying the grocery bill, and buying supplies and a little bit of finery at the Fair Store.

When I was growing up, children were to be seen, not heard. At meals family stories were not told in either my Mom's or my Dad's homes. At Dad's house, talk of our family before he left would have probably made both Dad and Marjorie uncomfortable, and on the few occasions that I was alone with Dad in a car, going fishing or to a river to train his dumb but exuberant Golden Retrievers, he didn't talk about the past.

So all of the stories of Mom's growing up, her high school and college years, her courtship with Dad? I never heard them. It was as though there was an unspoken conspiracy in both families that the time before the divorce—Mom and Dad's childhoods and their marriage—were not discussed in my presence.

The few things I know about Mom's childhood took place in Glasgow. I know from finding the gear and seeing a few old pictures that there were camping trips to western Montana even before Grandpa bought the land to build his Flathead Lake house. I heard stories about the times of boom and bust that were told as parables, as a warning to not waste my time, to garner my earnings, to take care of home and tools and cars, but I did not hear the stories of their experiences—or perhaps they told those stories and I wasn't paying attention.

There were few third or fourth generation Montanans in the 1940's. Montana was full of European immigrants and many of the parents of Mom and Nonie's schoolmates spoke with European accents and brought with them some of their Norwegian or Latvian or Polish or Scottish heritage. A generation later many of my friends' grandparents had accents, but we didn't know or care of what country their accents were vestiges. Never once when I was growing up was the subject of my friends' or my grandparents being immigrants discussed. It was not that it was avoided, or suppressed when it came up—it just never came up in my presence. The harshness of life on the western mountains and prairies—the poverty of the times, the hardships of two wars, the need to put dinner on the table and raise children—left people with little time to reminisce or mourn for what they had gladly left behind in Northern Europe or in the mid-west or the East Coast. Almost everyone was from somewhere else just one or two generations earlier.

CHAPTER

FIVE

TORN APART

WHEN I WAS learning to drive, my brother Sammie was pressured by Mom to go with me one Sunday morning so that I could I practice shifting and turning. He directed me on a tour of the houses that Mom and Dad lived in when they were first married. The first was just a few blocks from the University, and the second was in an old section of town where they moved when he was born. They were tiny one-bedroom cottages with faded shingle siding and dismal-looking shrubbery that for decades were temporary homes for newly married couples. Mom and Dad did not move to the McLeod house until after I was born, when Sammie was almost four.

There are pictures of me at that age sitting in a wagon or a tiny tricycle out in front. There is still a large currant bush where I sat picking currants and stuffing them in my mouth while red ants climbed into my shorts and I came wailing into the house with the fierce critters hanging on, refusing to give up their meal. When I couldn't

PART ONE

play outside I used to sit on the kitchen floor banging Mom's pots and pans, watching Beulah, Mom's maid, ironing and cleaning and cooking. I remember homemade cottage cheese hanging in a cloth bag from the faucet of the kitchen sink while the whey drained out of it, and I can call up the exact tangy, pleasantly sour taste of that cottage cheese, which I have tried to find in grocery stores for six decades without any luck.

I must have been about four when my brother Sammie and Roland Trenouth's sister Cecily and I picked handfuls of orange and red berries off of the flowering bushes that bordered the Trenouth's large backyard. Lacking kitchen utensils, we stirred the berries with sticks in a red American Flyer wagon, adding dollops of dirt and a few dead bugs and a bit of water from a backyard hose. Having created a noxious witch's brew, we needed a victim and decided to feed it to Rollie, who was minding his own business in his back yard. We all but convinced him that he had to eat the dirt-n-bug-n-berry stew if he wanted to be in our club. I have no idea what the club was or why Sammie and Cecily, who were three and four years older, would have allowed either Rollie or me into any club unless it was to exploit us. All properly raised children in those days had been warned not to eat anything picked off a bush, especially if it was red or orange, or handed to them by a stranger; our assumption was that unless it was parent-sanctioned, it was poisonous, so I think that we must have intended to do Rollie in, although it puzzles me that even the powerful inducement of being in my brother's inner circle for a few minutes would have led me to try to poison my best friend. Rollie and I still tell this story when we get together, our first experience with forbidden fruit: our older brother and sister the snakes, I the guileless dupe, and Rollie too cautious, then as now, to be drawn in.

A few months later Rollie showed me how nice a velvety pussy willow catkin felt sliding along my cheek and finger and tried to persuade me that it felt even better when he slipped it up his nostril. A few hours later he had to go to the hospital when neither he nor his father could retrieve the catkin and in their efforts kept pushing it in further and further. They gave him ether to pluck it out.

Rollie informed me that if I swallowed my gum I would get appendicitis; Mom had also told me that, but Rollie's father was a doctor and so I believed it when he said it. It must have been true: I have never swallowed gum since then, and I have never had appendicitis.

Just after my fifth birthday Sammie and Rollie and I took off on an expedition on our tricycles—me standing on the back of Sammie's trike, Rollie on his own, pedaling furiously on a route that took us dozens of blocks away through the University and to the Van Buren bridge where the Clark Fork River was roaring over its banks with the spring floods. On the way a bunch of boys jumped us in front of Jimmy Pramenko's house and tried to choke me but we managed to get away. We parked the trikes on the bridge above the river and scampered down the steep bank where sandbags had been piled, just a few feet from the furiously churning and muddy brown torrent. Within minutes the police showed up with their red light flashing. They snatched us away from the water and brought us home, each of them holding a tricycle out his window. I cried the whole way, "I don't want to go to jail, I don't want to go to jail," but they only wanted to keep us from drowning. Perhaps the jail cell for five year olds was already occupied. I have no idea where our mothers were or what they thought we were doing—we must have been away for hours.

One night I was shaken awake by Mom, who was frantic and angry. Sammie had taken an envelope from the top of Mom's bureau and buried it as pirates' treasure in the back yard. I stood by and watched as he took it, but I doubt I knew what he was up to. After we went to bed, Mom discovered that the envelope was missing and woke Sammie, who told Mom that I had buried it behind the house. Yelling at me, she dragged me outside by the arm like a rag doll and began to dig where Sammie told her I had buried it in the black, gritty dirt beneath the window where coal was delivered, using the first thing at hand, a spinning metal top shaped like a flying saucer and painted in bright yellow and blue and red. She found nothing in the cinders and dirt. She asked where I had put the envelope, but I was incoherent and blubbering. She gave up and made Sammie show her where he had buried it. I never forgot this story and when I was a teenager told it to Mom and Sammie. Sam laughed—he always got a kick out of the stories in which I described how he had pushed me around in one way or another or blamed me for things. Whether the money was an alimony payment from Dad, or a check from Grandpa, it was what Mom had to live on for a while and its disappearance clearly drove her wild. I cannot remember ever being scared of Mom before or after.

I was a frequent bystander in Sammie's assaults on adult rules: "thou shalt not play hooky from school; thou shalt not paint the dog white with a red head; thou shalt not try to put a firecracker up a cat's ass; thou shalt not steal money and bury it." I quickly learned that money was limited and important and that it was best to stay close enough to Sammie to enjoy what he was up to but far enough away to have clean hands and an innocent look when the jig was up. The buried treasure was my first memory of Sammie's substantial record of transgression as a child. I would develop my own as the years passed, but Sammie's always seemed more outrageous.

When I was 5 Mom took me downtown to a matinee she wanted to see at the Wilma Theater, across from Dad's bank. Sammie was in school, as were all the potential babysitters. I chatted loudly the whole time, asking what happened when the scene changed and a whole house and all the people in it suddenly disappeared, or how daylight could change instantly to night. Other people began hissing at us and we left early. She complained about the money she had wasted the entire walk home. She didn't take me to a movie again for years.

As with my initial participation in religion at the Congregational Church, in disgrace when I could not memorize twelve words for the Christmas pageant, I failed the first day of my formal education at the University Kindergarten. I was taken into the brown-stained shingle building behind the Forestry School at the University by Mom, who told me I would be brought home in the afternoon and then left me, bewildered, in the middle of twenty strange kids. We were told to find our cubbyholes and get our pads of paper and boxes of crayons. While all the other children were soon at small tables scribbling on their pads, I was lost. How did they find their cubbyhole and paper and crayons? In confusion and then in tears I wandered around until a teacher spotted me.

"Why haven't you found your crayons?"

"I don't know. I don't know where they are."

"Your cubby has your name on it."

I looked blank. I was unable to explain that I could not read my name, because I did not know about reading.

"What's your name?"

"Gordy."

She led me to my cubby and pointed out my name. I didn't know that was my name. I was helpless and humiliated. In a very short time it was also clear that I could not tie my own shoes and laboriously I learned that the rabbit came out of the hole ("what hole?"), went around the tree ("what tree?"), and back down the hole. My overalls didn't have a zipper fly and had to be taken down, but I couldn't do that without help; I had never seen paste, didn't know about finger painting, had not learned any of the organized games that other kids had already mastered.

Morning Graham crackers and milk went very well right from the first day and week after week were my absolutely favorite part of the day. In those years butter, cream, and milk were delivered to front porches every morning. You could see the cream layer on

PART ONE

top when standing thirty feet away on the sidewalk, the thicker the layer the better the milk. In winter a bottle left out too long froze and sprouted a long, arching neck of frozen cream rising above the bottle with the paper cap perched on top. I never knew how they got that frozen cream neck back in the bottle. Our bottles were miniatures of those, a half-pint glass bottle with a paper tab that could be pulled off after the bottle was shaken to mix the cream with the milk. We were taught to shake the bottle before we pulled the tab; we drank the milk with a straw. Slurping the last bit from the bottom of the bottle was lowbrow and we got a nasty look from a teacher if we did it. Girls never did it. Boys couldn't resist doing it, and the best of us did it again immediately after we were corrected, looking sideways to see if the teachers and other kids noticed how naughty we were.

After milk and crackers came napping, which went poorly. Napping was definitely a dull interruption of playing and seemed totally unnecessary. I was scolded frequently for violating the many rules about sleeping and sitting still and being quiet. I rarely went to sleep, but if I did I had to be shaken awake and was groggy and disoriented and sullen for an hour.

Playing outside went well. Unless there were three feet of new snow or a driving rainstorm, we always were sent out to play. There was no such concept as "too cold." Ice was an invitation for sliding and broom hockey. Montanans, along with much of the rest of the country, believed in the virtues of fresh air. At night in the middle of winter we slept with our storm windows cracked open even when it was thirty below zero outside: at the bottom the window sash there were three holes an inch in diameter and a wooden bar that could be rotated up to unblock the holes, rotated down to cover them up if ice began to form on the inside of the windows. The cost of the coal bill mattered less than the fresh air. During all of my childhood there was often a thin sheet of ice on the inside window when I woke up, my breath steaming up from my heaped covers, I pretended I was smoking and blowing smoke rings like grownups.

My favorite activity at kindergarten was lining up the dozens of large, one foot square brightly colored wooden blocks to create rooms and walls, houses, and forts. I learned about finger painting and using tongue depressors to spread delicious-smelling white paste—only half of which I ate—from huge screw-top jars onto scraps of paper. I could find pennies and marbles in the dirt that collected along the curb at the edge of the playground and I could find bloated worms on the sidewalk after it rained and carry them around in my pockets. The worms dried out and Mom found them and carefully separated the dried-out corpses from the pennies and marbles, which she returned to me. I could go down a slide and ride a teeter-totter and swing sitting but not standing. Eventually I learned to tie my shoes, and to read and write, but just a little bit.

We rode to and from Kindergarten in a green Army convoy truck with curved steel struts that supported the green canvas top. We sat four or five abreast on board benches in the truck bed; one of the teachers rode alongside the driver and hopped out at every stop to help us get in and out of the high truck bed. The truck stopped in front of my house to pick Rollie and me up and drop us off. We made a dozen or more stops between the University and my house.

The first ride back from kindergarten I remember must have been in the fall of 1946. It was a gray day, but not yet winter. I got down from the back of the truck and ran up the front stairs and into the front door. Inside, what was always a bright house during the day was so dark I could barely see, the heavy winter draperies pulled across all of the windows. I could make out very little, but I heard Mom crying and spotted her lying face down on the couch along the right-hand wall. I had never seen my mother cry. I asked what was wrong, why was the house dark, why was she crying. Without sitting up, turning her face away from me, in a hoarse whisper she told me to go next door to Dr. Clark's house and tell them I needed "a handout."

"What's that?"

"They'll know."

That was it. I was bewildered: what was a handout? I did what she said, and Mrs. Clark seemed to understand. She made me a sandwich and a glass of milk. I spent the rest of the afternoon in her living room, fascinated by the Victorian furnishings and the large Boston fern drooping over the edges of a pot on a small table near a bow window. I spent the night under a blanket sleeping in the bow window. I could see our darkened house next door where my sad mother slept by herself.

That was the beginning of my life as a divorced kid, the beginning of Mom's life as a single mother—a divorced, working mother—at a time and in a place where being divorced was considered, silently, a moral failure for both Mom and me, although it was Dad that broke the marriage.

That morning Dad had moved out, and in a few months he would take Sammie with him. Raising two boys by herself was too much for Mom. The decision to separate us, for her to keep me and send Sammie off for a life with Dad must have torn Mom apart, although she never talked about it.

Mom went to work for Mr. Campbell, a lawyer, as his secretary and assistant. I know that she admired him and when he died a half-year later, she brought home a dark green pot that had a latticework of gold wire wrapped around it. That pot and its durable pothos plant moved from place to place with us. It was still in her house sitting on a wall bracket in her living room when she died forty years later.

In the spring of 1947, when I came home in the troop truck on May 5th I didn't know that I wouldn't return to University Kindergarten and that it was the last time that I would walk in the front door of the house on McLeod Avenue.

The house was completely cleared of furniture. There were a few boxes scattered around, and several packed suitcases. I looked in my bedroom and found it emptied of bed and toys and clothes and my collection of sticks.

Mom told me we would be driving to Butte in an hour. Rollie had been sent back by his mom to say goodbye. Mom gave me a handful of pennies. We walked a few blocks east on McLeod to University Grocery and I bought hard, red cinnamon cubes about the size of sugar cubes, covered with sugar the way a lemon drop is. I gave one to Rollie, took one myself, and carried four or five more home in a small, white paper bag. Years later I would go back to the store looking for that candy, but I never found it again. I can still taste it, and feel the rough sugar on my tongue. I made the remaining pieces each last for a week, sucking on them for a few minutes, and then taking them out of my mouth and saving them for another day.

It was years before I saw Rollie again.

Six-year-old boys don't have prolonged goodbyes. I had no sense of "future." We didn't promise to write or be friends forever. I didn't cry or feel sad. I didn't ask Mom any questions about why we were leaving.

Mom put me in Arnold Beatty's grey coupe and we left Missoula.

I was a few hours older than six.

Arnold and his wife Gen lived in Butte. After Mr. Campbell died, they had persuaded Mom that she could find a job and a new life in the wide-open town of Butte, away from the daily, painful remainders of her old life with Dad and their college friends. Arnold was a

PART ONE

traveling salesman for the Burroughs Office Machine Corporation; he drove the winding, empty roads of Montana from one small town to the next servicing and selling adding machines and cash registers. He had a short, bristly mustache; he once told me that the reason he had a mustache was so that he could suck water out of it when he was picking spinach in the hot, dry spinach fields. I never doubted for a moment that Arnold could suck water out of his mustache, because he could take pennies and nickels right out of my ear lobe, and once even a dime. Of my Mom's friends, Arnold was my favorite. It puzzled me for a long time that a man who could produce money out of ears and supply himself with water from his upper lip needed to work, but I decided that he liked to travel.

The drive to Butte was the first car trip I remember. It was evening by the time we left Missoula. Soon I got tired of listening to Mom and Arnold talk about grown-up things that I didn't understand and I stretched out on the back seat, my head on the passenger side, and watched the telephone lines fall and rise between poles, imagining that they lived in arcs like upside down black rainbows because they wanted to and failing to understand that the poles or the weight of the lines or gravity had anything to do with it. I was asleep long before we arrived in Butte.

Arnold moved our few suitcases and boxes into our new home and drove away leaving us alone in a place where I knew no one.

Mom had taken me out of the University Kindergarten and moved us to Butte in May as soon as she found a job that could support us. Her planning included being sure she had a place for me to be while she was at work. The morning after we arrived was also her first day of work. She got me up early and helped me dress. Holding hands, we walked up Butte's long main street that connected the School of Mines nestled in the foothills of an extinct volcano—Mount

Butte—with the downtown area. Explaining as we walked, Mom said that it was too late in the school year for any of the public schools to accept me into kindergarten, but that St. Anne's School had agreed to take me, more or less on the principle that they would not turn away any of God's children. Mom's application process must have been pretty informal, as it appeared not to have covered some critical information about Catholic kindergartens. She walked me down a dark, varnished-wood hallway to an office where we were met by a woman dressed entirely in black, wearing a black hood. I stared at her with astonished terror. Mom placed my hand in Sister Felicity's hand and let me know that she would be back in the evening to get me. I, however, knew my "Hansel and Gretel," and I was terrified that I would be in the oven by the time she returned: Mom had left me firmly in the grasp of a scrawny witch from whom there would be no escape.

As I anxiously watched Mom disappear, Sister Felicity inspected me sternly from above—standing up straight I barely reached where a non-witch would have had a belly button. Even with the extra bulk of my OsgoshByGosh overalls and t-shirt there was not much to me. I needed a haircut and my fingernails were dirty. I almost certainly had the look of the unrepentant nose picker that I was.

I also inspected Sister Felicity. She had no ears and no hair that I could detect. Where you or I would have had eyes she had flat octagonal crystals that glinted a cold, hard light sparking off in random directions as she bobbed her head. The crystals were held to her face by thin, silvery wires that disappeared beneath her hood in the direction of where ears might once have been. Her nose was thin, blue, and horny; her lips were the texture, size, and color of drowned worms. Here and there her tight white skin was blotched with cobalt blue patches, black wiry hairs bristled on her chin and from her nose holes. Her chin was lost behind the hood that framed her bloodless face and fell over her shoulders. The only other flesh that was

PART ONE

exposed was on her claw-like hands. One claw held my hand the way an eagle might hold on to a rabbit that it was about to eat. Her other claw held a thin, black book from which dangled frazzled black ribbons. I looked around the office to spot where she had hidden her broom. There were more witches observing me intently from the other side of a glass window in an inner office, checking out their dinner victim.

Having not yet acquired unshakeable composure when faced with imminent death, I did the natural thing and began thrashing about and yelling and crying. Sister Felicity had the tenacity of an eagle and at the end of my first attempt to break out I was still firmly in her grip. She dragged me out of the office, down a long, gloomy hall into a musty classroom of scrupulously scrubbed but indifferent children who stared at me blankly. They all seemed to have become Sister Felicity's tamed and compliant captives. She placed me in a tiny desk at the front of the class and, never relaxing her grip on my wrist, began to talk with the other children. The mood in the room suddenly became somber. She said strange words; the kids looked down at their folded hands and mumbled the same words back to her. Back and forth this went for what seemed like a very long time. She watched me out of the corner of her eye and nodded her head after she spoke, apparently expecting me to mumble along with all the other kids. When she was through she commanded the kids to take out notebooks and to copy something written on her blackboard, which they did, the same words over and over again in rows down the page. I had seen an occasional child my age who could write a few words, but never a whole class that could write in unison. Sister Felicity turned to me.

"Who is your Lord and Savior," she asked.
"Huh?"
"Who is your Lord and Savior?"
"Uhh..."

Now her crystal eyes were flashing. "Have you been Baptized?"

"What?"

"Why were you put on earth?"

"I . . I . . ah. . ." I looked around the room to find the way out.

"Do you pray to our Holy Mother?"

That question totally boogered me. I had no idea what Sister Felicity was asking me, but I knew she was not getting the answers she wanted. I figured this was the test that she used to select who lived and who got roasted. Apparently the little automatons in the room were the survivors who knew the answers to this quiz and that anyone who did not would become dinner. I began to scream and thrash around, and then I bit her hand. This time I got away. I was out of the classroom and heading for the front door when my path was cut off by a second witch, who spread her skirts like a black toreador's cape. I diverted up a staircase. For the next few hours several panting witches worked in shifts to corner me in one or another hall way or classroom. No one said a word. Only Sister Felicity had claws: the others had stubby, puffy mittens of hands and would quickly let me go if bitten or scratched. They were chubby and out of shape and too well fed to be hungry enough to want to work hard to trap me. Ultimately there was a stand off. I sat on the top step of a stairway that led to some unused rooms on the darkened third floor, and a very fat witch sat in a chair on the landing below, blocking my way to the front door.

In the evening Mom and Sister Felicity came to an understanding: I would never darken the doorway of St. Anne's again. Although every child converted was a child saved, there were limits to how much of their own flesh St. Anne's nuns were willing to sacrifice for a heathen. I didn't know if Mom was humiliated or simply out of options, but she was silent on the walk home, brooding about something.

The next day I was sent into exile. My Butte academic debut had lasted less than eight hours. I can still smell the aromatic varnish and wax of St Anne's ancient wooden hallways.

CHAPTER

SIX

FLATHEAD LAKE

I HAD BEEN thrown out of the only kindergarten in Butte willing to admit me, with just a few weeks of the school year left. Mom had to work to support us but now she had no way to look after me during the long summer before I began the first grade in the close-by public school. She was in a strange town with few friends and no money for baby-sitters. A phone call was made. I could live with Grandpa and Grandma at Flathead Lake until the fall. I would travel alone on an eight-hour journey on three different buses.

The trip started at the Greyhound bus terminal in Butte. I was very excited. Across from the bus terminal I got a breakfast of hot dog and an Orange Crush at a tiny restaurant called the Donald Duck Inn. This became my favorite Butte restaurant, and to this day my invariable beverage of choice with a hot dog is neither beer nor Coke, but orange soda. Back at the terminal, Mom talked with the driver and pinned a note to the front of my jacket with my destination

PART ONE

and her telephone number at work. Grandma and Grandpa did not have a phone, but she put their names and address on the note. I was wearing neat short trousers and a plaid sport jacket. My hair had been combed wet with the hope that it would stay in place; my nails were clean and I had been scrubbed to within an inch of my life, even the insides of my ears reamed out over my howling protests. Clearly Mom was more concerned about how I looked when I arrived at Grandma's house than she had been about the nun's impression of me the day before. I carried my clothes in a black cardboard suitcase with worn corners that was almost as big as I was. Mom had told me not to let it out of my sight and, as usual, to beware of strange men. The driver put me in the front seat on the passenger side where I had a commanding view of the road and put the suitcase in the rack above me. I cheerfully waved goodbye, and Mom waved back. I wonder how much she worried as the big bus swung out of the terminal and out of her sight; I wasn't worried at all.

I never once heard what it was that strange men might do, but I suppose it was worse than what nuns might do since I had gotten no warning at all about them.

The telephone wires still made their endless arcs up and down, as they had 36 hours before, but there was much more to see through the bus's large, high windows and in the bright May morning sunlight. I tried not to miss a thing: fields full of cows and surging streams at the verge of their banks with the milk-chocolate brown water of spring run-off, the barns and corrals and modest houses of ranches and farms, the intense light green of meadow grasses and stream-side willows, the bunches of sheep that did not even look up as the bus rumbled by, the pot-hole ponds with ducks and flashing magpies and red-winged blackbirds. I craned my neck to study the little combination grocery store-post office-service stations that served as bus stations at the intersections of local roads and US Highway 10. We stopped at all of these. Usually there were two or three people standing outside, gazing up the road, impatient for our arrival. The driver would slow and pull off onto the gravel in front of the store, calling out the name of the stop: Warm Springs, Deer Lodge, Drummond, Garrison. Somebody in the back of the bus might stand up and begin making his way to the front. The driver had a handle on the dashboard in front of him connected to the door by a long, chrome-plated bar. When he pushed the handle away from him with his right hand, the door opened. He climbed out and took the hand of anyone who looked shaky climbing down from the bus. Then he checked the tickets or collected money from those boarding. In two minutes he closed the door and we were off again in a spray of dust and gravel.

At Garrison, near where the highway from the state capitol in Helena met Highway 10, the driver called out, "This is Garrison. Everyone back on board in fifteen minutes." People scurried to use the bathrooms or to buy a Coke or a candy bar. A half a dozen people got out to catch the waiting bus from Missoula to Helena, and another half dozen got on. A skinny man with yellow fingers who smoked continuously sat down next to me and for the rest of the trip piled up cigarette butts in the little armrest ashtray. I scooched down to try to keep my head below the clouds of smoke fanning out from his cigarette.

At Missoula the driver told me to stay put while the other riders got out and he unloaded bags from underneath the bus. Then he grabbed my suitcase from overhead and took me into the terminal and ordered me a Coke and a doughnut at the coffee-shop counter and the waitresses in black dresses and little white caps made a fuss over me for the next three-quarters of an hour. The driver of Inter-Mountain Express's Flexible Flyer bus took over for the trip north on US Highway 93 to Polson. We stopped a half dozen times at the tiny reservation towns to unload or pick up a few passengers—Evaro, Arlee, Ravalli, St. Ignatius, Charlo, Ronan, Pablo. These towns were not planned with building a highway in anyone's mind, so the highway zigged to the east and zagged to the west to connect the towns together. The reservation stores where the bus stopped were smaller and shabby, their paint peeling and peanut and popsicle bags and empty cigarette packs and match books strewn on the gravel in front. There were dogs lying in the dusty gravel near the gas pumps. Fewer people got off or on the bus.

The gigantic, deep purple Mission Mountains, still capped with snow, loomed over the wide spring-green valley. Having never lived anywhere else I was used to a landscape of mountains and valleys, but there was something about the scale of this valley that felt different and exciting. I must have driven through it every summer since I was born but this is the first memory I have of feeling the grandeur of the broad lower Flathead Valley.

After Ronan the driver said, "Look ahead, Sonny, and you'll see Flathead Lake pretty soon." As the road curved and descended I could see a broad swath of green fields and on the horizon a narrow band of blue backed by distant purple mountains, then gradually the lake lengthened and broadened and filled the entire horizon. All along the right side there were more mountains, heavily forested, more deep greenish-blue than purple. Beyond where the lake seemed to end, barely visible in the haze, there were snowy peaks that looked far, far away.

We entered a town a few minutes later, bigger than any we had passed since Missoula. All the stores and houses were one-story. Back a block or two from the road I could see green lawns and white fences and sprinklers at work. There were no sidewalks; most of the streets were dirt. Broken-down cars and trucks littered the side streets. A few kids in dirty shorts and t-shirts and bare feet rode bikes, weaving in and out of the parking lots in front of the service stations and drive-in restaurants that bordered the highway.

This was Polson, my next transfer. The driver turned left in the center of town, went around the block, and pulled in at an angle in front of Eddy's Drug Store. He took me into the drug store and told a girl at the long soda fountain counter that he was parking me on a stool and that she should be sure I got on the east shore bus. He lifted me up on the stool and spun the seat around a few times. My feet hung down two feet short of the floor.

The waitress asked me if I wanted a piece of pie. I accepted. "Cherry. And a glass of milk, please." It must have been free, because I certainly had not been sent off with any money. Maybe scrubbed up I was more appealing to bus stop waitresses than to nuns.

In a while a smaller, cream and red Intermountain Express bus pulled in. The driver had just come down the east shore from Kalispell and was heading back. The waitress pointed me out and when he had gotten the few other passengers on board he put me in a seat behind him, so that I would be on the lake side for the trip. The east shore road had just been paved. Unlike the road from Missoula that had some long, straight stretches, the east shore road was curved and hilly. We drove mostly in trees that abruptly descended down ridges to the lake. Here and there the land was less steep; cherry and apple orchards still cloudy with pink and white blossoms descended sloping benches of gravelly land. There were a few houses along the road but no towns and only a few stores. When the road dropped close to the level of the lake at Blue Bay and Yellow Bay, I could see a few people in small boats slowly trolling for salmon. It was now early evening and I was tired, excited, and very hungry. The driver knew more or less where I was going in Woods Bay from the instructions pinned to my jacket, and when he spotted Grandpa and Grandma standing beside the road in front of their house he blew his air horn enthusiastically. He could not have mistaken who they were waiting for. He stopped the bus in front of their house and like a puppy I bounced off the bus with the driver right behind carrying my cardboard suitcase. The few passengers in the bus grinned and clapped.

PART ONE

At six years plus three days I had made a 200-mile bus trip alone. But I was always in the company of friendly, helpful strangers. I was too excited to be afraid and although I never knew of another six-year-old who had made such a trip, I have an idea that the drivers had seen many kids being shipped alone across the country during the Depression and War.

I did not think of my Grandma as short when I was six, but now that I have to bend over the bathroom sink that Grandpa installed at a convenient height for her I know that she was a small woman, even for the 1940's. Both she and Grandpa, who must have been about five and half feet tall, were slender in their sixties, with none of the pudginess that older Americans tend to develop now. Except when she was going into town to shop, she always wore the same clothes—a simple cotton dress, usually with a pattern of small flowers, stockings, sturdy black shoes with low heels, her long gray-brown hair up in a tight bun. Grandma was a warm woman, but not effusive. She did not fold me into a capacious bosom or suffocate me with a bear hug. When I stepped off the bus she gave me a little hug, Grandpa patted me on the shoulder and back and called me by his pet name, "Gorgie Porgie," over and over again. The bus was already disappearing around the curve at the Mickens' store when we turned and walked up the long front walk to the house, each of them holding one of my hands, Grandpa carrying my suitcase. On both sides of the walk, Grandpa had planted peonies between the rock garden down in front and the top of the walk where it separated into paths leading to the back door on the left, the porch straight ahead, and the garage on the right. The slender, graceful peonies were propped upright in their wire cages, but they were still entirely green, with tight buds showing only a sliver of color, still a full month away from blooming. The air smelled like spring—cool, earthy, slightly perfumed by the early lilacs, with the strong scent of wet stones and driftwood from the shore where low waves were gently running in just a hundred feet away.

The main floor of the house was really the second floor on the front side, and we went up the steep stone front steps on this first day—the entrance to the house used only by guests. I would not use that doorway into Grandma's spotlessly clean front rooms again until the day I left. Inside the house, the front sleeping porch where Grandpa and Grandma slept in the summer was neat as a pin, as it always would be. On the right their bed was partly separated from the rest of the sleeping porch by a cloth curtain that pulled across the porch on a wire. On the left was a gliding swing, a couch set in a stand that allowed it to swing back and forth without being hung from above. A giant green-painted iron frog squatted next to the swing, waiting for me to ride him. Grandpa's Keystone springwound 8 mm movie camera and his binoculars hung from a hat rack that stood on the floor just to the left of the wide door into the living room. A table at the far left end of the room held recent magazines—*National Geographic, Time, Reader's Digest, Life Magazine, Coronet, Saturday Evening Post*.

The house was warm, heated by a giant old oil furnace in the basement; from its enormous plenum heat rose through a large square grate in the floor into the living room. The kitchen, dining room, and bathroom got their heat through the open doors to the living room; hot air rose from the grate through registers in the living room ceiling to heat the two bedrooms upstairs. It was a house built for summer, but with enough heat to make it comfortable in the cool—and sometimes below freezing—late springs and early autumns.

The living room—an open, airy rectangular room with knotty pine walls and a large fireplace made of big round stones from the beach—was huge compared to the tiny parlor in Butte. Under the

PART ONE

high window at the back that looked out over the orchard was a sofa covered with a bristly dark blue fabric and beside it on the floor towered a large console Philco radio half again as tall as I was. Beside the fireplace was a chair with bamboo arms and a back that could be adjusted to different positions but never was, and beside it on a wooden stand was a brass ashtray in the form of a stork standing on one leg who I liked very much, whose bill accepted ashes and whose head could be tipped up to empty the ashes into its belly. The living room floor was wood, with an oval rag rug in front of the hearth. Behind the bamboo chair was a corner table with a large vase, empty now, but over the next few weeks full of lilacs and then irises and peonies. The vase was a source of much suffering for Grandpa, who cut the flowers and brought them in for Grandma all the while complaining that they made his hay fever worse, although he never stopped bringing her flowers.

To the left a door led into the kitchen, bigger than any kitchen I could remember, the first place I would look when I was searching for Grandma, who seemed to spend nearly all of her time there. The kitchen had white walls and white cabinets and a wonderful sliding window that allowed food to be passed from the kitchen to the front porch and that gave Grandma a view of the lake and the benefit of the lake breeze through the front porch windows.

On this night the kitchen was full of the smell of cinnamon and baked bread. I jumped up and down with excitement and Grandma, recognizing that I had discovered her surprise, reached into a low cupboard and removed an enormous black enameled soup pot. She took off the lid and tipped it so that I could see the three dozen cinnamon rolls nestled there, arranged in layers separated by waxed paper, the tops bristling with black raisins baked to a golden brown, the bottoms sticky with brown sugar and butter caramel.

"Can I have one now?" I was hopping up and down with excitement.

"After dinner."

"Oooh . . ." I made my most appealing, coaxing face, but there was no arguing with Grandma about saving my appetite for dinner.

Grandma took me upstairs to put my suitcase in my room to unpack later. The front bedroom was saved for guests and used by Grandpa and Grandma in the early spring and late autumn when it was too cool to sleep on the front porch. The back bedroom was always mine when I was at the lake. It had two identical small beds, low, painted white, one on each side of the doorway that led into the front bedroom. I took the bed next to the hallway. Over each bed there was an elaborate white-and-gold framed print of forest glades with gardens, packed with cherubs and seraphim and goddesses floating through the air in gauzy, fluttering pastel gowns. Perhaps the goddesses were saints, but there were no halos, nor were there any grownup men. A few had wings, but the others had no visible means of flying. They looked like plump, sleepy, normal people with curly blonde hair and no purpose other than to evoke a sense of contentment. I had no idea why they were floating or where a garden like that might exist. I never grew fond of the pictures and tried never to look at them. The beds had flowers stenciled on them, and I did not like those either. Now I imagine that the beds and pictures and chests of drawers in the rooms had once belonged to Mom and my aunt Nonie when they were children in Glasgow.

In spite of the pictures and furniture, I loved this bedroom: it was very big; I had it to myself; and it had large windows that opened out onto the hillside leading up to the orchard through which cool evening breezes came down from the mountains after hot summer days. There were two doors and abundant light and a closet big enough to hold a lot of shoes and boxes, and two chests of drawers full of interesting things that Grandma stored there, that in secret I rifled through from time to time, looking for treasures but finding only old clothes and strange smells.

PART ONE

After dinner I got the cinnamon roll and a glass of milk. I felt totally cared for. Grandma was a wonderful cook; she never served me too much and she avoided foods that I didn't like to eat. By eight I was tucked in and asleep, two hours before nightfall.

CHAPTER

SEVEN

BUTTE

I WAS AT Flathead Lake for three and a half months with my grandparents, away from Mom, away from Sammie, Rollie, and Dad, away from my home on McLeod Avenue. There were weeks when I was sad and teary: there were no other children to play with and Grandpa and Grandma had no experience or skills for playing with a little boy or keeping him entertained. I barely could read, so books were not interesting to me. Most of the time I played alone in the rock gardens or the orchard with the few toys I had, or with the sticks and rocks that I collected on the beach. Finally, at the end of August, Mom took a short vacation and joined us. We took walks and played on the beach. She also read to me. That was when I met Peter Rabbit and Farmer Brown. My Grandpa was a gardener and my sympathies were entirely with Farmer Brown. We returned to Butte together, me talking the entire way, showing Mom what I saw out the window, while she feigned interest and kept nodding off to sleep.

PART ONE

Our apartment in Butte was snug. During the Depression, the owner of the house, Conrad Benson, converted the front rooms of the two-story Victorian house into a small apartment to make a little extra cash when his work as a carpenter fell off. They lived in the back half of the first floor—a small living room, a dining room, and a kitchen—and in four bedrooms on the second floor.

Before the conversion our tiny apartment must originally have been the house's front parlor. Our living room had only enough space for a couch that served as my bed; a towering brown enameled gas heater; two small end tables and two worn upholstered chairs. The bedroom held Mom's double bed, a bureau, and a bedside table. There was not much room for anything else. Already very small, the kitchen was further crowded by a tiny table with two chairs.

With a small window in the kitchen and a bigger one in the bedroom, we had a total of four, enough that the apartment, with its faded beige wallpaper, did not seem dark. One living room window looked out on Galena Street over a tiny grassless front yard no more than four feet deep, separated from the sidewalk by an iron fence. On the side a smaller window looked out on a porch that ran from the front of the house the full depth of the parlor, with a door straight ahead into the Benson's, and a door on the right leading directly into our apartment.

Butte was carved out of a mountain and few streets were level. A long railing on the porch prevented a fall from the porch, which was only a few feet above the sidewalk in front, but quickly became six or eight feet as the sidewalk descended the steep hill beside the house—steep enough that at the back of the house the door to Conrad Benson's basement carpentry shop was at ground level.

Across a tiny, barren backyard was a garage where Conrad kept his truck and ladders and piles of wood. Above the garage was a small apartment rented by the Gentrys, a young couple with a new baby who I visited often.

The Bensons were a happy family that quickly adopted Mom and me. Traffic flowed between our apartment and their house easily but infrequently. Their daughter Sondra was a few years older than I and became a babysitter without the formality of times on a calendar or the exchange of money. I came home after school several hours before Mom did and she knew that someone was always home next door if I needed something. Although I was home alone without a parent, technically I was not a latchkey kid because we never locked our front door.

Conrad Benson—a blue-eyed Swede with a prominent accent—was busy as a carpenter by the time we arrived in Butte; even during the Depression, as a mining town Butte had lost fewer jobs than most of the rest of Montana. The War had made Butte, with its rich veins of copper, gold, lead, and silver, a vital source of war supplies and the city was bustling with prosperous businesses. In the post-war boom, houses were going up and Conrad had plenty to do: a house took two years for one man to build. Conrad did all of his own cabinet and finish work and made the doors and windows. Very little was pre-cut to standard sizes, and every house was a little different than any other. His basement was a wonderful place for a little boy. I loved to shuffle around in the sweet-smelling sawdust—did anyone work in a better-smelling world than a carpenter, unless maybe it was a baker or a candy maker? Conrad made me my first set of wooden blocks and every once in a while when I was hanging around in the shop, if he was not too preoccupied with what he was working on, he would let me saw up scrap wood or hammer nails into boards to make fantastical shapes that I imagined to be boats and fighter planes and houses.

The day after we returned to Butte I began grade school at the McKinley School, just a few blocks from our apartment. Mom had to be at work at eight, so our landlord's daughter walked me to school and took me to my classroom.

McKinley was big: there were no junior high schools in Montana until decades later, so McKinley had children ranging in age from six to fourteen, with the first and second graders on the first floor, and upper classes above, with the seventh and eighth graders on the fourth floor. I remember almost nothing about school except the punishment meted out for my various infractions: cleaning blackboards and erasers after school if I talked when I was not supposed to; being made to sit in the corner after I was caught in the cloakroom outside my second grade class being kissed by a girl named Joan; being forced to sit on a stool in front of the whole class for a full hour side by side with Gail Golubin when we were caught chewing gum, with the offending gum stuck to our noses. Other than chewing gum in school, Gail and I had nothing in common; the prosperous Golubin family owned a flower shop that still is in business in Butte.

Mom and I struggled every day over whether I was or was not going to eat what was put in front of me. As a little boy I was a finicky eater and had a tiny appetite, surprising to anyone who knew me later. The game I played was to move whatever I did not want around my plate in such a way as to fool Mom into believing that I had tried it (usually not true) and that I had made a significant dent in it (never true). Long after she had finished eating I would still be sitting at the table, chin on hand, hand propped on elbow, rearranging the lettuce and canned peas and mashed potatoes into new landscapes in which the items which I hated most but which were least negotiable to Mom (vegetables and meat, for example) were hidden under what she considered optional (mashed potatoes) until in exasperation she would finally scrape the whole mess into the garbage, too late to discover the subterfuge or to care. The truth is, I doubt that she was fooled; after an hour of watching me play with my food, more likely she was tired and wanted to get the dishes washed. Food also walked out of the kitchen to a storm sewer in front of the house in my pockets, in the cuffs of my pants, in my armpit, stuffed into my underpants. Until she stopped the practice, in the morning I would sometimes take a bowl of Kix, a particularly offending cereal that she insisted was healthy, into the bathroom with me ("it's efficient, Mom"), close the door, and dump the cereal in the toilet: she would tolerate my reading while sitting on the toilet as a useful combination, but eating while sitting on the toilet and reading stretched the bounds of what she thought it was normal for a small boy to do, especially one who seemed fated to never weigh more than 50 pounds. The subterfuge ended abruptly one morning when my incomplete flush left a few dozen insoluble, spiny Kix globes spitefully bobbing on the surface. This was disgusting enough that she stopped buying Kix. For years I shuddered when I walked by a Kix display in grocery stores.

She despaired that I would ever begin to grow. When I was about seven, I was awakened by three flashlights shining on my face a few hours after I had been put to bed. My Mom and two of her friends were looking to see if worms were crawling out of my face because one of them had read in the *Readers Digest* that worms could keep a little boy stunted and they could be discovered out for a stroll at night by examining the child with a flashlight. No worms were found. The thought horrified me.

She and her friends agreed that I was "high strung," which seemed to satisfy them as a definitive explanation for all of my deficiencies and peculiarities.

There was no television in Montana in those days, and if there had been, we would have not had the money to buy a television set. But we did own a radio and radio shows were our perpetual companions during meals.

PART ONE

We listened to *The Arthur Godfrey Show* during breakfast, and we listened to *Ozzie and Harriet*, *The Jack Benny Show*, *The Life of Riley*, and *The Great Gildersleeve* during dinner. Probably *Life with Luigi* was my favorite. The show painted the daily life of an Italian immigrant in Chicago through letters back home to his mother captured in scenes of his life as an immigrant bachelor learning to speak and write English and stumbling through American culture, targeted as a potential suitor for a series of unappealing daughters.

Although I was pokey and fussy, I remember these meals as being a warm and pleasant time together with Mom, her long day completed, my long afternoon of waiting for her to come home over. The radio substituted for family dinner-table conversation—most of the programs were about families, and probably my sense of what a normal family was came more from these radio programs than from knowing other families, or having one of my own. Divorce was never mentioned.

Our few memorable meals during the Butte years were eaten in restaurants. Because Butte was a blue-collar city with a rich collection of ethnicities among its miners and smelter workers, there were Welsh, Cornish, Italian, Irish, and Chinese cafes. On Mom's tiny salary we couldn't afford to go out to eat often, but occasionally she went out with friends to eat ravioli and chicken livers at Lydia's café, leaving me home because she had no luck in getting me to eat any of those strange foods. Occasionally she would bring home half of a Cornish pasty and stick it in my lunch bag.

A few times a year we would go out. My favorite meal out was the hot dogs at the Donald Duck Inn across from the bus station. Once a year we went to an ice cream parlor called Gamer's where I had an ice cream sundae, vanilla with fudge sauce, which I spent an hour eating, savoring one spoonful at a time, while Mom patiently waited. That place is still there, white-painted gingerbread trim, velvet-curtained booths where young couples could smooch in private, and square tables with twisted ironwork chairs exactly as they always were.

The Montana Cafe was thrilling, less because of their menu than its proximity to one of the biggest mines on Butte Hill. If we got there at 4 pm I could see the miners coming up in a cage-like elevator from a mile below and the next shift descending in the same cage, whistles blowing to indicate the end of the shift and bells clanging to warn everyone that the lift was starting down.

All of Mom's friends said that the best meal in town was served at the Rocky Mountain Cafe on the far edge of Butte Hill in Meaderville. Slot machines were legal at the Rocky Mountain Cafe and competed for attention with the thick grilled steaks and with the breadsticks with which small boys were expected to entertain themselves while the adults drank highballs and laughed while waiting for dinner. I never saw wine with a meal in Montana until I left for college, and beer was most often a picnic and outdoor sports drink. Mom rationed the breadsticks so that I would not fill up on them before the first course arrived. No matter what was ordered, every table got a huge antipasti platter of fresh green spring onions and radishes that we dosed with salt, slices of salami, white and yellow American cheese, sweet green peppers, and green beans pickled in vinegar, which I found disgusting—and still do. There were also three kinds of olives that made me gag and even throw up, to Mom's great annoyance.

By the time the steaks arrived I had filled up, exasperating Mom, not because she was out the money—her friends always paid for these dinners—but because she regarded steak as both a luxury and as the mother lode of nutrition that might add a few grams of muscle to my skinny arms and legs. She said that I looked like a war orphan. I wasn't sure what was special about being a war orphan, but I knew that being an orphan was about the lowest rank a child could descend to, although perhaps being called a ragamuffin was even worse. I got

PART ONE

a kids' steak, with a side of baked potato filled with butter and some kind of green vegetable that left no memory at all. I sat pressed into a corner of the booth, boosted up on a box, legs dangling way short of the floor, my head supported on my left hand, my fork pushing around the bites of steak that Mom sawed off, wiping them in the congealing red juices so that the increasingly inattentive adults would think I was actually eating. After that there was a huge bowl of salad, more drinks, and my deeply anticipated dessert—always vanilla ice cream with chocolate syrup streaming down its sides, a bright red cherry on top, and a long spoon so that I could get out the last few milliliters of melted ice cream and chocolate sauce from the bottom of the pressed glass tulip sundae dish. Sticking my tongue into the dish was forbidden, but by this time no one was paying any attention to me, or noticing the small pile of vegetables I had dumped on the floor beneath the table, about which I felt temporarily guilty because Mom always talked about the starving kids in Europe who didn't have enough food. I told her that I would be glad to send them my food, an offer she declined by changing the subject.

At some point long after I had passed out in the corner of the booth I was carried from the restaurant to a car and driven home to Galena Street and would awaken the next morning on the sofa in the bright light of the living room without remembering how I got there.

The evening after dinners at the Rocky Mountain Cafe we ate tamale pie or hash made from the leftover steak. There were no bread sticks and almost no tulip dishes with ice cream and chocolate sauce in my life at any other times. The steak we could afford was cube steak and round steak, made tender by hammering with a corrugated wooden meat mallet, and then braised. Tenderizing tough steak was my job—Mom thought it would build up my biceps. I loved the noise and violence.

I was carted along whenever Mom got an invitation to go out to a restaurant or to a friend's party, often the only child, knee high in a room full of adults. If I stayed low enough I could keep my face beneath the stinking, eye-stinging fumes that drifted up from the Chesterfields and Camels and Lucky Strikes: everyone smoked, everyone drank, everyone was glad to see me and then promptly forgot me. By the end of the first grade I brought along a supply of books and found some deserted corner where I could read. There might be a spot in the kitchen where the host had set out a little food for me. Sooner or later Arnold Beatty would take out his accordion and everyone would start singing the songs they had sung in the thirties and through the war years. As the evening crept toward midnight the laughing and smoking and drinking would intensify. Around eight I would be put down to sleep in the grown-up's bedroom among the perfumed fur coats and purses and fedoras and top coats and ladies' hats topped with bird remnants. Sometime after midnight Mom and I would be taken home; I was an easy bundle for one of the men to carry out to the back seat of whatever car was to serve as our taxi.

These were among the few times I saw Mom happy and relaxed. She was a drinker, but a slow drinker. She said she could nurse a drink for two hours. So probably it wasn't just the alcohol at work, but the singing and the gaiety of her friends that made her vivacious and warm. Her friends laughed a lot, sometimes glancing at me in a way that made me pretty sure they had told a joke I was not meant to understand. She was a great singer and seemed to know the words to any song anyone suggested. She was slender, about five-feet four, with pure black hair and eyebrows, brown eyes, and an inviting smile. She was also vain: she wore glasses, but always took them off for pictures; she frequently excused herself to freshen her makeup; she used perfume liberally, which I hated, and a lot of what she called "costume jewelry", which I also hated.

She managed on a small budget to always look nicer than any other woman at a party.

I made few friends during our three years in Butte. Because there were no yards in our blue-collar neighborhood of crowded wood frame houses and two-story brick row apartments, I never played outside. There were no parks nearby, and the streets in this neighborhood surrounded by ravines channeling yellow and blue and red mining run-off were too dangerous for street games with other kids. Every few hours day and night we could feel the dull shock of an explosive charge being set off to extend a tunnel a mile below us. Every year kids found the blasting caps that were used to fire the dynamite lying in the street and blew off their hands or faces. In Butte we were not told to avoid red berries—there were none—but rather not to ever touch anything red and cylindrical.

Even walking the three blocks home from school was dangerous. One afternoon near the beginning of the second grade I walked on my usual route east on Park Street and then down the steep hill a block to our house. As I got to the corner across the street, two boys jumped out from behind a brick wall and blocked my way. They were a lot bigger than I was. I recognized them. I knew that they lived a block away and they had sometimes yelled names at me. Now they told me that they wouldn't let me go home. One of them shoved me backwards, knocked me down, and sat on my chest beating me with his fists. The other kicked the bag that I was carrying into the street. The best I could do to protect myself was to cover my face and flail with my legs to try to get free. After a minute of this the one sitting on me got up and threw dirt on my face and they walked away. Shaken and sobbing, I limped home, let myself into the apartment, and waited for Mom to come home. Every few minutes I would start sobbing. When Mom got home and saw what I mess I was she put me into the bath tub and, sitting on the toilet seat next to me, tried to calm me down by telling me why sometimes boys picked fights and that I would be alright in a day or two.

After that, every week or two I was jumped by these guys, whose names I learned were Brian O'Boyle and Tommy Sullivan. They attended St. Anne's Catholic grade school and their main mission in life seemed to be figuring out which of my several routes home I had chosen as my best chance to avoid being beaten up by them. They guessed right about once a month and I came home punched and scraped and bruised. Once the two showed up with one of their little brothers, and they stood back, giving him instructions on how to knock me down and pound his fists into my chest and face. The kid was no bigger than I was, but he was already in training to carry on his brother and friend's work. Mom walked across the street to talk to their parents. Nothing changed. She didn't say anything about fighting back. Conrad Benson told me that I was so little that there was probably no way I was going to win a fight with them and that I should learn to run fast and change my route home every day. Every day I walked home without encountering them my terror increased, as I knew that the time was running out until they beat me up again.

Years later I heard that there were similar problems between the older boys in Butte High School and Butte Central Catholic High School and I formed the fixed belief that the Catholic Schools let out their students fifteen minutes earlier than the public schools so that the boys could take up street and alley positions to jump the Protestant boys.

After school I was alone for two hours until Mom walked back from downtown. Some of the time I listened to the afternoon radio programs aimed at kids—*The Lone Ranger, The Green Hornet, Sergeant Preston of the Yukon,* and *Sleepy Joe's Uncle Remus Stories.* Mom knew I was safe indoors. Although the door into the Benson's house was always open, I rarely left our apartment unless Sandra was desperate to have someone to play with and beguiled me into playing house or

PART ONE

school. But she was bossy: she took all the major roles and I always was the naughty little boy or the bad student. And she cheated, changing the rules to her advantage. After she put me in jail for refusing an order to wrap a towel around my crotch like a diaper and cry like a baby I avoided her.

In the meager space between the main house and the garage over which the Gentrys lived, there was a scruffy lilac bush. Migratory birds heading north returned to Butte late—the town is a mile high and winter hangs on there until April, with snow coming as late as June, as it does in much of Montana. The last spring I was there—the year in which I broke my arm falling while trying to walk the Benson's front porch railing eight feet above the sidewalk—a neighborhood boy came down that hill with a Daisy Red Ryder BB gun and shot at a robin perched in the lilac. There were not a lot of places for birds to rest in Butte or lawns on which they could troll for worms. I saw the boy go by and envied him for having a BB gun, but I didn't go out to watch what he was up to. A few minutes later Ann Gentry came to our apartment and took me to the back yard to see the bird. She was very upset: the robin was alive, shuddering, its feathers puffed up, both of its eyes shot out, making a wobbly last stand on the meager grass. She was horrified and wanted me to see it and told me never, never to do that. It was my first experience of seeing the deliberate and pointless torture of an animal. I stood deathwatch, the bird cupped in my hands, but it soon died. Ann and I hacked a little trough in the harsh, unwelcoming earth behind the Benson's house and buried it. Laying out the robin—still warm but now unnaturally limp—sent shivers up my spine. I put it down tenderly and with my shaking fingers made a little heap of dirt on top of it. That blinding, the robin's suffering and its death, remain as vivid now as they were in 1950. I was eight.

Once I learned to read I exhausted my teacher's supply of take-home books. She told me that even first graders could take books home from the Butte Public Library. One afternoon Mom came home early and we walked back down town to the library where, with some ceremony, I was entered into the library's register. I don't think a lot of seven year olds frequented the library so the staff was very cordial and showed me the shelves of books for beginners. I immediately chose one called *Reading Orally*. I was devoted to a radio program that featured the bandleader Fred Waring who frequently read stories about a redheaded boy named Little Orley who was in constant trouble but was always irresistible to his parents, teachers, and friends in spite of it. I loved the stories and I was excited that it was the first book I took home, expecting to be entertained by more Little Orley stories. Unfortunately the book was nothing more than a collection of simple paragraphs for children to practice reading out loud. I was very disappointed. After that the librarian helped me pick out books until I had cleaned out the beginner's section and moved on to the children's section. I didn't mind that the librarians always made a fuss over me when I showed up to get more books.

As the smallest and most defenseless kid around, I made every trip uptown in a state of high anxiety until I had cleared the boundaries of our neighborhood and entered the safety of the business district where I trusted that adults would keep anything bad from happening to me. By the age of seven I was negotiating Butte's tough precincts with one eye on the concealing shrubbery and the other on the world of goods displayed in the shop windows, beyond our finances but not beyond my dreams. I spent hours prowling the aisles of the giant Woolworth's Five and Dime Store scheming about finding enough pennies and nickels, maybe even gold nuggets, to buy a

PART ONE

cap pistol or a lizard or eight jumbo gum drops at one cent each, in all the colors of the rainbow plus black.

Mom sometimes brought home *Holiday Magazine* that friends gave her. In the spring of my second-grade year, on long, boring, chilly Saturday afternoons, I cut out coupons from ads suggesting that I write immediately to receive the exciting details of a vacation in Jamaica or a safari in Kenya. I could not respond to the ones that required me to enclose a dime, but some were free and I wrote letters using Mom's envelopes and stamps. Impressive numbers of glossy brochures poured in. One Saturday in March I also came across an invitation to sell seeds. It was a ship, sell, and repay proposition: without my sending them any money they would send me by the next mail the "Anyone Can Have a Garden" kit: 30 packets of seeds that I could sell for fifteen cents each. When I had sold the seeds I would send them three dollars and clear a hefty profit of a buck-fifty. This was irresistible: the entry level repeating cap pistol with a roll of 50 caps cost only one dollar and sixty-nine cents. The seeds came about the first of April; I hid them under the couch before Mom got home. The next afternoon I headed out to peddle brightly colored paper packets of marigolds and radishes and parsley and lettuce and beets and carrots and zinnias. The houses surrounding ours on Galena were small bungalows or brick row houses of three apartments, a basement apartment a half flight down and two more above. At three in the afternoon no one seemed to be at home to hear my pitch—"do you want some seeds??"—although from time to time I thought I saw the flutter of a lace curtain where perhaps someone pushed it slightly aside to see what I was up to.

I walked this route every afternoon for two weeks, always keeping an eye out for Brian O'Boyle and Tommy Sullivan. I didn't sell a single packet. I gave it up and hid the seeds under the couch. A few weeks later I was confronted by Mom who had a letter from the seed company demanding their three dollars. She had no idea what I had been up to and she was furious when I showed her my stash of unsold seeds under the couch. She told me I needed to sell the seeds, and I told her that I had been trying for two weeks. She offered some of the seeds to friends and a few people at work, but growing vegetables and flowers in Butte where the growing season only lasted two months was practically impossible, and beyond that, almost no one had a yard in which to make a garden. In the end she had to buy all the seeds and send in her hard-earned three dollars. In Butte Montana in 1949 three dollars bought sixty candy bars, twenty slices of pie, or fifteen hamburgers. Or one and a half cap pistols with enough change to buy ten rolls of caps.

I eventually got the cap pistol after Mom began to date a man named Mr. Green, from my perspective the most promising of a luckless succession of suitors with whom Mom and I double dated over the next ten years. Mr. Green had three striking attributes: Mr. Green wore a gray, pin-striped suit to work every day; Mr. Green walked with a limp in spite of an amazing shoe that added at least six inches to his right leg; and Mr. Green was no less than the manager of Woolworths' Five and Dime and had spotted me in orbit around the cap pistol I so desperately wanted. By then I knew Mr. Green and I made sure that I circled around the cap gun four or five times when he could see me. Mr. Green got at least a half hour alone in our front room with Mom the night he gave me the cap pistol and turned me loose on my front porch to noisily pick off black-hatted desperadoes and vicious Irish bullies who died agonizing deaths in the dusty gutters of Galena Street in the wild and wicked mining city of Butte, Montana, circa 1949.

I got the gumdrops too, but a lizard was beyond even Mr. Green's powers. A Woolworth's turtle named Myrtle did make the trip in his pocket to our bathroom one Sunday. Myrtle had a short life and an inglorious death when Mom—she says by accident—flushed him (or her) down the toilet when cleaning the nifty plastic bowl

PART ONE

that had a spiral ramp that allowed him to have a drying cycle when he needed it.

When I started begging Mom to let me have one of the chicks that appeared in Woolworths a few weeks before Easter, Mr. Green was sternly warned about any further border crossings of immigrant animals into the sanctuary of our tiny apartment. Desperate for an Easter chick—rabbits were as much out of the question with Mom as they were for Grandma, who regarded them as dinner and not pets—I decided to create my own chicks. Every few days I stole an egg from the icebox and hid it in a nest made of a winter scarf under the front-room space heater, which I took to be a pretty good incubator. After a few weeks the eggs had made no progress toward becoming the cuddly, chirping, fuzzy yellow chicks that I had coveted at Woolworth's; Easter passed, and I forgot about the eggs. A few months later, just before I left for Flathead for the summer, Mom became aware of a terrible rotten smell in the front room after she had swept the vacuum's corner-cleaning nozzle under the heater. When interrogated, I put on my confused but innocent look and told her that I knew nothing about rotting eggs or bad smells and certainly I had nothing to do with it. She was surprisingly skeptical about my speculation that perhaps a fecund chicken had wandered into the house, laid a clutch of eggs in a warm place, and wandered out again, although that seemed plausible enough that I thought she might buy it.

The alley cat that I coaxed into our living room and then imprisoned for three days in a box holding Mom's skunk-fur coat in the top of the closet was harder to explain away. I could not tell who was more frantic, Mom or the cat, when she discovered and opened the vibrating, meowing box. The cat shot off the shelf over Mom's head and hit all four walls of the front room, knocking over every table lamp on its way to an open window. Mom flatly rejected my argument that the skunk coat must have smelled worse before the boxed cat peed on it for three days.

Butte still had a few streetcar lines in the late 1940's. In cities all over western America where space on the edges of towns was plentiful and cheap, amusement parks had been built for the summer entertainment of families. People with wealth could take trains or private cars to resort hot springs or bigger cities where the attractions were more numerous, but a consistent stage in the development of a smaller town was creating places where people of more ordinary means could picnic and ride a roller coaster or Ferris wheel or merry-go-round. In Butte that place was Columbia Gardens, and because many families did not have cars during the depression and the war when money was scarce and gas was rationed, the street car lines could get them from their neighborhoods to the park in the foothills of the mountains east of Butte.

The park had been built by William Andrews Clark, one of the legendary "Copper Kings" who became extraordinarily wealthy extracting the minerals of what was dubbed the "Richest Hill on Earth". Clark gave the city the park and refused to charge admissions, as a way of making his workers feel that his mining company was interested in their welfare and their city.

Free was a price Mom could pay, and at least once a year at the end of the summer we spent a half-day there. Mom mostly skipped the rides but stood by while I worked my way through the long lines of kids waiting for the roller coaster and carrousel with its brightly painted ponies and piping band organ. I liked the Ferris wheel least—too tame—and would ride the roller coaster two or three times, each cycle taking 15 or 20 minutes of standing in line. I was barely big enough to meet the seat requirement so that the lap bar would actually keep me from falling out.

Columbia Gardens was beautifully planted with summer annuals in large patterns like flags and animals and children, with rolling green lawns between the rides and flowerbeds. Mom loved gardens and, finding few in Butte, we strolled for an hour before we left, bending down to sniff the flowers. Her favorites were the roses.

My last trip to Columbia Gardens was sad, and yet I think of it more frequently than the many happy trips to the Gardens. Friends of Mom who had no children knew a family that was giving a birthday party for their son at the restaurant on the grounds of the Gardens. They wangled an invitation for me, but we arrived late because Mom and her friends stopped several times on the drive to have drinks. We entered the restaurant and one of the waiters took me to the room where the birthday party was, but the food had been consumed and everyone was finishing their cake and ice cream. All the tables were filled and I was put in a side room and given cake and ice cream and silently ate it by myself. When I finished the other children were outside, set up in some kind of game. I sat on the porch and watched. No one noticed me. I went looking for Mom, but she was in the bar with her friends and I was told I couldn't go in. After another hour or so Mom found me and we went home. That was the only birthday party I had ever been to. I was not invited to another for five years.

In the third grade Mom got me into a Cub Scout pack. Cub Scouts were the only after-school activity that Mom felt was safe for me to attend. The pack met at school and I finished about when she would be walking home from downtown, so she could swing by the school and walk home with me. It was just a small handful of boys and a rotating cast of mothers who brought in games to play or led us in some kind of craft activity. My only strong memory was going to the annual Cub Scout banquet in the Miner's Union meeting hall in the downtown business district. Mom took me and when we got there discovered a room full of boys from many different Cub Scout packs running around, their fathers standing in small clumps talking with each other. I think that Mom either had not understood that this was a father-son banquet, or she had decided that I shouldn't be left out and simply braved showing up. In any case we stood off to one side while the boys and their fathers lined up at a table to fill their plates. We went through the line last when there wasn't much food left. The two of us sat at the end of a table, ate quickly and skipped out as soon as we were done. After that I drifted away from the pack.

A few times Mom took me walking along the tracks of the Butte-Anaconda rail line that was used to haul ore from Butte to the smelter in Anaconda. The tracks were just a few blocks up Galena from our apartment, on the edge of the campus of the School of Mines. We walked for a few hours in the dry heat of late summer, the flats along Silver Bow creek winding below us. There were strange volcanic rock formations here, the ancient remains of the last eruptions of Mount Butte. The attraction for me was the thousands of glittering rocks streaked with "fools' gold," iron pyrites. It was gorgeous to look at and fun to pretend that it was gold and that we would have endless wealth just for the work of picking up a few rocks. At a large flat rock where we could dangle our feet and look at the distant mountains Mom would open a paper bag of crispy, salty fried chicken that we ate silently, inhaling the smells of sage and creosote bushes and licking our fingers clean. It was always just the two of us—we had no friends with children my age. Those few walks are the happiest times I remember in Butte.

When I was sick Mom had no choice but to leave me at home, with Gladys Benson and Mrs. Carter next door. She would set me up in her big bed for the day and I listened to the radio and played and read.

PART ONE

In February of the third grade I was home for four or five days with the mumps. The rule for mumps was that boys must be keep inactive, since if we exercised we might get mumps in our testicles and never be able to have children. Of course I didn't know the word testicles—those body parts were not mentioned, ever. So I was just told I might not be able to have children, which didn't seem like a big deal to me at the age of eight.

On the third day, bored, I lay on my stomach and hung over the edge of Mom's bed. Beneath it, hidden by her white bedspread, was a large, unopened box in a bed of fluffy dust bunnies. I got out of bed and tugged it into sight. It was addressed to me and had been sent before Christmas by Dad, so I cut the tape sealing it with the tip of a pair of scissors and found inside a complete American Flyer train set. By the time Mom came home I had emptied the box, read the instructions, assembled the sixteen sections of straight tracks and eight sections of curved tracks that formed an oval in the living room that took up the entire space between my sleeping couch and the chairs shoved against the windows. I had linked the transformer to the tracks with the wires included, plugged it in, and run the engine, box car, gondola car, and caboose for an hour when Mom walked in and saw my possibly sterile body hunched over the transformer intently watching the forbidden train go around and around in the middle of the living room

She was annoyed. It was a Christmas present from Dad and she didn't want me to have it. She had told me he hadn't sent a present this year. She could never have afforded a train set, an expensive gift that she knew I would have been grateful for. And she was angry that I had taken it out of the box and put it together by myself, angry that I had caught her in a lie and an act of selfishness.

She made me take the tracks apart and we packed the beautiful engine and cars back in the box. She hid it away for another four years.

When I was a teenager I worried about my testicles when they had become more apparent to me, but in time I forgot about not being able to have babies. Maybe she had made up the story about sterility so that I wouldn't get out of her bed and find the train hidden beneath it.

Mom had found the refuge she needed in Butte among friends whom she had first met in Glasgow or as a college student in Missoula. Because they had moved to Butte years before in search of a better life in Butte's booming, war-driven economy, they had not been a part of her post-college married life with Dad and she was free to be seen with them in public: in a free-wheeling Butte that knew a little something about fallen women, she was able to go to work at the Ford dealership without feeling that everyone was judging her as a divorced woman who had failed to keep her man.

As a self-absorbed six and seven and eight year old, I accepted our life and didn't think about the grief and humiliation she must have experienced during those years. I never learned what demons might have kept her awake during the three Butte years, after her marriage and dreams fell apart and she had to learn to make a life for herself and for me on her own. She never got over her anger that Dad had divorced her to marry the daughter of the president of the bank in which he worked as a cashier, that he left her on her own to earn a living and to raise a son and to play out her solitary hand as Dad became quietly prosperous.

Sammie had another theory: that Mom was deeply in love with Dad and crushed when he abandoned her. Sammie thought that she had never gotten over him.

By the time I finished the third grade she must have healed enough to feel that she could return to Missoula. Her explanations in later years about why we went back had to do with me, not with her: she was afraid that I would be killed in Butte, or at the very least that I would grow up having never played happily in streets and yards,

PART ONE

having never been free of the fear of being beaten up. Later she told me that she wanted more space and privacy than our little apartment with the Bensons allowed, and that she missed the gardens and yards and maple-tree-lined streets of Missoula, the "Garden City," as it called itself.

Perhaps she had a score to settle, but she never told me.

40th Anniversary of Edwin & Hannah Noel, Clarence MO, 1907. My grandfather Bert Noel back row far right; my grandmother Carrie Noel in second row far right; my uncle Lloyd is in the front row second from right

Dad around 1937

Mom and Dad with his family. My grandfather and grandmother Noel are on the left; next to Mom are my Aunt Ruth and Uncle Lloyd. Around 1937

Mom camping with Grandpa and Grandma Orvis around 1920. Grandpa is obviously doing well with his Glasgow store

Mom seated, with her sister Nonie and Grandpa and Grandma Orvis. Late 1920's

Grandpa and Grandma with Mom; on the right Nonie with Grandma's mother, father and sister. Couple on the left unknown

The house on Mcleod Avenue where I lived until 1947

Sammie and me, about 1942

Mom with me about 1943

Dad with Sammie and me, about 1943

Sammie and me off on another tricycle adventure

Mom with Sammie and me at Flathead Lake, Grandma looking on

Grandpa and Grandma at Flathead Lake, about 1947

The Flathead Lake house and Grandpa's rock garden

Sammie and me on Galena Street Butte, about 1949

PART TWO

CHAPTER

EIGHT

STARTING OVER

IN THE SPRING of 1950, at the end of the third grade, I left Butte to spend the summer at Flathead Lake. When summer was done, Grandpa and Grandma flagged down the bus to Polson in front of their house. I changed in Polson for the Missoula bus that meandered through the lower Flathead Valley, framed by the snowless, jagged Mission Mountains to the east and the lower green-forested mountains to the west, the flat valley gorgeous in the summer, ripe with golden wheat, yellow alfalfa and glowing brown hay and sprinkled with the small pot-hole lakes left behind when the glaciers melted 10,000 years ago. I sat in the front on the right where I could see through the windshield and the side window, hoping to spot ducks startled into flight from the ponds, ponies or deer—equally wild—grazing near the road, or logging trucks heavy with huge tree trunks from virgin forests lumbering by on their way to the mills in Missoula.

PART TWO

Mom met me at the bus station. She didn't own a car during the years I was growing up in Missoula, so one of the mechanics at the Chevrolet dealership where she had started to work during the summer drove us. The trip from downtown Missoula to our new home took five minutes. I was excited to be living in a real house—although it was only the basement of a real house. From what Mom had described, I was sure that we had taken a step up from Butte.

Our house was a low white stucco box with red roof tiles that was called "Spanish Style," appropriate for Tucson or Santa Fe. In Missoula its flat roof was at risk of collapsing with heavy snows or turning into a lake during a chinook thaw because the drainage ports were frozen closed. The house was built in the pre-depression 1920's when Missoula had overrun the original city plan that included grassy strips between the sidewalks and streets planted with stately maples and elms. My first home on McLeod Avenue was on one of those gracious streets near the University of Montana, but our new place was outside of the University District and the houses were distinctly less attractive, many looking like they had been built from kits—assembled elsewhere then taken apart and shipped by train and truck and put together quickly. Mount Avenue had sparse strips of worn-out grass and no canopies of trees. Most of the houses were small and run down and some looked like old farmhouses that had been swallowed up in Missoula's expansion. Most of our neighbors were old, rarely seen, waiting out the remainder of their lives.

We entered our apartment from a side door that connected the owner's kitchen to her garage. At the bottom of the stairs there was a laundry room that we shared with her and that also served as an atrium leading to our kitchen on the left and to the other rooms on the right. The kitchen, while again tiny, had a counter where two of us could sit side by side to eat under a basement window high above our heads that gave us a glimpse of the sky.

Next to the kitchen was a big room containing a huge furnace and a sawdust bin. Along one side there was a long, wide varnished pine table mounted on the wall that I could use as a desk for schoolwork and reading.

Off the furnace room was a good-sized living room that had French windows looking into a window well that was a perfect place to perform a (small) play or pretend that I was in a foxhole. The bottom of the window well was a good four feet below the side yard, but it gave us the illusion of having a living room window, even though our only view was grey concrete and the collected bugs and detritus that blew in off the street; if we got on our knees and looked up we could see the sooty eaves of Walter Jorgensen's house next door.

I sometimes played in that window well, although the first time I jumped in I realized that the top of the wall was barely reachable. With my puny arms I could just manage to jump up, grasp the top edge, and, using my feet, throw my leg over the edge and climb out, my heart pounding from exertion and the fear that I would not be able to get out, that no one would hear me yelling for help and that I would die there and no one would find me until I was just a pile of bones. The cowboys in the double feature matinees I watched at the Fox Theater on Saturdays were always stumbling on piles of bones in cavey places.

Connected both to the living room and to the atrium was a bedroom, large enough for both Mom's double bed and a rollaway cot that served as my bed for the next three years. This room had several windows at ceiling level from which we could view a narrow slice of the tall trees in the back yard. Having spent my Butte years at the level of adults' knees, now I was living below the level of a Cocker Spaniel's belly. I didn't mind: I pretended that I was living in a submarine.

An early mystery was why the owner's full name was Lady Lucille Bailey. Even in the fourth grade I knew that Americans didn't have names like that. She was a rather grand old woman of 48 who processed from room to room in her main-floor chambers as though she were attending a state occasion. She wore large, flowery kimonos and kept her silver-streaked golden hair swept up in various arrangements evoking an earlier but now faded glamour. When she spoke, often with flowing gestures and an upturned face, it was clear that she expected to be attended to. Her skin glowed like alabaster rubbed with cold cream—or at least what I imagined alabaster to be like. Occasionally when I was playing in the back yard she would walk around with her kimono unfastened, her face upturned to the sun and her arms spread wide like an uncensored Roman goddess, while I snuck peeks with guilty fascination; if she noticed my gawking she made no attempt to cover herself up.

It was quickly made known to me that she had allowed a small boy into her presence with great reluctance: she suspected that all small boys sooner or later tried to burn down whatever quarters they occupied. I did not fail her: within a year I had set fire to the dried-out vacant lot across the street, which she suspected, Mom denied, and I kept uncharacteristically unconfirmed. Lady Lucille was either divorced or widowed—the details on that were murky. It was said that in Sweden, where her ancestors came from, she would have been royalty, but in Missoula, Montana she was merely eccentric, which put her in the company of most of the people who befriended us.

The set-up on Mount was perfect for us. Mom could catch a bus half a block away on Higgins that took her uptown to within a few blocks of Kraabel Chevrolet. She had found a job similar to the one she had in Butte, in the service department with the mechanics, deciphering the notes they scribbled with greasy hands on cheap paper work orders and translating them into neatly written bills when customers picked up their cars.

Every neighborhood in Missoula was safe for me. Paxson grade school was only two houses away. Mrs. Bailey almost never left the house—where would royalty visit or dine in Missoula in 1950?—providing Mom with a little cover for me in the hours between the end of my school day and when she got home from work. The little basement apartment provided a place where I could invite my friend Rollie to play.

It was Rollie who taught me how to ride the bicycle I discovered on the day I moved in, a J.C. Higgins picked out from the Montgomery Wards' catalogue by Grandpa and shipped to our home in a flat cardboard box. The box stood unopened tipped against the wall in the garage waiting until Mrs. Bailey's son could unpack and assemble it for me. I was assured that I was too little and a bike was too complicated for me to put together, but I could watch Bill Bailey do it in a week or two. I had a few days before I would begin the fourth grade and I couldn't wait. The next day, as soon as Mom left, I tore the box open. There were no instructions, but I figured out how to attach the handlebars to the stem above the front wheel fork; I mounted the seat; I put the pedals on the crankshaft. On a grimy shelf I found rusty pliers to tighten the nuts. I walked and ran the eight blocks over to Rollie's house to get his help in learning how to ride it, and he pedaled us back on his bike with me sitting on the handlebars.

Rollie belonged to the point-and-shoot school of bicycle training. He instructed me to get on the bicycle and pedal while he ran alongside and steadied me by holding onto the seat. When I had developed a fair head of steam he simply let go and yelled, "keep pedaling!" This worked fairly well until I realized that I was not supported any more, lost confidence, and wobbled off down a small slope and across the neighbor's lawn, stopping only when I crashed into their birch tree. I thought the bike was ruined. None of those nuts had been very tight and the handlebars pointed north and the front wheel south. We found the pliers and using all four of our hands we cinched the nuts down tighter. On the second try, I rode off the curb and crashed in the gutter. More handlebar and seat straightening. On the third

PART TWO

try I made it a hundred feet down the sidewalk before I tipped over. On the fourth try I stayed upright, with Rollie shouting instructions about how to turn around and how to brake, details hitherto unaddressed. As soon as I figured out the brake and the bike stopped abruptly, I fell over again. But by the end of the day I had mastered the basics.

On my new bike, all of Missoula quickly became accessible and familiar to me. I could bike to the neighborhood where my Dad and uncle Lloyd lived, explore the University, go uptown and visit Mom or check out the model trains at the Missoula Mercantile. If I could rustle a nickel I biked to the Spudnut shop across from the high school for a chocolate glazed cake donut or maple bar or, if I was in luck and there were "day-olds," I could get two for a nickel. On my allowance of twenty cents a week for making my bed and doing the dishes and emptying the wastebaskets, I could buy eight day-old donuts a week, or four ice-cream cones at Hansen's, licorice when they had it, otherwise maple walnut or chocolate, but never vanilla or strawberry.

My ability to bike immediately got Sammie and me into trouble. In reality, Sammie got into trouble; I went along for the ride and got off clean. For all the fact that he knocked me around roughhousing, or took us off on illicit adventures, it was always Sammie that got in trouble.

Post-war Missoula was growing rapidly: before the war it was a town of about 18,000; when I was in the fourth grade it was more than 22,000, the population swollen by vets who had come to the university to study and then stayed instead of returning to their small towns and farms and ranches. By the time I finished high school the population was 27,000, the third largest town in Montana. That meant new neighborhoods in what had been vacant lots and farms on the edge of town, and it meant new schools. Just before we moved back to Missoula, a line had been drawn down the middle of North Avenue. In January, those to the north of that line would stay at Paxson Grade School, and those to the south—including Sammie and my cousin Eddie—would go to the new Washington Grade School. Until Washington opened after New Year's day, Paxson was too crowded and the school was divided into two shifts through the fall, Paxson kids in the morning, the future Washington kids in the afternoon. The North Avenue line divided us forever: Sammie and Eddie became Washington kids and always ran in a different crowd, and I became and remained a Paxson kid: all but a small handful of my friends in high school were from Paxson and some of them have remained my friends for more than a half-century.

A few weeks after school resumed, Sammie took advantage of his overworked, confused teachers and began to play hooky from school, claiming complicated dental problems. Every few days, as soon as my morning school was done he would appear on his bike at 119 Mount, a hundred yards from where his classmates were lining up to enter Paxson, and we would head off on an adventure. September was warm and many afternoons we biked the three miles to the old Maclay bridge over the Bitterroot River, where we stripped and played in the water, built stone dams, wiggled our toes in the backwater sloughs' succulent mud, searched for toads, and made chains of brittle snake grass. It took an hour to bike there. As a beginner with only a few weeks of biking I struggled to keep up with Sammie, who was better conditioned and much bigger that I was. Mom never suspected that I had been out with Sammie; if she asked how I had spent my afternoon I would tell her that I just messed around, or hung out at Rollie's house. I was already pretty good at lying.

When the weather got too cold for wading we biked to the University, stashed our bikes in the bushes beside the Clark Fork River and walked on the Milwaukee Railroad tracks a mile or so up

PART TWO

Hell Gate Canyon, scampering by the scary hobo camp where there were always a few ragged men sitting around a fire. Most days they yelled at us, but we didn't understand and we didn't hang around to make inquiries. Our destination was the almost vertical, talus side of Mt. Sentinel where avalanches had swept the trees away. We climbed the rockslides, prying loose big rocks that we hoped would roll all the way to the tracks. We clawed our way up to a cliff five hundred feet above the tracks where we sat waiting for the electric locomotives to come roaring by pulling long strings of box cars heading for the West Coast, always a bum or two basking on the open flat cars. On the best days Sammie would steal a handful of Dad's .22 caliber bullets and we placed them on the rails before trains came by. When the caboose passed out of site we rock-surfed down the steep slope to the tracks and searched for the flattened bullet casings and lead slugs, the metal burning hot. If we didn't have bullets we dug pennies and nickels out of our pockets to flatten. Once I flattened a quarter to the size of a jar lid, almost transparently thin. Johnny Butler loved George Washington's long face and Pinocchio nose and gave me two quarters for it. As soon as he bought it he showed it to everyone at recess, surrounded by his admirers and acolytes, and then traded it for a Whamo slingshot.

To provision these half-day expeditions, while I waited outside a neighborhood market on my bike holding Sammie's bike ready for a fast getaway, he would light-finger packages of pastries. I remember the little fruitcakes best, full of orange and yellow and green candied fruit and raisins and nuts, fragrant with cloves and cinnamon and nutmeg. He took more than half because he was bigger and had done the dangerous work of stealing them.

We took a dozen of these hooky-days over a month and a half, but finally Sammie's excuse of endless afternoon dentist visits struck his teacher as fishy. Dad was called and confirmed that he hadn't signed the permission notes that Sammie gave to the teacher and that his teeth were just fine. The next time he didn't show up at school, Sammie was nabbed in Mrs. Bailey's driveway by Mr. Blakeslee, the Paxson principal. Sammie went on detention and had to stay after school every afternoon for a month to make up the time he had lost. Since I missed no school, the powers of correction passed me over. The great fruitcake robberies went undetected as far as I know. The bullets exploding under the train wheels appear not to have harmed anyone, although later it seemed like a dangerous thing to be doing. The rubber on Johnny Butler's slingshot broke almost immediately and Johnny asked for his flattened George Washington quarter back, but didn't get it.

Mrs. Bailey's house on Mount provided other diversions. As many homes were before a natural gas pipeline was built, it was heated by the sawdust that sprayed out as logs were sawed into boards at the many lumber mills on the outskirts of Missoula. A sawdust delivery meant that I had a job that earned me a little cash. Two or three times a year a giant truck would dump two tons of steaming hot, fragrant chips in the driveway. Mrs. Bailey gave me 50 cents to shovel it through a window next to the driveway into the bin in the furnace room. The shoveling would take me a few afternoons, but since Mrs. Bailey rarely took out the pre-war Packard limousine that she kept parked in the garage, having the drive clogged while I scooped was not an issue.

Once the bin was full I would talk Rollie into coming over to swim in it. We took off our clothes and tunneled two feet down, throwing armloads of it at each other when we surfaced. We filled buckets and tried to bury each other until our arms were too tired to throw any more. Swimming in sawdust should have resulted in terminal cases of splinters but didn't. Mom complained about finding sawdust in my ears and up my nose and between my toes for days afterwards. I never heard if Mrs. Trenouth called Mom to complain when Rollie shed a pile of chips when he undressed those nights.

Most of our fourth grade class had a crush on our teacher, the delightful, beautiful Miss Jones, freshly graduated from the University of Montana, full of joy and mischief, and tolerant of the bursting energy and misbehavior of fourth graders. She laughed at our jokes, even when they weren't funny or even understandable. She corrected us by telling us that we almost had it right, and then gave us three suggestions about the right answer, two of them plainly ridiculous, although Johnny Butler often chose a ridiculous answer to get a laugh. She wore classy clothes, not the dowdy threadbare black and brown suits and polka dot dresses that the graying veteran teachers cycled every five days. She had long, silky brown hair that softly twirled down to her shoulders and that dangled enticingly in front of our faces when she was helping us at our desks. She had deep blue eyes. She smelled faintly like lilacs one day, roses another. We took turns volunteering to stay after school to clean the blackboards. That had been a punishment in Butte.

When we resumed full-day classes after the New Year we saw that inkwells had been inserted into holes in the top of our desks and that straight pens with steel nibs were laid out for us. Our inky experiments in learning longhand script included a ban on ever again printing—from that day on we were only to scrawl Gregg-method characters, and always with a straight pen. Ballpoint pens were forbidden because we might be spoiled and never learn the precise nib positions required to create the round, lovely B's and Q's and D's blazoned on a frieze that wrapped around the walls of the room. Pencils were allowed only for math. Our desks, our sleeves, our schoolwork were all spotted with ink. Twice a day we used wet rags to clean ink from our desktops and hands. Our mothers struggled to remove the washable ink from our clothes without spoiling an entire load of laundry. The first time Mom missed a patch of ink on my shirt sleeve and turned her favorite white blouse to gray she unloaded an astonishing heap of invective on me, on Miss Jones, and on ink manufacturers who claimed their ink was washable when clearly it wasn't. I was in the doghouse for days and I really hadn't done anything wrong, although most of the many things I deliberately did wrong she never discovered.

We were seated alternately boy-girl, so that the boys would have girls on all four sides and girls would have boys on all four sides. If the girl in front of us braided her hair into a pigtail, sooner or later we could not resist and we would dip it into our inkwell. Girls seemed rarely to retaliate, but they howled and pointed to us and Miss Jones, suppressing a smile, would scold us and sheer fondness for her made us obey for a few days.

Johnny Butler taught us all how to flip ink across the room by holding the base of the pen while pulling back the top just below the wetted nib and then letting go. Ink trajectories were uncontrollable and victimization unpredictable. That behavior quickly was snuffed out too—writing "I will not fling ink" after school with chalk on a blackboard in perfect script one hundred times was amazingly effective: there were few repeat offenders.

Johnny was the official bad boy in our room. His archrival Mike "Mickey" McCullough had been assigned to the other fourth grade room because of their history of fighting in class. Johnny was the second biggest boy in our class, blonde, energetic, fidgety, talkative, and a continuous show-off who would say anything for attention. Mike McCullough seemed to be his only enemy, so most of us weren't afraid of him and a lot of us enjoyed his comic disruptions. One day he showed up with a small pocket mirror pasted to the top

PART TWO

of his shoe; at recess on the playground he told a bunch of us boys to watch. He slipped up behind two girls talking and moved his foot under their skirts, announcing when he returned to us that he could see their underpants. He offered to give us turns with the mirror, but I didn't see what the big deal was since girls often turned upside down on the jungle gym, with their skirts briefly inverting over their chests and heads. And, anyways, what was so interesting about underwear? Johnny was just a bit ahead of all of us in his choice of hobbies, but all of that changed in a few years.

One day Johnny arrived in class with a pocket-full of mechanical pencils and ballpoint pens and gummy erasers. He told us that he had swiped them at Sprouse-Reitz, a five and dime store about a five-minute bike ride from Paxson. After school that day Dick Ainsworth and I rode there and supplied ourselves with as many Scripto mechanical pencils (yellow, blue, red) and ball point pens and gummy erasers as we could stuff in our pockets when the clerks weren't looking. Hearts pounding, we moved deeper into the store to throw off any suspicions by carefully studying a shelf of small upholstered pillows and knitting materials. Then, when the store was momentarily busy we strolled out and hopped on our bikes and headed for a favorite big tree in Bonner Park, climbed it, and compared our loot.

We revisited Spouse-Reitz, and the much bigger Woolworths, many times over the years to shoplift fishing lures and office supplies. Only their candy seemed to be guarded; no one seemed to think that kids would be coveting office supplies. I still hoard office supplies against the day when I might need brightly colored paper clips or fine point pens in five colors, only now I almost always pay for them.

In the winter, after the Washington kids moved into their new school and we had full-day classes, Miss Jones told my mother that I sometimes couldn't see what she wrote on the blackboard, even after she moved me to the front row. Both my Mom and Dad wore glasses and it probably didn't take more of a prompt than that for Mom to take me to an optometrist.

He told me that I was very near-sighted. A few days later I went back and got my first pair of glasses. It was already dark when I left the building and turned into the street: I was blasted with crystalline beams of intense, pure light from every lamppost and traffic light and car. I was astonished to see that stores had names on the signs above their doors, that license plates had numbers, that mannequins in the Mercantile's men's shop windows had hair and were wearing plaids and that their shirts had small buttons and that there were eyelets in their shoes for laces. Of course I had seen some of this when I was close to signs and window displays, but now I could see these things twenty steps away. In class I could read the blackboard and the frieze of script letters above the blackboard; I could read the title of the comic book that Johnny Butler was hiding in his lap and the word "Art Gum" on his erasers two rows away.

That night when I was brushing my teeth I looked at myself in a mirror and with clear vision I saw that I was a big-eared geek who wore pink, plastic-rimmed glasses, a geek with crooked buck teeth who had to stand on a chair to see himself in the mirror. I was embarrassed, for years so ashamed that I rarely studied my face in a mirror or wanted my picture taken.

In the spring, without advanced notice a substitute teacher took over our fourth grade class for a few days. When she returned Miss Jones had a new name, Mrs. Metki. Miss Jones no longer belonged exclusively to us, and it dawned on us that perhaps we were not the cause of her joy and energy the previous autumn. As the year wound down we must have worn her out: she began to utter dark warnings

PART TWO

about how tough the fifth grade would be and that we were not nearly grown up enough to be promoted. But usually she relented and some of her old energy returned. We totally missed noticing that she was putting on weight and didn't know that she was having a baby until autumn when she didn't return to teach the fourth grade.

In the fourth grade we had group singing and in the fifth grade song flute lessons. Although I was nothing special on the song flute, I had a good soprano voice and big lungs and if a song had a high note at the end I would hold it for an extra four or five beats so that everyone would notice. The girls who were rule-obeyers glared at me, but the only person I really cared about impressing was Mary Kraabel. I had a crush on her from the fourth grade until a year or two into college. Mary was the daughter of Mom's boss at Kraabel Chevrolet. She was beautiful, with light brown, slightly wavy hair, a willowy athletic body, perfect teeth and lovely pink gums that showed brilliantly when she smiled. She was shy and tomboyish, but when I left a note on her desk in the fifth grade telling her I liked her and asking her if she liked me, she turned around as soon as she read it, looked at me, smiled, and nodded her head. That was the absolute peak of our relationship. From that day on I bicycled by her house at least twice a week hoping to run into her, but I never once saw her. In the seventh grade I gave her 28 valentines, one for each day of February and was heartbroken that among the twenty or so valentines in my decorated shoebox there was not a single valentine from Mary. I didn't even bother to look at the others; they meant nothing to me and I threw them all away.

Once we returned to Missoula, still alone most of the time and not out playing with other kids very often, I developed the habit of continual reading, fueled by weekly bike trips uptown to the library. I was allowed to take out fifteen books or magazines at a time from the children's room, which I carried home in the basket on the front of my bike. I quickly exhausted the kid's department and when I was twelve was rewarded with a card to the adult collection on the upper floors. I had become comfortable with school as a task and a community in which I could get some of the attention and rewards missing at home. In the sixth grade I read sixty books a month, which I would not have done if Miss Egan, who looked like the cartoon character Daisy Mae and who was the one other teacher for whom I developed a crush, had not required us to post our lists in the front of the room where everyone could see them. Half the books I read were about submarines and battleships and the Second World War or dogs or the Yukon, and half were speedily read Hardy Boys mysteries or manuals on how to customize a Chevy or build a tree house that your parent could not get into (dreaming did not require that we own either a Chevy or a tree). I posted twice as many as any other kid and felt proud when Miss Egan singled me out as the best reader.

In the summer of 1953 we moved out of the basement apartment on Mount and into a house a few blocks away where Mom lived the rest of her life. A house of her own had become a goal for Mom when my impending adolescence demanded something more than a shared bedroom. However, puberty was the farthest thing from my mind when I first saw the house: of much greater interest were having my own bedroom, windows that put us on the same level as the rest of the world, a tiny dining nook off the kitchen where we could eat dinner at a table, a basement with a workbench, a large willow tree in the backyard that I clearly could climb and that Mom clearly could not, and an empty garage in which someday I might park a Chevy.

CHAPTER

NINE

SUMMERS AT FLATHEAD LAKE

I SPENT ALMOST my entire summer at Flathead Lake during the six years we lived in Butte and in the Mount Avenue basement apartment in Missoula: Mom did not want me cooped up all day playing by myself or reading. And so as soon as school was over I rode the bus from Butte and Missoula and was dropped at the Wood's Bay house where Grandma and Grandma were waiting. Grandpa and Grandma would walk up to the house slowly while I pranced around, describing my trip and asking questions:

"Are there cinnamon rolls, Grandma? Can we go fishing? What are we having for dinner? Can I go down and see the lake? Are there strawberries in the garden? Are we going to town on Saturday?" And on and on.

Grandma and Grandpa were not playful people. I was a burst of wind shaking up their calm, well-ordered lives. They smiled as I ran around the house checking to see all of my favorite things, just on the edge of finding me a bit disturbing but also pleased by how much I appreciated them and the house and the gardens.

For all but a few hours a day Grandpa quietly toiled in his flower and vegetable gardens or worked on one or another small house repair. His days never varied up to his death. He was always out of bed before Grandma, usually before seven. In the morning he pruned or weeded or hand watered in his gardens in the pure, cool, high-Rockies air scented with a thousand blossoms and a million trees. At eight Grandma would be in front a low mirror weaving her long gray-streaked brown hair into a braid and then winding the braid into a chignon. Grandpa would come into the kitchen, pour himself a cup of hot water and, putting four sugar cubes into his mouth one at a time, sip the water through the sugar cubes. Then he would go out and work more strenuously in the garden, hand-plowing, hoeing, digging, harvesting, thinning, planting. The winds during western Montana's frequent thunderstorms spread tufts of pine and fir cones and broken branches promiscuously and Grandpa would fight back by removing them all by mid- morning.

At ten Grandma would serve us breakfast, always the same: hot cereal, toast with her jam (never store-bought), a soft boiled egg. Once a week she fried eggs and two strips of hand-cut local bacon for Grandpa, one for me. I asked, but never received, two strips. He drank one cup of Maxwell House instant coffee. Usually he would read the newspaper as he ate. Meals were mostly silent. Grandma said that breakfast did not agree with her and she never joined us at the table.

After breakfast Grandpa worked outside until one, when he had lunch. In the afternoons he went upstairs for a short nap. Around four he would return to his outside chores.

Montana is dry in the summer. Occasional thunderstorms can bring a deluge lasting minutes or at most an hour or two, but days and weeks can pass without a raindrop. Grandpa had boxes of geraniums beneath the first floor front windows. I never saw how he planted them—getting to them would have required a tall ladder. To water them he had created a pipe system that dripped water into the boxes until it ran from their bottoms. In the rock garden he had created a bird fountain to which he brought water by burying an underground pipe, and another underground pipe brought water to two heart-shaped sprinklers on pipes four feet high that watered the prolific flowers in the rock gardens and peonies along the front sidewalk. Other pipes carried water to the orchard and vegetable gardens. He laid all of these pipes in trenches that he gouged out of the ancient rocky beach upon which the gardens were created—pick and shovel work that he was doing in his sixties and seventies.

Our house sat halfway up the hill from the lake. Grandpa had created an attention-commanding rock garden at the front of the lawn beside the road. Dozens of peonies lined the sidewalk up the hill to the front porch. Above that he had a large rose garden separated by small paths into beds in the shape of a four-leaf clover. Where the yard edged into the dense thicket of lodge pole pine beside the house, thick as dogs' hair and witchy dark to walk through on the stone path, he had a bed of succulents—hens-and-chicks, cactus, creeping sedums—in a bed shaped like a star. I loved to walk on the paths through these gardens, sitting on the lawns to read, my back against a pitchy pine, distracted from my reading at times by the laboring ants making a harvest from the insects trapped in the sticky bark. A constant stream of tourists' cars flowed by. Most slowed to look at the thousand blazing flowers stretching up to the house from the road; many stopped to take pictures, attracted by nature's overflow like insects to pitch. Grandpa knew how to make flowers and gardens seductive.

His orchard was so prolific that Grandpa could not pick all of the cherries after he had shipped crates of them to family and friends—there simply were too many ripening at the same time. At the beginning of the harvest season he posted a red-lettered sign on a white

PART TWO

background: "Cherries—U Pick'm". Beneath that was a blank spot where each year he would tack a square of cardboard with the current price. In 1950 the price was 3½ cents a pound, which even then seemed cheap: a 1¼ ounce Hersey bar cost a dime. When tourists stopped, Grandpa equipped them with harnesses and buckets and led them up the hill where he had placed orchard ladders beneath the most heavily laden trees. When they were done he weighed the buckets on the spring scale he used to weigh fish and they would drive off with five pounds that he discounted to 17 cents. Occasionally a family of Mennonites in their homespun clothes stopped and picked the trees clean. Grandpa would give them a discount, take down his "U Pick'm" sign, and put away the three-legged orchard ladders until apple season.

Every night after dinner I helped Grandma with the dishes, carefully drying plates, glasses, or utensils and placing them on a counter so she could put them away in cabinets too high for me to reach. Grandma didn't ask questions about my day—she already knew the answers—but she listened attentively to my chattering about events real and imagined while Grandpa sat in the big chair next to the fireplace in the living room reading *Time Magazine* or *Newsweek* or *National Geographic*. If something he read startled him, he read it to Grandma, who responded by clucking her tongue and saying "can you imagine that," with a downward deflection, more an exclamation than a question. If the information verged on scandalous, every few minutes she would repeat "can you imagine that" to herself as she finished up her chores.

They seldom listened to the weekly radio shows. If they did it was on Sunday evenings, when Grandpa might tune into *The Jack Benny Show* if he was in the mood. Jack Benny and he had met once or twice in Waukegan when Grandpa worked for Benny's father in his cousin's furniture and clothing store. One of the rare family stories was that Jack Benny and his wife visited the Flathead Lake house after he had become a famous radio comedian. Grandpa sent him back to Hollywood with a crate of Bing cherries.

At eight o'clock I was put to bed, under protest, and by nine Grandpa and Grandma had bedded down on the screened front porch, the windows thrown open to catch the cool breezes off the lake, all the lights out, just the sound of waves and the shimmering, scratchy wind in the tall firs and pines and the occasional rumble of a passing logging truck. Grandpa parked his teeth in a glass of fizzy water beside the bed.

I played alone at Flathead on most days. There were no games in the house; television in the mountainous west was ten years in the future. The radio was turned on only for something important, like a speech by President Truman or a world championship boxing match, and once for the *Miss America Pageant* when a Montana girl was a finalist, although I can't imagine that radio would have been an effective broadcast medium for a beauty contest, especially if the finalists danced or threw a lariat. For reading there were the news magazines and the *Saturday Evening Post, Look Magazine, Coronet* and *Readers Digest*, but no children's books. Grandpa had two books, *The War of the Copper Kings* and *Not as a Stranger*. I tried reading *Not as a Stranger* and decided that doctors had sad lives and put it down after reading a hundred pages.

I had few toys at Flathead. I stayed busy building something, or pretending to be a cowboy or pirate or soldier. Behind the house, a stone walk and stairs led up the hillside and crossed the grassy path along which the ladies of the neighborhood walked to visit each other or to drop off groceries requested from town, or to borrow a stick of butter or a lemon or two eggs. Between the path and the house there were remnants of an earlier, terraced strawberry garden, overgrown with wildflowers. The hill was crisscrossed with fallen

PART TWO

branches and short logs that I turned into gymnasium equipment when I reached that stage of early puberty when some boys notice their pathetic inventory of manly muscles. I found slender logs and used them as splintery, buggy barbells, lifting them above my head ten or twelve times or curling them two-handed from thigh to chest. Big rocks substituted for free hand weights.

I watched my progress by "making a muscle" in the tiny mirror in the basement bathroom to which I was assigned because I was always too dirty for the upstairs bathroom. My progress in muscle growing was unimpressive. A popular advertisement in boys' magazines at that time was for the Charles Atlas body-building course. The ads depicted an attractive girl in a bathing suit talking with a skinny teenage boy. In the second panel he was pushed out of the way by a brawny, square-jawed bully a foot taller, or the bully kicked beach sand in his face and walked off with the girl. The next panels showed the skinny boy reading a Charles Atlas book, exercising, sprouting muscles, growing a foot taller, and a few weeks later chasing off the bully. I was definitely the skinny little kid, and Grandpa's hillside was the workout program that would, in Charles Atlas' words, bring me "Fame instead of Shame." As of yet there was no one with whom I wished to demonstrate my breath-taking body, but grade school and high school were full of bullies that I knew I could never stand up to in my current condition.

Once a week Grandma prepared my favorite meal, the one she also served to guests, salmon broiled with butter, served delicately pink and flakey, the skin still on but the heads and tails removed. These were small Kokanee salmon—landlocked Sockeye salmon that were planted in the lake about the time that Grandpa and Grandma settled there, that Grandpa was an expert in catching and Grandma was an expert in cooking. We would troll for these in the late afternoon when Grandpa could see that the fish were rising to feed a few hundred feet off shore, their splash creating widening concentric circles when they rose to scoop bugs off the surface. When this happened Grandpa would ask me if I wanted to go fishing. Of course I always wanted to go fishing. I would be dispatched with a hand trowel and "Bob's Bait Box," a green tube about the size of a can of soda with a curved lid in the side, to get worms from Grandpa's worm garden, a deep bed in which he continuously dug in coffee grounds and other worm comfort foods. After I dug up a dozen or so fat worms, we assembled our equipment: the rods and tackle boxes, the net and stringers, the gas can, and a life jacket for me. We walked along the road that ran in front of the house to the Micken's dock, where Grandpa and all the other neighbors kept their boats. I had no happier moments than these short trips walking with Grandpa, each of us carrying fishing gear, heading for the boat shed, filled with fishermen's optimism. Fishing was a man's job and I felt like a man with an important mission, walking side by side with the most expert fisherman in the world.

I loved Grandpa's boat. I was secure in the knowledge that it was the most elegant of the twenty fishing boats packed into the boat shed. The boat was very heavy—made of mahogany, with a dark brown, varnished hull, bow deck, and rails. Under the deck Grandpa stowed his seat cushions and a gas can, an extra mooring rope, and a belaying pin that he used to thunk salmon on the head after he caught them, so that they would not struggle so hard that they would tear loose from the stringer he towed behind the boat to keep them cold and fresh.

Everything in that boat smelled of varnish, gas and fish. I loved the smell of the boat, although Grandma didn't like it and never went out with Grandpa. The boat and his orchard and flower gardens—Grandma also didn't like to go out in the hot sun—were Grandpa's refuges.

PART TWO

The boat was powered by a Johnson five horsepower motor, which of course made me loyal to Johnson's Outboard Marine and hostile to the inferior (in my view) Evinrude and Mercury motors for the rest of my life.

The boat could seat four on two plank benches—Grandpa sat in the stern on a small metal chair that gave him back support, his feet forward, his left arm extended back on the motor's tiller. I sat up front on the opposite side, ostensibly to balance the boat, but I barely weighed sixty pounds, just enough to counterbalance a Springer Spaniel.

To get out of the large shed dock through about twenty boats, we pushed the boat backwards and away from the boats beside us, occasionally nudging a boat out of our way. When we floated into the lake-end of the dock, Grandpa pulled the starter rope hard a few times, adjusted the throttle and choke until the spark caught, and then backed us the rest of the way out. Beyond the breakwater that protected the maw of the boat shed, he turned the bow into the oncoming waves and pointed us toward the west end of Woods Bay and throttled up. I believed we were the fastest, jazziest fishing boat on the lake.

We fished in long loops just offshore where Grandpa had seen the fish rising to feed. Our gear was simple: metal poles, level-wind reels, and cowbells—long strings of eight hammered silver or gold metal spoons, attached to a rubber snubber that stretched when a fish struck the hook so that it would not tear out of the salmon's soft mouth. We put a worm on the hook, or sometimes corn, or maybe chicken skin. We could troll for an hour or two and not catch anything on some days, and on others when the salmon were actively feeding we would catch a fish every five or ten minutes. Small ones under eight inches were tenderly separated from the hook and thrown back in the water, to hunt again another day. The biggest were 14 inches, but most were 11 or 12 inches. Their scales were shiny and so slimy that the fish sometimes slipped through our hands when we removed them from the hook to put them on the stringer. Grandpa would bend over the rails to rinse his hands, then hold me by my life jacket so I could do the same.

Once when we had both caught salmon at the same time and were floating quietly with the motor off re-rigging our lines, a huge bull trout attacked our stringer of five fish and tore away the two bottom-most fish. I was excited. Grandpa was disappointed because we had just enough fish for the company expected that evening. We had to work for another hour to make up for what the bull trout stole, although the trout might have seen us as the thieves.

Grandpa was a patient man: it must have been a lot of work for him to have me along—because of my questions, because I frequently thought I felt a tug on my line and had a fish, requiring him to kill the motor so that we could both reel in when there was no fish, not even evidence that the worm had been abused. From time to time when I was not paying attention our lines crossed and tangled and Grandpa would spend an hour untangling them. My pole control was shaky and more than once I hooked grandpa's big straw hat or his sleeve and he had to spend five minutes backing the snelled hook out of the woven material. Grandpa muttered through his efforts to untangle the lines or pull out the hook, but I never heard him swear or get angry with me.

When we got back Grandma always asked, "Did you catch fish?" If we did, she changed her dinner plans. Grandma felt that salmon deserved fresh peas from the garden. She would climb up the hill behind the house to the vegetable garden in her sturdy leather shoes, stockings, house dress, sun bonnet, and apron, return with a pan of peas that she cooked in a little sauce pan on her stove side-by-side with a pot of new potatoes—and that was dinner: silver salmon alive in the lake just an hour or two before, buttered and broiled, slices of lemon, and peas and new potatoes mixed together with black pepper, salt and butter.

For me fishing wasn't utilitarian—a chore done to put dinner on the table. It was the embodiment of a successful life. And Grandpa's boat was never just a fishing boat. I dreamed about it for many years, long after it had been sold and disappeared to whatever other-worldly lake old boats bob in through eternity. I never imagined Grandpa in heaven, cavorting with cherubs like those in the gold-framed prints in my bedroom. I pictured him sitting in his boat in the late afternoon, his left hand extended back to the tiller, his tanned face turned forward, scanning a placid lake for the tell-tale rings that announced that the salmon were striking. Just on the edge of his field of vision there would be a little boy in a striped t-shirt and sneakers, sitting on his feet dangling a fishing pole over the other side, contented just to be fishing with his Grandpa.

The houses in Woods Bay had been built and settled by couples who retired from jobs in the Hi-Line towns like Shelby and Glasgow and Malta on the prairies of eastern Montana, moving west when US Highway 2 was built during the Depression and people from the east could drive across the mountains. Their houses were small and their own children grown up. I remember few visits by their grown children and rarely did grandchildren stay long enough for us to become friends.

The exception was Jack Agen's family. He was an oilman from Shelby who spent the summer in Woods Bay with his two sons, in a house adjoining the houses of Mrs. Agen's sister and her parents. Jerry was three or four years older and several feet taller than I was, then as now. Sometimes I read comic books at Jerry's house or played with him on his beach, since there was no beach in front of our house. Occasionally Jerry would propose an expedition to Castle Rock to capture snapping turtles at one of the ponds back in the mountains, or a pirate excursion down the buccaneer east coast of the lake in the small boat that he captained.

In the summer after the second grade I nearly died at Jerry's place. There were a lot of hazards when I played there, the lake itself and even more the highway that ran in front of our houses, busy with huge logging and transport trucks and rubbernecking tourists. During the first three summers I spent with them, my grandparents would not let me cross the road alone, but by the time I was eight I would let them know where I was going, and they would tell me to be careful, and I would go by myself north to the Micken's dock where all the boats were moored or south to Jerry's house to play with him. Grandpa and Grandma told me I couldn't go in the water by myself. Neither were swimmers, they had never raised a little boy at the edge of a lake, and they didn't teach me how to swim. So I only waded.

One evening after dinner I ran out of the house and along the road and crossed over to where Jerry was fishing on the Birmingham's log dock adjacent to theirs. It went far out in the lake and from the end Jerry could catch a big squawfish or sucker or sometimes perch or sunfish. I ran out to the end of the dock to say hello, watched him a little, and then, bored just watching, wandered back toward the shore. Somehow I slipped off the water-slicked logs at the edge of the dock and was immediately in water over my head. I thrashed frantically in the water but sank to the bottom—I was too skinny to be buoyant. When my feet hit the bottom I pushed myself up and my head broke above the water for a second. Gasping, I took in as much water as air and immediately sank again. Even in a light wind, lakes are noisy from the breaking of the waves on the shore and on the dock and Jerry didn't hear a splash when I fell in. Later he said that maybe he heard something but thought it was his dog jumping in.

I bounced off the bottom a second time, and then a third, becoming more and more frantic. My lungs were screaming in pain. I must have realized that I had moved toward the shore a bit, that the water was a little less far above my head. I pogo-sticked off the bottom seven or eight more times until I could actually hold my mouth above the water long enough to take a small breath. In a few more hops my feet were on the bottom and my face above water and I crawled out on hands and knees to the shore and lay there for a long time, panting and coughing. Jerry still knew nothing, and I did not tell him.

Now I had the dilemma of having to go home soaking wet at eight o'clock at night. I told the truth. My grandparents knew that it was more likely that I would have drowned than survived.

They grounded me. Literally. I was forbidden to go near the water without a life jacket and an adult with me. Neither Grandma nor Grandpa liked to spend time on the beach, and neither could rescue me if I fell in again. The beach was my favorite place to play, and Jerry, my only Flathead playmate, spent much of his time on the water—building and sailing little wooden boats, skipping rocks, fishing, rowing out on the lake twenty or thirty feet offshore to jump in and swim to shore or dangle worms for fish.

All my years in Butte I was a fatherless kid who didn't know how to play street games or hit a ball, and now I was at Flathead with grandparents who probably had not played in their childhoods, and certainly were not going to play with me now—or teach me how to swim.

When I was spending my summers at Flathead, most of the shore along Woods Bay was still what we today call "wetlands", with trees and shrubs growing right down to the water. For two hundred feet on either side of our house there was no rock beach: the waterfront was marshy woods completely filled with cottonwood trees and maples. At the water's edge the waves undercut the tree roots creating shallow crevices and leafy overhangs full of frogs and snakes, minnows and water skeeters, snake grass and turtles and dragonflies. The smell was wonderful, and although we could not wade or bask in the sun, we could explore for everything that had evolved in a hundred centuries. If I were offered a time-trip to the past, it wouldn't be to watch gladiators fight in Rome or to a hilltop looking down on grazing dinosaurs, but to 1950 and this stretch of beach, to spend a day sitting on the edge of the water on a hot, sunny day, bare-footed, knees pulled up to my chest with my arms wrapped around them, watching and smelling this little patch of the world with nothing on my mind other than what was in front of me.

In those years when I crossed the road to the beach barefooted, I shivered and got goose bumps on the back of my neck because of the countless squashed reptiles I had to walk over—huge frogs as green and flat as a dollar bill; snakes half smashed with tail or head still writhing; sad, sad turtles splayed out in perfect silhouettes, their cracked shells driven down into their punctured guts. I never liked to find dead animals, especially not ones I loved to hold and play with. I was philosophical about the dying snakes, but my love of turtles was—is—irrational and I grieved. Sometimes I had to move them away so that I did not pass by them every day: I returned them to the water and let the waves take them home.

Over the next decade all of this would gradually go away now that there was a highway with heavy traffic and a booming post-war economy bringing in families with money who were replacing the wetlands with docks and retaining walls.

The summer before Sammie began high school and I began the sixth grade Mom thought it would be a good idea for him to come to the lake while I was there, since we were rarely together and he saw much less of Grandpa and Grandma than I did. Almost always this resulted in trouble. We fought constantly, and although I was the loser of the physical battles, here as in Missoula I won most of the blame mediations since I was an effective crier, was far smaller than Sammie, and was much less likely to cause Grandpa and Grandma problems.

After just a week Sammie decided we should run away because he was in trouble for setting off firecrackers that he wasn't supposed to have. He rounded up a small gang of kids who were summer visitors and herded us up the road toward Bigfork, barefooted and without provisions. With logging trucks and freighters rumbling by just feet away from us throwing up clouds of dust, we managed to walk along the edge of the road for about two miles. Where the road curved down to bisect a fecund swamp of cattails and algae and dragonflies, the roadside gravel beside the ponds was paved with smashed frogs and snakes, crushed ducklings and red-winged blackbirds smashed in flight. We tried to step around the skins, dried like jerky, each in the perfect two-dimensional form it had in life. The carnage of the war of cars and trucks against reptiles and amphibians and birds was awful, too great to toe-dance our way through. We turned around and barefooted it home in time for supper. No one ever knew we had run away.

Those Montana summers when I was in grade school were my only experiences of living in a family with a man. My grandparents were serious, quiet people. I later wondered what their childhoods in Lithuania had been like and wished that I had heard stories about their coming to a strange country from a difficult one. It was common in those years for children to be reminded of how lucky they were to not have been in Europe during or after the two World Wars, or to have experienced the Depression, and I knew that Grandpa and Grandma felt humble and fortunate not only to have come to America but to have had modest success in establishing a business and founding an American family.

Most of what I learned about the life of a grown-up man I learned from Grandpa, and what little I grasped about relaxations like fishing and gardening I knew because of our time together.

They were kind people. At a time when few mothers worked and few children were raised without both a father and mother in the home, they gave me undemonstrative affection and warmth during long summers when I might otherwise have been entirely alone.

Every summer Grandpa set up a cloth hammock near some leafy trees between our and Doc Reimer's house, where, shaded from the scorching afternoon sun, I would be sent to nap but instead read or daydreamed, conjuring the clouds into empires and the unfathomable blue sky into oceans swarming with mythical creatures. When a couple of those trees got old and died Grandpa cut off the stumps at table height and built a little tea-tray where I could sit, grandly, in my private shade and have lunch. The lake and its shore, the gardens and orchard and woods supplied me with endless adventures. A few times the first few summers I was homesick, but after the third grade being with Grandma and Grandpa in the Woods Bay house felt like home.

I spent most of my days by myself, but I was no longer lonely.

CHAPTER

TEN

THE LITTLE YELLOW HOUSE ON BEVERLY AVENUE

MOM LEARNED ABOUT the house on Beverly Avenue from a college friend, Marge Dickson, who owned a real estate and insurance company downtown. I don't recall knowing about Marge before we moved out of Lady Lucille's house, but from that point on she was a frequent visitor in our life, partly because it was her house that Mom and Grandpa were buying when Marge and her husband Snuse decided to adopt a baby, partly because I did some of her lawn work as I grew up, and partly because she always made sure that Mom and I had a family to be with for Christmas and Thanksgiving dinners. Marge had thick, flaming red hair that suspiciously continued to flame when the heads of the rest of her generation had faded into gray or lilac-tinged white. She dressed expensively and ornamented herself with turquoise and silver. She was the first business woman I knew, more successful than Snuse, who barely covered his expenses in the small high-quality men's clothing shop he maintained in the Florence Hotel lobby.

Our house was a few blocks south of the University district, five or six blocks from the base of Mount Sentinel, and just three blocks from Paxson School. Most of the houses had been built in the thirties and were one-story ranch houses of wood and brick, or modified colonials, simple, unpretentious, neat, well kept up. We were a few blocks south of the gracious University District, and like the Mount Avenue house, there were no big trees along the street to cast shade in the bright, hot summers or to shed piles of leaves in the autumn to play in. To kick through golden, fragrant maple leaves in the fall we walked down to the University.

In the Calvinist Missoula of the 1950's, among a hundred absolute sins there were two that pertained to houses: having a dirty car parked in front, and not keeping an immaculate front yard. On the first sunny weekend day of spring, everyone celebrated the return of warmth by dragging their garden hoses out of storage, and, with buckets of hot, soapy water, washing the grime of a long winter off their car while the lovely smell of last autumn's leaves being burned in the alleys behind the houses drifted through. Lawns were raked, fertilizer spread, front porches washed, lawn mowers pushed clacking back and forth through the uneven early grass. We could hear the first resonant pocks of bats connecting with softballs a few houses away in Bonner Park, the slap of balls in mitts. But in Montana steadily warm temperatures came late, and even then winter could hold on: as late as Memorial Day there was a risk of frost, and every few years we would get a heavy snow after the trees and shrubs had leafed out, bringing brilliant white-frosted green branches crashing to the ground and turning lilac bushes into arching purple-flower-spotted ghosts of the winter past.

The house had been built with only one bedroom, a very small living room with a dining nook, a tiny kitchen, and a single bathroom so small that I could sit on the toilet and dangle my feet in the bathtub under Mom's drying underwear. Marge and Snuse had converted their garage into a second bedroom that became mine, and then built a new garage, now empty but big enough for a Chevy. There were three plum trees and a giant willow in the back yard. As typical of Missoula, we had a lot of space for lawn and flower gardens. Along the rear driveway, between our house and the Porters, clotheslines stretched between two poles; we had no clothes drier and laundry was hung out to dry, sheets and towels and jeans and underwear frozen board stiff in winter. A white fence enclosed the backyard, the kind of fence that a boy was expected to paint every few years as a family expectation, like raking leaves and shoveling snow and mowing the lawn. I complained but was told that it was better than having been sent to an orphanage when I was born. I believe this was meant to be ironic, but I knew enough about orphans and orphanages to understand that my deal was better.

I was excited that for the first time I had a room of my own. Grandpa and Grandma had shipped twin beds of "rock maple" from the Fair Store, and they also bought me a large maple bureau and a small desk. The heavy, faux-colonial maple furniture filled the room, but there were lots of built in shelves where I stored toys and clothes and books and hidden treasures that I did not want Mom to know I had, like twenty Scripto mechanical pencils in four jewel-like colors, a half-dozen Art Gum erasers, a stapler, boxes of paper clips, bundles of rubber bands, and a foreboding but prescient hallway sign that said "No Exit".

Mom sprang for decoration, converting the green walls to calamine-lotion pink—the color of old women's corsets—and green drapes of Grandma Moses' country scenes that for a decade were most of what I knew about the New England landscape.

PART TWO

Once we moved to Beverly Avenue our life together developed a rhythm that lasted until I left for college. My school, a ten minute walk away, started at 8:45. Mom had to leave for her job at Kraabel Chevrolet early to check in customers waiting to drop off their cars and trucks for service at 7:30. I dressed and ate breakfast alone in our little kitchen. Every kitchen had a built-in pastry board because every mother made her own pies and cookies; I pulled our pastry board out to use as a table and, sitting on a red step stool, ate the hot cereal Mom had left keeping warm in a double boiler on the stove. I loaded the cereal with sugar and raisins and drowned it in milk. Hot cereal in the school months was another Calvinist tenant in Montana: serving cold, sweetened packaged cereal to children was looked on with disapproval, a sign of being a bad mother. Dry cereals were allowable only in the summer, along with popsicles and Kool-Aid, when standards were relaxed.

There were no lunches in Paxson grade school because we all lived close-by and could walk to our houses at noon. Most of my classmates' mothers were at home and had lunch waiting for them. I made myself lunch, usually Campbell's soup and a sandwich: bologna, lettuce, and mayonnaise on white bread was my favorite, but sometimes Mom bought salami or thinly sliced ham or American cheese. Peanut butter was for emergencies.

Mom cooked dinner for the week on Sunday afternoons, usually a roast that could be used as leftovers for a few more meals. The roasts alternated between pot-roasted beef, baked ham, roasted or fried chicken, and pork roasts. She served pot-roast with mashed potatoes; I always made a lake in the top of mashed potatoes that I filled with thick, dark brown gravy made from the pan juices. She thought my engineering in the potatoes was uncivilized: "What if you were eating with the Queen?" I thought that the arrival of the Queen at 412 Beverly was a remote possibility at the moment and continued to play with my dinner, carving canals down the heaped up mountains of potatoes, draining gravy into the chunks of well-cooked tender roast. During the week Mom would either heat up leftovers or cook something quick, since she rarely got home before six or six-thirty.

My Montana vacations with Grandma and Grandpa after we moved to Beverly Avenue were a month or less. By the end of the sixth grade Mom knew I could take care of myself and that a full summer at Flathead Lake alone would have been boring. I spent long summer days in the tree house I had dreamt of. I scavenged old boards out of alley trashcans and the scrap piles outside of construction projects to build a platform, cutting them with a hand saw I bought at Montgomery Wards. One hot July morning I climbed a rickety ladder and hauled the boards up to the wide crotch of the willow about twelve feet above the lawn and cobbled them together with nails driven at random angles into the tree and to each other. I made a crude hanging ladder of rope and sticks that could be pulled up, making the tree house unimpregnable.

I rushed to finish before Mom got home. An extension cord drooped in a long arc from an outlet in the garage to a branch above the platform and powered a light fixture I crafted from an unused table lamp, shadeless and hanging upside down like a forlorn duck in a Chinese restaurant window. A radio with a broken case a friend had been about to throw away was playing staticky Perry Como and Rosemary Clooney ballads. I had found a long rope in the garage and created a bucket hoist by which I pulled up survival rations and my current reading.

I wanted to impress on Mom the perfection and permanence of my summer quarters and my amazing ingenuity; I posed myself desert-island aloof, barefooted and barechested, at leisure on the platform.

When she finally arrived I pretended not to hear her as she walked through the house calling for me. She came out the back door, looked around the lawn and flowerbeds but not up. She was about to go inside without seeing me. I pushed a book overboard that landed with a smack on the picnic table beneath and, startled, she looked up and took it all in.

"How'd you do that?"

"Just did."

"I see that."

This was followed by a series of questions about the origins of the lamp, ropes, bucket, radio, and a couch pillow that I had purloined but claimed to have found in a trashcan. Then she went inside and fixed dinner. I never heard further from her about the tree house. Most summer evenings she had to come out and tell me to turn off the light and radio and get ready for bed. One night I told her I wanted to camp out on the platform. She said I might fall off and refused. She rarely put her foot down like that, so I didn't argue; I rolled out my sleeping bag and slept on the lawn for the rest of the summer.

Montana has a long and harsh winter. Once warm weather began in June or July everyone spent as much time as possible outside. We ate in the backyard every night unless there was a thunderstorm. Picnics in the many parks around Missoula were out of the question since we had no car; Mom had bought the picnic table and benches as soon as we moved in and most nights we ate under the big willow tree.

A few minutes before five on Sunday nights I turned on my little outside radio so that we could hear *The Jack Benny Show* and Mom set out dinner. When Jack Benny was done cracking us up, we listened to *Amos 'n' Andy*, whose malapropisms and complex situations we relished. There was only one black family in Missoula at that time and very few in all of Montana. We knew nothing about black people and had no sense at all of the irony of two white men playing black characters living in Harlem—I didn't know until I got to college that Freeman Gosden and Charles Correll were not black, and that all the hundreds of other characters' voices in the program were theirs.

Sunday dinners were our banquets, especially in the summer. On the last Sunday of August Mom served my favorite dinner, fried chicken with mashed potatoes and gravy and local corn on the cob and fresh pickles of cucumbers and sliced white onions from uncle Lloyd's garden, soaked in vinegar and a bit of sugar for a few hours. The crowning touch was a lemon meringue pie, which took much of the afternoon for Mom to create. A lemon meringue pie baking in the oven kept no secrets and hours in advance I knew that we were celebrating the end of summer and my return to school. This was as close to perfection as my life got in those years, even though the willow was buggy and when the wind blew, tiny green aphids sprinkled down on our heads and shoulders and food.

We did not have the money to eat in restaurants often. Occasionally we would make a trip to the Golden Pheasant, Missoula's decades-old Chinese restaurant; the absence of a car made almost any other restaurant out of range. Not until I bought a car at sixteen was I able to drive to the drive-in restaurants on the highways at the edge of town to bring home hamburgers, or drive downtown to pick up Elmer Shea's Special Formula Batter Fried Chicken from his Double Front Restaurant on Railroad Street. A few times a year when she was going out for dinner, Mom sent me off on my bicycle with fifty cents. At my favorite cafe—the Chimney Corner, on the edge of the University—fifty cents would buy a hamburger on a fresh, puffy bun with lettuce and tomatoes and a handful of French fries and a thick chocolate malt that required two straws. I would have fifteen cents left over if instead I headed uptown for the Florence Hotel on

PART TWO

Higgins Avenue and ordered egg salad on white bread with a Coke in the coffee shop, where the waitresses wore pale pink uniforms with little white aprons and always asked if my sandwich was okay, as if I were a regular hotel customer. In the summer the Dairy Queen on the corner of Higgins and Beverly was also an option, although we had standards and none of us kids thought it proper that an ice cream place was trying to horn in on the hamburger and hotdog business.

After moving, life looked up in many ways. In the fall I began the seventh grade. As sixth graders we had heard from the class ahead of us that every spring Mrs. Johnson took her students to her house and taught them how to bake bread. Mrs. Johnson divided us into groups and showed us how to mix the flour and water and salt and yeast. We took turns kneading the sticky dough. We ate lunch and while the bread rose she told us (for the third time that year) about her trip to Kenya the previous summer, about the Mau Mau uprising against the British colonizers and army, and about her expeditions to see animals that were to us almost mythical: zebras, giraffes, elephants, rhinoceroses and hippopotami. The boys wanted to hear about crocodiles, and the girls about impalas and flamingoes. Everyone wanted to know if she and her husband were scared.

When the bread had risen and baked we ate thick warm slices slathered with butter and honey, with milk chasers.

Baking bread with Mrs. Johnson turned on some latent gene that I didn't know I had, the ability to cook if I was hungry and there wasn't anyone around to cook for me. I had discovered that cooking and baking were something that someone as ordinary and unskillful as a seventh grader could do if the ingredients were at hand, no harder than putting together a train set or a bike.

My first experiments began almost immediately. Mom was committed to sleeping in on Sunday mornings. Although, like any kid,

I could sleep late when the occasion called for it, by and large getting up always offered more interesting possibilities than staying in bed and by 8 AM on Sundays I was wide awake. The comic pages of the *Sunday Missoulian* were not extensive and by nine o'clock I was starving, waiting for Mom. By the time I was twelve I realized that the odds of a breakfast earlier than ten o'clock on Sunday were better if I did the cooking. I learned to read the instructions on the back of the Aunt Jemima Pancake Mix box: how to measure out milk and Wesson Oil, how to crack a few eggs, how to stir up the batter without leaving large patches of dry flour in the bottom, how to oil and heat a frying pan. I still had to wait until Mom got up, but I did everything in my power to move along her return to consciousness, from fits of loud coughing in the living room to heavily dropped shoes to noisily rattled newspapers—all without actually violating the rule of not deliberately waking her up.

Like Grandma, Mom was a good cook. Once she had made a recipe she cooked by instinct, figuring out alternatives if she lacked an ingredient. Her recipe box had a hundred neatly written or typed recipe cards. Decades later the cards are spotless and appear practically unused, but all these dishes appeared regularly in front of me. Most of the recipes were probably what Grandma had cooked when Mom was growing up. Mom must have written these and the accompanying cards filled with household hints—how to remove stains, rescue scorched food, eliminate odors—as she was starting up married life with Dad. Mom was clearly following the best advice to a housewife of the time, recorded in her *Better Homes and Gardens Cookbook*: "Meal-planning is a game that's fun if you play it with imagination and zest. If you play it well, you win satisfaction for yourself and cheers of enthusiasm from your family."

PART TWO

It certainly didn't work out that way for Mom, but I don't think that Dad's decision to abandon her was due to a failure in her cooking.

I still relish and can call up the smells and tastes of her meals. Food was a source both of comfort and a way of expressing affection, and eating dinner together, often with the radio playing in the background, was our most constant shared activity.

CHAPTER

ELEVEN

LITTLE WHEELS

FROM THE FIRST week after our return to Missoula I explored Missoula's neighborhoods on my bicycle. In the valley a heavy bike with fat tires wasn't hard to pedal through the streets that we shared with cars and trucks without any thought of hazards or fatigue. At the edges of Missoula the flat land yields to the encircling mountains and as I grew older I began venturing up the steep dirt roads that ascended the narrow canyons of the Rattlesnake Mountains. Multiple speed bikes with gears and handbrakes were rare until a decade later; when we climbed the steep dirt roads we stood up in the pedals. It was hard work going up and exhilarating heedlessly speeding down, skidding around sharp turns and throwing up a tail of dust.

What drew me to tackle those mountains was the possibility of catching fish. My first mountain trips were with my cousin Eddie, when I was in the seventh grade. Eddie was a year older than I was, a bit bigger and a lot tougher. Although he had polio when I lived in Butte and wore leg braces for a few years, he recovered completely. In high school he was an effective halfback because he was fast, wiry, elusive, and mean. His face was spattered with freckles and topped with wavy black hair. If he hadn't been my cousin—if I had encountered him turning a corner in Butte—I would have been afraid of him. But as my fishing coach, I merely struggled to keep up with him. On the six mile bike rides from our houses to the dam that confined Rattlesnake Creek's crystal clear water in a reservoir that was Missoula's water supply, Eddie just kept grinding away, sitting when I was already standing in the pedals, never dismounting when—stripped to the waist, panting, and complaining of aching legs—I desperately wanted to walk the last few hills and push my bike up the dusty gravel road. I was too embarrassed to wimp out.

The trip took an hour. We dropped our bikes in the bushes and scrambled and slid down the steep rocky banks just below the dam. With telescoping metal poles that could be collapsed and carried on our backs for the ride, we tossed hooks baited with worms or grasshoppers into the swirling pool at the base of the dam. Between bouts of daydreaming we watched the ripples and the pools downstream of the boulders for the barely detectable shadows of loafing trout resting from the swift current. When we saw a trout we felt all the intensity of a hunt, but more often than not we couldn't tempt them to bite and caught nothing but their fleeting beauty.

The creeks I biked to when I first began to fish were not the bountiful trout streams where I learned to fly fish years later—and a worm or grasshopper on a hook dangling in the water was not a Royal Coachman or grey-hackle yellow that could be cast twenty or thirty feet from where we were sitting. I didn't care much if I caught a fish, but I was thrilled when I got a sharp tug and watched my line zigzag across the water as the fish tried to escape. I had no net; if I worked the fish close to the edge of the water without losing it I just jerked it out onto the bank where it lay gasping and flopping until, with hands shaky from the excitement of landing it, I banged it on the head with a rock.

These were days that I dreamed about in the years after I left Montana: on the edge of our surging adolescence, we were full of excited anticipation of all that lay ahead; we were off on our own where no adult or other kids could bother us or even know where we were. We had done a hard and satisfying piece of work to get there. What I missed later wasn't so much catching fish but the scent of the hot, dry, resiny pines and the dust from the road and the pleasure of eating my lunch with my bare feet dangling into the cold stream and my back warmed by the sun. The only sounds in that windless canyon were the clicking of grasshoppers that sailed yellow-winged from one clump of weed flowers to the next and the crashing of the water down the face of the dam into the pool and around the boulders dropped there by glaciers thousands of years ago.

I made my usual lunch, sandwiches of bologna with iceberg lettuce and Kraft mayonnaise on white bread, and maybe a few cookies, but after the ride in and a few hours of fishing, they tasted awesome. Aunt Ruth made Eddie's enviable lunches with thick slices of their leftover breakfast bacon layered on slices of Uncle Lloyd's tomatoes and the crisp leaves of his lettuce between two pieces of toast.

Later, when we were in the eighth grade, Dick Ainsworth and I would make the long, difficult ascent of Pattee Canyon beyond where there were any houses and fish the creek with dry flies that we had shoplifted from Montgomery Wards and catch little trout that we cleaned, skewered with a bank-side willow branch, and roasted over a fire made from dry sticks left behind as the spring floods receded, the fish only minutes away from where they had been sheltering under the branches that shaded the creek. We always carried matches and a Boy Scout knife, all we needed to prepare the meal. We usually burned the fish but lied to each other and said they tasted terrific.

PART TWO

When I started the seventh grade in 1956 the University was still catching up with the doubling of the student body that followed the World War Two and the Korean War. While cheap housing was rapidly built about twenty blocks south of the campus for the married GIs who might never have gone to college except for the GI Bill that paid for their tuition and expenses, the Republican legislators delayed funding new classrooms, athletic facilities, and administrative buildings at the University because they thought that it was too liberal. They steered funds to the State College in Bozeman to expand the more practical and apolitical agriculture and engineering schools. When funding finally was shifted to the overcrowded Missoula campus and a rash of building broke out, the old heating plant near the river had to be expanded. Huge tunnels were constructed to connect the new buildings to the heating system. For a few months Rollie and I biked to the University to watch the construction. The concrete pipes were big enough for a full-grown man to stand up, and soon we figured out where we could enter the tunnels and explore the entire system, often as much as a half mile away from where we had entered. The uninsulated cast iron pipes that would carry steam were attached in brackets along one side of the concrete tunnels; we did our explorations in the summer, before the new sections of the heating system were turned on.

We explored in the total dark with only a flashlight and the occasional bright streaks of light beaming in from widely spaced openings in the tunnel where manholes would be installed. In our imaginations, we were American soldiers sneaking up German escape routes to mount a surprise attack, or submariners stalking battleships, or spies communicating with secret agents behind enemy lines. We lived in constant, low level fear that the whole heating system would suddenly be turned on or sealed up and that we would be roasted before we could get out, or that a pipe would blow up, or that we would be trapped like miners in a cave-in. That only added to the excitement and sense of discovery. We never told our parents. And we never met other kids in the tunnels: perhaps they had more normal ways of spending their summer.

A childhood in Missoula afforded us many benefits that would have been hard to come by in, say, Los Angeles or Philadelphia: Rollie and I were a ten-minute ride away from our own river and island.

As the Clark Fork passes through the center of Missoula, it divides around several long and narrow gravel islands during the spring run-off flood that were much wider through the dry summer and fall. The biggest of them was right under the Higgins Bridge where a small pedestrian bridge made it accessible, and anything one might do there was fully visible to anyone standing on the bank or crossing the bridge. But our stretch of the Clark Fork and its island were inaccessible except to the intrepid. At the upper end of town where the river widened as it came out of Hell Gate Canyon was a long gravel bar jammed with willows and cottonwoods and aspens lying under the old wood-decked Van Buren Street Bridge, cut off from both shores by the swift current. The only way to get on the island was wading the sometimes-lethal current or climbing down the steel girders that supported the middle of the bridge. We had to climb over the safety rails on the side of the bridge and then dangle from the stringers that supported the deck until we got a toehold in the girders that angled away from us at 45 degrees and then climb down about thirty feet, one handhold, one toehold at a time, until we were on the island.

By the middle of summer, when the river was down to probably a third of its peak flow, we could wade across from the southern shore through waist deep water, trying not to lose our balance on the slippery rocks or be knocked over by the current and washed into the main channel, where we were almost certainly too small and too poor swimmers to avoid being drowned.

PART TWO

This was the exact spot where a decade earlier the police had picked up Sammie, Rollie, and me when we tricycled from McLeod Avenue to visit the river at the roaring spring flood stage.

We believed that other kids had never figured out how to get on the island before us, but animals certainly had—the only paths through the trees and wildflowers and brush were deer and beaver trails. The deer crossed from the shore on the ice during the winter. The beavers were permanent residents. We never saw another person—or a deer—on our island adventures, and the beavers eluded us and our traps.

We built a hut from driftwood and dead branches and reeds. The first visit we built the walls. We came back to complete the hut a few weeks later. Rollie brought a hatchet tucked in his belt to cut leafy, low-hanging branches from cottonwoods for a roof and camouflage. Toward the end of our construction, I was inside smoothing out the sand and pebble floor and Rollie was tossing branches on the top. I complained that he was going to knock the place down, but he assured me that the hut was "strong enough to hold an elephant." Then he threw on a long piece of driftwood and the roof collapsed and the sides followed and I was buried in sticks and leaves and tent caterpillar webs and dust. He was laughing so hard that it took a long time for me to persuade him that he had to dig me out.

We mostly just explored the island, finding old sand bags piled years earlier when a flood threatened to wash out the foundation pier. We found rabbit trails and created clever traps of bent willow branches with a loop to catch a foot, and baited the trigger with carrots stolen from home. We brought matches so we could roast what we caught. The carrots disappeared but we never caught anything. We found clothes and fishing lines and empty cans still bearing the faded labels of extinct brands of tobacco and beer and corned beef that had washed up on the island and then been left behind when the water levels fell in mid-summer. We lay on the sand, shoeless and shirtless after swimming in small, calm backwaters, letting the sun bake our wet jeans dry and tight. We spied on a couple of college students trying to find a few private minutes together in the brushy banks across the channel on the shore abutting the University's arboretum; Rollie gave a running commentary about what he thought they were doing, but neither of us fully understood how sex worked, and just the thought that they might be kissing left us giggly and breathless.

We spotted birds and declared them eagles, and stirred up snakes and pronounced them serpents. We felt fearless and brave and wild, but our mothers complained about the sand and feathers and little white bones that fell out of our pockets when we undressed after a day of exploring.

At Halloween I went trick or treating with other kids who lived close-by, racing from house to house.

"Trick or Treat!"

"Who are you?"

"Gordy Noel," I said, and whoever I was with would shout out at the same time "Dick Ainsworth," or "Rollie Trenouth," or "Hal Woods."

"What are you?"

"Hobos!"

Always we were hobos, dressed just in our old clothes. Our masks cost a dime or we had no masks and we smudged our faces with fireplace ashes. No one spent money for manufactured costumes.

If the people who came to the door didn't know us they asked where we lived or guessed at our mother's names or our father's business:

"Dick Ainsworth? Then Bud Ainsworth who has the drugstore on Broadway is your dad, isn't he?"

PART TWO

We would double back to the houses that were giving out bigger treats—full size Hershey Bars that sold for a nickel, or Mounds Bars that sold for a dime. For the repeat visits we tried to change our appearance enough not to be caught; we didn't always succeed and were shooed away. The local Coca Cola dealer Mr. Small gave out bottles of Coke and cinnamon donuts and we always got there early: on Halloween that was our dinner. Dr. Zimmerman, my dentist, handed out toothbrushes. We went there once and never went back. I hated him, and so I decided to hate his bossy daughter, Mary Anne Zimmerman, who had perfect teeth and was always good.

When we moved to Beverly Avenue after the sixth grade I was the only boy within several blocks of suitable age to be asked to mow and water neighbors' lawns when they left for their two-week summer vacation. My lawn jobs did not turn up much cash—25 cents to mow a lawn, a dollar a week to both mow and water. I started to make real money when I took over Joe Monger's evening *Missoula Sentinel* newspaper route that fall. Joe had moved up to the coveted *Daily Missoulian* morning route—many more customers on each block and less territory to cover. Readership for the evening paper was skimpy, 105 customers spread over 100 blocks, just one or two on any block. I delivered the evening paper six days a week and the *Sunday Missoulian* as well. On Sundays I got up at 5 AM to deliver the paper, but the rest of the week I rushed home when school let out at 3:45 PM to begin my deliveries. A bundle of 107 papers was thrown on my front lawn around 3 PM. I "boxed" the papers into a shape that could be sailed twenty-five feet onto the front porch and stuffed them in a large canvas bag that I carried in a basket attached to the handlebars of my sturdy bicycle. I rode as fast as I could on streets and sidewalks and front lawns, zigzagging from one house to the next, tossing the paper on the front porch or steps. When it was raining or snowing I got off the bike at houses without covered porches to put the paper inside the front door so that it wouldn't get wet.

Most of the time I was home by six o'clock to do homework and eat dinner around 7 when Mom finally got home. For half the year I rode from dusk to dark—the winter sun sets early in Montana. My bike lamp did no good because the newspaper bag obstructed it. But the streets were lit and there were not a lot of cars on neighborhood streets until people began to come home around five-thirty.

No one walked dogs in those days; the owners opened the door and let their dog out to sniff around the neighborhood until they decided to go back home. Sometimes one would chase me. The herding dogs were bred to chase anything that moved and nipped at my ankles and feet, but every kind of dog from Dachshunds and terriers to hefty Springer Spaniels and retrievers took off after me. To avoid getting bit I would raise up both feet to the level of the handlebars and coast for a few dozen feet hoping that I had enough momentum that they would drop the chase before I had to pedal to stay upright. After a year of battling or evading dogs, I acquired a belaying pin from the set of an opera in which I was performing and carried it and a Captain Nemo squirt gun filled with soapy water to bop the dogs on the nose or squirt them in the face, which deterred all but one cranky Cocker Spaniel that would first savage me and then tear the paper into shreds. That dog's owner complained that I was delivering slobbery papers and I told the manager of the delivery boys, Jim Rambo, that it was their dog and not me chewing up the papers, that they could avoid the problem if they kept the dog inside in the afternoon. Mr. Rambo called them, and after that they mostly kept him in, but every few months he would be lying in wait for me behind a hedge next to the house and race toward me snarling and barking. The hair on the back of my neck stood up, my heart raced. I raised my feet, bopped him with the belaying pin and coasted. He was determined to catch me and I could never get away from him without pedaling. He chased me a half block, foamy saliva flying out of his mouth and then, having fulfilled his mission, he trotted home proudly and shredded the paper into confetti.

The *Missoula Sentinel* had to be delivered in all seasons and in all weather. Like dairy farmers, paperboys did not get vacations: the summer after the seventh grade I missed going to Flathead because of the paper route, and there were papers to be delivered on every holiday evening except Christmas Day and the Fourth of July, when the publisher figured no one would be reading the evening news and the stores would not be advertising.

In the winter I rode on the ice and snow, careful not to turn corners too sharply or to try to plow through drifts. Temperatures could plunge to minus twenty—sometimes to minus thirty. When the lawns got covered with snow I could no longer arc from sidewalk or street through the yard to get closer to the front porches—I had to sail the papers further, from the sidewalk or street. If I missed, I got off the bike, put down the bike's kickstand, walked through the snow, found the scar where the paper had incised the snow and reached deep to find the square package. I tossed it on to the porch and remounted my bike, my hands and toes getting progressively colder as I got further and further into the route. The winter gear I could afford was not very effective: at the end of the route, and often much sooner, I would feel frozen to the bone, worried that I would get frostbite. Mom said my lips and nails were blue for an hour after I got home. Sometimes I had to take a hot bath to get thawed out.

A few times every winter the snow would pile up to two or three feet during an overnight blizzard and biking the route was out of the question—in two feet of snow I could not even get the bike out of the garage because the door would not open; no one would have shoveled their sidewalk; and not enough traffic would have gone down the streets to create a hard-packed track I could ride in. On those nights or pre-dawn Sunday mornings I trudged the route, carrying the heavy bag over my shoulder, catching snow flakes on my tongue, wiping at my tearing eyes to keep the lids from freezing shut, my squeaking rubber boots making a fresh track on the walk and lawns and streets. Walking in deep snow, I would get the last papers delivered at 6:30 or 7:00 pm and still have a mile to trudge back home.

Some winter nights, finger-frozen, I would stop at a grocery store to warm up, slapping my hands together, stomping my feet, as most of the customers did as they crossed the threshold, their breath steaming. A few times when the owner wasn't looking I kyped a package of Hostess cupcakes—I preferred chocolate, with the crème center; second best were the "Snowballs", chocolate half-globes with marshmallow centers, covered with coconut, one white, one pink. I didn't care for Twinkies. The cupcakes went down the front of my pants—I pulled the waistband out to make sure that the package went inside my underpants so that it wouldn't fall down my pants leg and onto the floor as I walked out, which was always hard to explain. Then I ate them as I biked the rest of my route, my hands immediately getting cold again as I unwrapped the package, but my mouth and stomach satisfied and thrilled by getting away with it. Sometimes I ordered ten cents worth of salami and waited while the owner cut from a long sausage ten thin slices that he would hand over on a piece of butcher paper in exchange for two nickels or a dime: he objected if I paid him in pennies because he knew that I was a boy who worked and had real money in my pocket, dimes and quarters and sometimes a silver dollar.

I made a dollar a day, thirty bucks a month, delivering newspapers. But delivering the papers was not the hardest part: collecting payment for them was. I had stiff beige cards in a canvas-covered binder three inches wide and 10 inches long, one for each house with the customer's name and address at the top and perforated rows and columns of chits with the date of each week running from bottom to top. Most customers wanted to pay for a whole month at a time, 30 cents for the six *Missoula Sentinel* papers, 40 cents if they also took the *Sunday Missoulian*. Almost no one paid ahead of time—they paid for what had been delivered. Because I was in school all day, I collected on Saturday mornings or afternoons, biking or walking from house to house, ringing the doorbell or knocking, waiting for someone to answer, often a dog having a tantrum on the other side of the door. Whoever opened the door peered down at me, usually with a disgusted expression. I was barely five feet tall and just over a hundred pounds, spectacled, freckled, buck-toothed, and very serious. I carried a moneychanger on my belt. I was never who they wanted to see at their front door.

"Collecting for the Sentinel."

"How much is it?"

"There were five weeks last month. Two dollars please." I tried to be chipper to help the customer through this difficult moment.

"I ain't got two bucks right now. Why'didntcha come last week?"

"I did . . . . last week you said you didn't have any money, I should come back this week."

"Well, I ain't got as much as two bucks. Let me go look." Then he would disappear for a few minutes to scrape up some change, returning with a handful of coins that he was still picking through. "Here, I have a buck forty-eight."

"Okay, well, I'll take a dollar twenty and you will still owe me for two weeks. I'll come back next weekend and you can pay me that and for this week."

I would rip off three chits from the bottom of the card and then move on to the next customer. The men were the grumpiest. Women just tended to take forever finding their coin purses and then claimed inadequate funds. The reluctant customers tried to make it seem my fault that they didn't have enough to pay me, my fault that I couldn't change a twenty dollar bill for an eighty cent charge, my fault that I didn't come last week or next week, my fault that the paper wasn't worth what they were paying me for it, my fault that I had bothered them.

Each week I collected from about thirty customers in two or three hours. Some insisted that I come every week and would never pay for two weeks. Some refused to pay at all and after a month or two when they ignored my knocks I would tell Mr. Rambo and he would either extract the money from them or tell me to stop delivering.

When I collected in the summer, I could smell cooking through the screen doors—bacon in the morning, cabbage at noon, or toasted cheese, at every time of day the smell of scorched coffee from percolators kept simmering on the back of the stove. In the winter the door was usually closed in my face and I stood shivering on the front porch.

For the *Missoula Sentinel* customers I got their paper on the porch or inside their front door 312 times every year, 363 times if I also delivered their *Sunday Missoulian*. At Christmas I would get tips from maybe a third—usually twenty-five or fifty cents; I considered a dollar a prize. Or I would be given a slice of fruit cake, or a cookie, or a Christmas card—the kind that came twenty to a box for a dollar—with the customer's name scrawled on it, but no gratitude, no flattering comments like "best paper boy in all of Missoula." I preferred the money or the fruitcake.

Every week I had to pay for my papers. For every paper Mr. Rambo took four cents, and I got a cent. If I could not collect, it came out of my share: Mr. Rambo never paid me back what the people who wouldn't pay cost me. He wrote that off as my bad luck.

I bought a small metal strong box and screwed it into the floor under a drawer in the bottom of the built-in closet in my bedroom. With the lid locked and the key hidden, my portion was safe and I felt rich, with money to spend for candy or pop or anything that my weekly allowance of twenty-five cents would not cover. Every few months I wrapped my coins in paper tubes and took them to the bank, in exchange for which they stamped in the sum of the deposit. Between the seventh grade and the end of my sophomore year in 1957 I had saved enough to buy a car.

Rollie was my most frequent playmate in grade school. There were two other boys in our grade who lived close to him, Stubby Wilcox and Bruce Sievers; Rollie had gotten to know them at Paxson in the three years I was away in Butte, and he often played with them. We all were in Cub Scouts and Boy Scouts together, but I never played with either. Dick Ainsworth was my closest neighbor and my other regular playmate. Dick had a tree house that his dad had made, reached by a ladder that could be pulled up to keep others out. There was a swinging rope for returning to the ground in a Tarzan-like arc with our best imitation of a jungle whoop. Dick had an enormous collection of comic books for which I could sometimes trade those few comics I owned that he had not already read—all of the Bugs Bunny and Donald Duck and Roy Rogers variety—for his much more desirable Batman and Superman and combat comics. My Mom censored violent subscriptions, except for the white-hatted cowboy variety, but I never told her about my swaps with Dick and she didn't go through my comic book pile looking for contraband crime and war "comics".

Both Dick and Rollie spent more time with other boys than with me, and while I sometimes felt lonely and envious when I knew they were playing with other kids, I also seemed to drift toward reading without any prompting from anyone. Most weekend or summer days I spent hours in my tree house or inside lying with my back on the floor, my legs propped above me on the seat of a chair, reading a Hardy Boy mystery or living two hundred pages underwater with the crew of a submarine stalking German transports and battle-ships.

After nearly drowning in Flathead Lake I was a non-swimmer from the third to the sixth grade. Flathead Lake was the logical place for me to learn to swim, but there still was no one there to teach me. I spent the summers playing on the beach or in the shallow water near shore in a humiliating life jacket. After moving to Missoula the situation remained the same: the Missoula municipal pool was closed for years because of the polio epidemic throughout the country; even the great wading pool in Bonner Park close by my house was dry for years. In the summer of 1952 the swimming pool was reopened, and during the summer before the seventh grade I was old enough to be allowed inside the pool by myself. Most young children went to the pool with a family member, but Mom worked. Having Dad go there with me was never a possibility. So one day I bicycled there by myself and entered into a strange world with no clue about what to do. I parked my bike in a vast rack of bikes, none of them locked. A high school student working in the locker room handed me a basket to put my clothes in. I undressed and he shelved my basket and gave me a large safety pin with the same number as the basket that I fastened to the leg of my swimming trunks. That was cool. So far, so good.

I looked around to figure out what to do next. I could not see where door to the swimming pool was. The dressing room was full of boys, almost all bigger than I was and aggressive in the noisy, pushy, blustery way grade school boys can be. I was none of those things. I watched what the other boys did and, trying not to be noticed, followed them into a shower room, and then through a foot bath, and then outside into the brilliant, blasting, heat of a Montana August after-noon. The world was blurry, since I had left my glasses with my clothes. There must have been a hundred kids running around the pool, jumping in, yelling, diving off the high dive, pushing each other in, ignoring the whistle blasts of the majestic, god-like lifeguards. Clumps of girls had claimed territory, sunning themselves on large towels thrown on the hot concrete skirt around the pool. A few were in the water calmly floating on their backs. I wondered how they did that. There were no boys sunning or floating: the boys were in constant motion, like ants whose anthill had just been poked with a stick, running around the edges, jumping in the pool, splashing water on anyone foolish enough to have parked themselves too close to the water.

The concrete was so hot that my feet were at risk of blistering. I climbed down into the shallow end of the pool and clung to a corner, watching. The water was almost as warm as a bathtub, and it reeked of chlorine. An older boy was showing a boy even smaller than I was how to dog paddle. I imitated this and immediately sank to the bottom: I was nothing but skin and bones, with no fat and no buoyancy. Hacking and spewing inhaled water, I tried again. In a few minutes I was paddling hard enough to move a little in the water and I figured out a way to suck in a gulp of air, although someone's wave occasionally arrived just as I was inhaling and I had to cough out the water. Swimming seemed like a slow form of drowning.

Over the summer, by imitation or an occasional suggestion from other kids, I progressed from the dog paddle to something like a backstroke, then a sidestroke, and then a crawl. By the end of the summer I was able to demonstrate to a lifeguard that I could swim across the deep end of the pool and I was allowed to jump off the diving board.

The next time I was at Flathead I told Grandpa and Grandma within two minutes of arriving that I no longer needed a life jacket to fish or swim. I explained that I had learned to swim at the pool in Missoula. I put on swimming shorts and took them down to the Agen's dock. Before they could stop me, I jumped in and swam about twenty feet into deeper water, and turned around and swam back grinning. Grandma said, to no one in particular, "Can you imagine that!"

CHAPTER TWELVE

OUR RETURN TO Missoula in 1950 posed problems that Butte did not, because of Dad's proximity: with whom would I eat Thanksgiving and Christmas dinners? How much time would I spend with Dad? How much time would Sammie spend with us? Because Sammie and I fought all the time when he visited in Butte, Mom had decided that my visits with my brother had to occur in Dad's presence; the presumption was that Dad could control the fighting, although when he heard me howling he simply assumed that Sammie had done something wrong and punished him; I retreated from the field bloodied but haloed.

There was just enough truth in Dad's presumptions to sustain this unequal arrangement for the rest of Dad's lifetime and well beyond. When I was eight Mom and I had made a short visit to Missoula a few days after Christmas. I hadn't seen Dad in more than two years and Mom turned me over to Dad for a night so that she could go out with friends. He and Marjorie—the "other woman," whom I had never met—were living in an old section of the downtown in a narrow, lightless three-story apartment, with a kitchen and sitting room on the first floor, their room and a bathroom on the second floor, and, at the top of a dingy, narrow, steep staircase, an attic room where Sammie slept. After dinner I was turned loose with Sammie to play. He took me to the third floor to show me his Christmas booty, which included a set of boxing gloves. Sammie laced me into mine and then said he was going to teach me how to box to protect myself from the Butte boys who made my life miserable. His first punch knocked me three feet across the room. I began to cry and he teased me from tears to laughter. He then knocked me stair by stair down the staircase, every few stairs teasing me into laughter, until I was laid out squalling on the second floor landing. Dad came whipping around the corner of the living room and up the stairs and slapped Sammie around. Sammie covered his face with his hands and cowered against a wall to ward Dad off. He was banished to the third floor and I spent the night on the living room couch.

 I didn't spend another night in any of Dad's several houses as he slowly moved up in the bank and into better neighborhoods and houses. When Sammie invited me to his house to play, Mom always checked to be sure that Dad or Marjorie would be there too.

Holiday meals were much more complex than the decision about where Sammie and I would play. Mom wanted me to be with her on Thanksgiving, which was fine with me because Dad used ten times too much sage in his turkey stuffing for my taste. Instead, Mom and I went to dinner with Uncle Lloyd and Aunt Ruth, an odd arrangement since Lloyd was Dad's brother and in many ways his hard-edged, Camel-smoking, whiskey-drinking twin. Lloyd and Ruth managed the difficult task of remaining on speaking terms with

Dad and staying good friends with Mom for the rest of their lives, although many years later Sammie told me that Lloyd never forgave Dad for leaving Mom, whom he adored, and splitting up the family.

Uncle Lloyd had the most beautiful garden in our part of Missoula. Kids could know that because we were constantly biking along the alleys that ran behind the houses, taking short cuts from one friend's house to another, or prospecting for cool trash in back yards. We knew in which yard there were apples ripening, where someone was hoping that the corn would mature before the first frost in September, where there were prize-quality pumpkins, and where the cucumbers were so big that we were tempted to steal them for one of our pickup games of vegetable football. We also knew where the friendly dogs were kept behind a fence that we could poke our fingers through and pet them, and where the dogs would just as likely bite our fingers off.

Uncle Lloyd's garden seemed huge to me at the time, although it was probably no more than about 30 feet on a side. He composted his grass, kitchen scraps, and autumn leaves and dug the compost into the deep, fertile Missoula Valley soil. The smallest weed didn't stand a chance. He was as protective of his garden as a surgeon would be of his operating room; he shooed us away if we ventured inside the surrounding fence to keep us from trampling anything. Outside the garden he had raspberries that Aunt Ruth turned into pies and preserves; crabapples that, pickled, found their way to the Thanksgiving and Christmas tables, and currants for jellies. He grew beans and cucumbers on strings spread between neatly implanted posts, with pole beans climbing to six feet. His tomatoes and other tender plants bore fruit long before anyone else's because he started them in hot beds in which rotting fresh cow manure and strategic alignment with the sun kept plants warm when the temperature outside still dipped below freezing at night.

There were a lot of stories about Uncle Lloyd, most of them involving gardening, drinking, smoking, and his trial-winning Golden

PART TWO

Retrievers and Labradors. Uncle Lloyd never worked in the garden without at least one Camel cigarette lit. He chain-smoked, lighting one cigarette with the glowing butt of the previous one. Sometimes he forgot that he had put a cigarette on a post when a chore required both hands. Once I found two cigarettes smoldering on separate posts, while another was burning down millimeters from his lips. I learned a lot about swearing from Uncle Lloyd: twice, when he was yelling at my cousin Eddie and me for an infraction of one of his many rules, he picked a cigarette off a post and put it in his mouth lit-end first. The invective stream was impressive. We beat it out of there as fast as our legs would carry us, trying not to laugh loudly enough for him to hear us.

Uncle Lloyd, or Uncle Did, as he wanted to be called, was a terrific gardener in a town full of terrific gardeners. Post-war Missoula was still a place where anyone with a little ground grew vegetables in sufficient quantity to put up a full pantry for the winter. At Lloyd and Ruth's, Thanksgiving really was a celebration of the year's bounty. The table was pulled out to its greatest length, which in the small dining room meant that the kids, once seated, were pinned against the wall until it was time for the adults to get up. Various card tables were set up for extra food and extra people that appeared at the last moment. At each place was a little crenellated paper party-favor cup full of peanuts and pastel-colored butter mints, an amazing concession to the otherwise total prohibition on sweets before dinner that we observed the other 364 days of the year. In clear glass dishes shaped like leaves and four-leaf clovers Ruth set out her best strawberry and raspberry preserves, pickled crabapples and pickled watermelon rind and bread and butter pickles and tiny sweet pickles and pickled tiny onions. There were plates of celery filled with cream cheese and scrubbed carrots and radishes and bunching onions with their greens curled if Lloyd had managed to keep the fall plantings of root vegetables going all the way through November by covering them with straw.

When we were seated at the table, Lloyd carried in the deeply browned twenty-five pound turkey on a platter and sliced off drumsticks as large as footballs for Eddie and me; it was an article of faith that small boys liked drumsticks and I was never given the option to eat white meat until 1959 when Rollie Trenouth and I, far away from home, ate Thanksgiving dinner in a restaurant, something unheard of in Montana, where almost everyone was with family or friends and only the Golden Pheasant Chinese restaurant was open. The drumstick was a source of great apprehension for me, weighing about two pounds and by itself adding up to about four times what I could eat in a single sitting. My plate passed hand to hand around the table as a progression of adults ladled on mounds of mashed potatoes, bread stuffing and sweet potatoes, peas, jellied cranberry sauce that still had the marks of the can molded into it, fresh baked clover-leaf rolls, and a great daub of yellow butter.

By the time the plate was set down in front of me it was piled so high with food that I was eye to eye with my potatoes and could only see the tops of the adults' faces from the nose up, even though I was sitting on a stack of magazines. Of course, the rule was that I had to eat everything placed in front of me, and Lloyd had the theory that I would not be so small if I ate more. At this point I regretted having eaten anything for the past three days, but I would diligently shovel my way through. I was always the last to leave the table and never had room for the fresh, thick apple pie and glasses of cold milk that were served when the adults had washed the last of the company China and silver and cooking pans and had put them away until Christmas. We were turned loose to play—there was no television to watch—and we ran around playing games of hide-and-seek and treasure hunt in the bedrooms and attic while the adults went to the living room to smoke and talk.

Before I went home Aunt Ruth—skinny as Uncle Lloyd and, also a chain-smoker, leather-faced—would sit me down in the kitchen and feed me one of her oatmeal cookies with a glass of milk. She leaned against the frame of the kitchen door, one bony arm crossed over the other, a Chesterfield between her second and third fingers, black hair hanging straight to her shoulders, asking me to tell her whatever was important to me at the moment, just the two of us. Turkey and stuffing and potatoes and rolls and an oatmeal cookie or two—there was never pie left over—always accompanied us home, because Ruth said that Thanksgiving without leftovers would not have been good enough for Mom and me.

Lloyd and Ruth never expressed affection for me in words—in Montana at that time neither relatives nor friends volunteered that they loved us—but the affection was clear none-the-less in including us in their family, in making sure we had leftovers to take home, in listening carefully to what we had to say. Mom called on Lloyd when she had a financial issue to discuss or needed guidance in fixing something that was old or broken in our house. And after high school Lloyd found good jobs for me in the sprawling Forest Service that he helped to manage.

At Christmas, Mom allowed a brief amnesty in her embargo against my going to Dad's house and I was allowed to eat dinner with Sammie, Marjorie and Dad and their daughters Arlene and Judy, but not until Mom and I had opened presents quickly and gotten the house ready for her one annual social event, an open house where she served Tom and Jerrys in white mugs used only at Christmas, cookies, fudge, and the prized fruitcake that took her three months to make from a recipe that had come down from Grandma. Getting me out of the house was a practical response to the crush of guests about to arrive: the front room only had seats for five people when there was no tree, so the ten or twelve people who squeezed in on Christmas afternoon took chairs from the dinette or sat on footstools. Their cigarette smoke and laughter filled the house for hours, progressively louder as Mom's annual bottle of Bourbon was drained into the Tom and Jerry batter. Just before her friends began to arrive around 3 PM I walked the six blocks over to Dad's house for supper. Mom wouldn't allow Dad to drive to the house to get me, especially when it was full of her friends.

Dad's Christmas table was not the overladen banquet of Lloyd and Ruth's Thanksgiving, but the staid and appropriate fine supper of a banker. No one in Missoula ate better on that day. We sat down to a five-rib roast of prime beef served properly rare in a pool of red juice, roasted potatoes that had baked in the pan drippings for the hour before the roast came out, bowls of cooked vegetables, and various pickles and relishes from Dad's modest garden. The amount put in front of me was negotiable: unlike Uncle Lloyd, Dad was considerate of how much I could comfortably eat. The supper was delicious and probably the only rare roast beef I would eat for a year. Wine drinking had not come to Montana and certainly would not have been shared with children. I think that Dad, for whom drinking was a problem, tried to avoid alcohol when I was around, if not so that I could carry a good report back to Mom, at least to avoid a bad report.

After dinner we would sit in the large living room for a half hour or so and he would give me my gift. This too was always a source of bitter displeasure for Mom, who resented the fact that Dad could give me memorable, "milestone" gifts that I would cherish and that she could not afford. When I was fourteen, he gave me a Remington .22 rifle with a five bullet magazine and then gave me a shooting lesson, an occasion which required Mom reluctantly turning me over for the extra time with him. Another Christmas he gave me my first fly rod. When I got older he just handed me a sealed envelope in a heavily embossed gift envelope from the First National Bank with a crisp new ten-dollar bill.

PART TWO

Dad and I hardly knew each other: he knew nothing of my daily life and didn't ask about school or what I was reading or how I spent my time. He always seemed ill at ease, as though he was on his best behavior. I was spared the angry and often disparaging comments that he made to Sammie and sometimes to his daughters, but for me there was never warmth in that house.

While Dad often gave me a nice present at Christmas, in other regards he was not generous. Sammie got braces in high school; when I got to that age Dad asked to look at my teeth. I clenched my jaw and pulled back my lips.

"Your teeth are really crooked," he said.

He asked me to open my mouth wide and he studied my many fillings, the legacy of living in an area without natural fluoridation and my fondness for sweets.

He said, "They aren't worth straightening," and he looked at me in a way that said I wasn't much to look at and that straightened teeth wouldn't make me look any better and would be a waste of his money. Perhaps he thought that my dental destiny was going to mirror his. He said that his teeth were taken out during a childhood infection and, like Grandpa, he had false teeth.

Dad did introduce me to fly fishing and between the seventh grade and high school graduation he took me with him four or five times. Before our first trip he took me to the Missoula Mercantile sports department. I biked downtown and met him across the street at the First National Bank, where he had a desk with the other loan officers. Dad had on tan gabardine slacks and a bold plaid sports jacket, a white shirt and tie, his usual work clothes. His wavy blonde hair was neatly combed and parted. He wore wire-rimmed glasses that framed his bright blue eyes against the ruddy background of his face. I was in jeans, striped t-shirt, and sneakers, my usual clothes summer and winter. He took me around to show me off to several women who were cashiers and secretaries. Marjorie's brother Randy

Jacobs, a bank vice-president, was seated nearby; Dad did not introduce me—the kid from the woman he had left—to Randy.

We jaywalked across Front Street to the Missoula Mercantile and into a large room full of sporting gear but empty of customers on a summer weekday morning. The only person working was a distinguished, silver-haired man in his fifties who was standing behind a glass-top counter full of pistols and expensive fishing reels. He had a nametag that stated that he was Les Colby, the sports department manager. He was wearing a grey suit and a tie decorated with small jumping rainbow trout. He looked like the father in "Father Knows Best," a TV program I had seen at Rollie's house. Dad introduced me as his son Gordie and told him that I needed some fishing line and a reel. Les looked at me with a surprised but friendly expression and asked Dad how much he wanted to spend.

"This much," Dad said, and held up a dime.

I didn't know much about fishing gear, but I knew enough to understand that Dad felt that my potential as fisherman and son weren't worth much. Les rounded up ten cents' worth of fishing line, a package of five snelled hooks for worms and grasshoppers, and a reel.

Dad asked Les what it all would cost. "Two bucks and two bits," a dollar-twenty-five.

Dad forked over a silver dollar and two dimes and a nickel and I marched out beside him with a mixture of satisfaction and disappointment, pleased with my new fishing gear, but humiliated. Lots of kids whose lumberjack or truck driver fathers wouldn't have been able to afford more than $2.25 would have walked out pleased that the budget had been squeezed a little so that they could outfit a fishing pole. But I knew that Dad wasn't just scraping by. Perhaps this was just the way men talked about their young children with each other—holding up a dime as a funny way of saying, "let's keep this inexpensive until we see if he's going to be interested in fishing."

But I had no way of knowing how men talked to each other and was embarrassed that this handsome friend of Dad's would know that my dad didn't give a damn about my feelings or about me.

It was through fishing that I became aware of Dad's drinking. Each of the next few summers he took me fishing with him on Rock Creek, even then a famous fishing destination. I would bike to his house with my gear in the early afternoon. He would be standing at a stove heating a large cast-iron frying pan in which he had cut up chunks of beef, carrots, onions, and celery, stirring them in a thick brown gravy. When I arrived he would spoon it all into a wide-mouthed thermos and pack some slices of white bread thickly buttered.

The drive to Rock Creek was about an hour. Dad would stop at a tavern about fifteen miles up the road and go in for a highball of bourbon and soda. He would order Seven Up or a ginger ale for me, and we would linger at the bar while he chatted with the bartender. Dad seemed to know everyone. Then we would continue the drive to the Forest Service road that ran along Rock Creek. There was a famous roadhouse there, the Rock Creek Tavern. Dad always pulled into their dusty parking lot and sat at the bar for another half hour or so, drinking one or two more highballs while he sent me off with fifty cents to buy us each a few dry flies at the sports counter, telling me which patterns to look for.

The drive along Rock Creek on the graveled, rutted road, occasionally blocked by grazing cattle, could be another half hour or so, until he found one of his favorite stretches of water where there were no cars already parked along the road. Boys splashing in water spoil the fishing for anyone downstream, so he went upstream of me. He stuffed his creel with fresh wild grass and I could see that he had two bottles of Highlander beer in the bottom. We probably wouldn't see each other for an hour or so as I worked upstream toward him, casting as best I could into the ripples and under the branches overhanging shaded, slow, deep water. I spent a lot of time rescuing my flies from the shrubbery when my cast went astray, sometimes risking drowning in swift, deep water in order to retrieve the ten-cent fly. Dad waded in khaki pants and shirt and hat and calf-high rubber boots. I waded in sneakers and jeans and was soaking wet by the end of the day. I was happy as a clam and caught about as many fish as a clam might have. Dad usually had two or three nice trout nested on the grass in his creel and he would give me one to take home for dinner the next night, which Mom would grudgingly cook. As the sun was setting we would sit on the tailgate of his station wagon eating the beef stew and buttered bread, Dad drinking a beer. I drank the Coke that he had brought along for me.

I knew Dad until I was thirty-five. These were my happiest memories of him. My fly-fishing skills ultimately developed all the way to mediocre; what I learned I picked up here and there. Dad never took time to fish beside me and coach my casting; if he knew how to read the bug hatches and match the fly he was using to what the fish were seeing on the surface or under the water, he never taught me. When I improved my fishing gear I bought it myself with money I earned from my various jobs.

Sometimes in the spring or fall when he didn't have anyone to play with Sammie would invite me over to play catch or throw passes. The first time I played catch with him he threw a hard ground ball that bounced and hit me in the face. The second time it happened the ball broke my glasses, which made Mom furious, because new lenses or frames were not in her budget plans. She forbade me to play ball while wearing glasses, but I disobeyed: without them I couldn't see well enough to catch or hit or even to throw accurately. I never acquired an ability to keep my eyes on a fast grounder coming toward me without at the last minute flinching, turning my head aside to avoid being smashed in the face. That meant that often the ball went between my legs or hit me someplace where my glove wasn't, to the dismay of anyone whose pickup team had been unlucky enough to end up with me, usually among the last few chosen. Until near the end of grade school I didn't even have a baseball mitt, a baseball, or a bat. When he moved out of Dad's house at the beginning of college Sammie gave me a useless catcher's mitt the size of a dinner plate that was too stiff to fold around a ball, and an old first baseman's mitt missing the webbing between the fingers. I managed to re-web the first-baseman's glove and it was passable, but by then all of my friends had been started in Little League years earlier and the good ones had moved up to the Pony League. In what few pickup games I encountered during the rest of my life my poor eye-hand coordination always betrayed me.

Without an engaged dad and with a working mom, I drifted through childhood without the experiences that people later on assumed would have been a big part of a Montana childhood. I had to confess, with embarrassment, that I was not an expert horseman because I never got close to a horse, nor could I talk about Montana's great powder snow or iced-over lakes: with neither a car nor money, skiing and skating were out of my range.

Cub Scouts and Boy Scouts were the after-school activities that I stuck with through grade school. Beginning in the fifth grade every few weeks I went to Steve Smith's house to do some kind of craft with Steve's mother who was the "Den Mother." The best of our projects was making puppets over several months, creating a playhouse and a script, and then putting on a very silly play in which the puppets mostly beat on each other until the strings by which we dangled and controlled them got tangled. My puppet lost a leg in the middle of the show. For a decade it hung lonely and purposeless in its blue tunic from a nail pounded into a ceiling joist in the basement, its separated leg ghoulishly thumb tacked to its right hand.

Our Boy Scout troop was even better organized. Starting in the sixth grade we met in the evening once a month in the Paxson gymnasium. The evening activities were devoted to learning skills like knot tying and braiding, use of knives and hatchets and axes, first aid, and woods craft. Our troop leader was Owen Bacchus, a recent graduate of the School of Forestry at the University, now working for the U.S. Forest Service. He was a tall, strong, cheerful, and unflappable guy who was born to teach the skills we were required to learn so that we could acquire merit badges and move up the promotion ladder from Tenderfoot Scout, to Second Class Scout, to First Class Scout, and then on to Eagle Scout.

There were about fifteen of us boys. Herding us required the help of several fathers who would show up for the meetings and join us on hikes and camping trips. Not all of the boys' fathers came—Dr. Trenouth and Hal Woods' father never did as I recall.

I suppose my father was never invited. I was used to him being absent from most things in my life, but one time Dad decided to accompany me to the annual Father-Son Boy Scout Dinner in Missoula. This turned out to be as awkward for my Dad and me as it had been when Mom came to the Cub Scout banquet in Butte. Dad drove me to the large Masonic Temple meeting room and we walked in together, but I felt weird being with a man that none of my friends had ever seen with me. All the fathers knew the other dads in our troop, but Dad didn't seem to know any of them, although we all lived in the same neighborhood. He made no effort to strike up a conversation with anyone, and none of other dads came over to talk to him. The two of us stood alone silently on the edge of the room, Dad smoking. During the dinner we sat alone. I left feeling disgraced: I knew how to navigate the dads and sons on my own, but having my Dad along felt like a burden and I didn't have the skills to deal with it. I didn't know polite manners—walking up to a friend and his father and saying with pride, "this is my dad; Dad, this is Bruce Sievers and his father."

As hard as it was for Mom to have been left by a husband who went off with another woman, my Dad's life after the divorce must have been uncomfortable for him as well. Dad probably avoided being in situations where others would see us together: it would have been a reminder of who he was and what he had done. I guessed that none of my friends' dads respected him enough to be friendly with him. I might as well have brought a bum to the dinner.

In the winter we spent one or two weekends camping in the snow. On one trip the snow was so deep that we couldn't set up tents and ended up staying in a Forest Service cabin, fifteen boys and four fathers crowded together in closely packed sleeping bags and all talking at once. After a day spent tromping around in the snow identifying the tracks of three types of rabbit and foraging for plants under the snow from which we could make soup if someday we were stranded, our drying clothes in the hot cabin created clouds near the ceiling. We all smelled like wet dogs. The fathers were heroic: we served as kitchen hands and they toasted bread and fried eggs and bacon on the wood-burning stove for breakfast, and grilled up greasy hamburgers and sliced potatoes for dinner. Hungry from the long day's exertion we chewed through the piles of food as if we had been served a banquet. The four fathers became all of our fathers and directed us with the expectation that there would be no back talk, and there was none. It was my only experience of seeing other boys with their fathers or seeing men together with each other.

In the early spring of my eighth grade year our troop took a snow hike up Butler Creek. As we hiked up from the road we crossed south-facing hills where the snow was melting off fast, creating dozens of small crystalline streams running down to the creek. In an hour of hiking we climbed a north-facing hillside where the snow was still a foot deep, completely burying the trail in some places. I was ten yards ahead bushwhacking on the edge of the snow pack, trying not to slip. Suddenly there was an explosion of snow and something moving fast up the hill and I was tumbling down the hill. I rolled to a halt against a tree and saw a black bear scampering into a patch of pines. The rest of the troop stared open-mouthed at the bear crashing into the trees, trying to figure out what had happened. We discovered that the deep snow had covered a small cave just above the edge of trail. The bear—probably three years old—had hibernated in the cave and as the snow melted, his nose, which was outside of the cave, had become exposed.

I had stepped on the bear's nose.

I was thrilled.

I didn't make much progress as a Boy Scout. Others in the troop got the necessary merit badges to advance to First Class Scout. Bruce Sievers became an Eagle Scout, and so did Mike Brown, and maybe Stubby Wilcox. Working on merit badges required a father or a brother to help with projects, to teach skills, to arrange outings. I barely made it to Second Class Scout, and then only because Mike Brown's dad agreed to take me along on a hike in which we were supposed to cook dinner for a father. Mr. Brown valiantly ate our greasy fried potatoes, greasy hamburger, and scorched butterscotch pudding. Mike and I were both terrible cooks, but it was easier for Mr. Brown to pass us than to expose himself to our cooking a second time.

In Boy Scouts I was an orphan. Because I was silly and talkative I often had to be pulled back in line by one or another father and I sensed that none of them liked me. Finally, Stubby Wilcox's perpetually stern, scowling father told me I had to shape up. He suggested that I become the quartermaster for the troop, in charge of all the troop's equipment, our flags, and whatever we needed to take along on a camping trip or hike. He had guessed, correctly, that given some responsibility I would feel valued enough to settle down. That worked pretty well and turned out to be something that my teachers and classmates also figured out once I got to high school: when I was asked to organize or manage almost anything I did a good job and enjoyed myself.

In the end, although I wasn't a dedicated Boy Scout, I learned a lot in scouts and for years I hiked and camped with skills and knowledge acquired over those grade school years, although, as it turned out, I hadn't learned enough to keep me out of trouble.

CHAPTER

THIRTEEN

SMALL TRANSGRESSIONS

IF ROLLIE AND I could have talked our parents into camping out in our backyards every night during the summer, we would have done it. In August, on moonless nights we knew that there would be a lot of shooting stars, often two or three in the same moment, a half dozen in a minute. We had ground cloths to block the dew, and sleeping bags. My kapok sleeping bag was so massive that I had to carry it on my head the ten blocks to Rollie's back yard. Full darkness doesn't arrive until very late in Montana in the summer; even in August it is not totally dark until after 10. We would lie on top of our sleeping bags watching for the stars to become visible as the dusk faded to night. We tried to see the constellations as they were shown on the map that Rollie had, but I wasn't good at imagining outlines when I only saw scattered stars surrounded by other equally bright stars. When we gave up we joked about boys we deemed even stranger than we were, speculated on how awful next year's teachers would be—speculation fueled by well-worn tradition passed down from our older brothers and sisters and the big kids in the neighborhood. We swore to stay awake all night. I was asleep in an hour and awoke hours after dawn with my dew-glazed glasses still on.

On other nights, when the house lights were turned off we crept away and roamed Missoula's sleeping streets. Few houses had lights on after 10:30 and there was no television at that time to keep those awake who in a few years would become the baggy-eyed late-night watchers of Steve Allen and Jack Parr and Ernie Kovaks. Our frequent cruises down alleys acquainted us with which yards had ripe fruit and vegetables. We all must have been continuously hungry as kids because we were always looking for free food—raspberry bushes planted too close to a low back fence; strawberries edging a lawn where it met the gravel alleys; apples ripening on branches overhanging the street.

We didn't deliberately head out with the mission of stealing fruit and vegetables, it just . . . kind of . . . happened. The urge to pull a fat carrot out of the ground was irresistible. We would grab the biggest carrots and run like crazy, as though each carrot was alarmed and that at any moment a watchman would appear with a shotgun. Perhaps we identified with Peter Rabbit and regarded our nameless, faceless neighbors as Peter regarded farmer Brown—as grumpy old people to be tormented. Perhaps it was a more general pushing back against grownups' expectations of respectable behavior, as when, on deep frigid nights walking home from Boy Scout meetings, we peed profanities on the pavement in front of the houses of people against whom we carried no important grudge. The letters were fully visible as black ice the next morning when we walked to school, barely hiding our secret ecstasy as we studied our artfully embossed three and four-letter words ("pee" and "poop" were still regarded as a vile profanities; anything anatomic was beyond our courage or knowledge). Perhaps transgression was the natural outlet for the pent-up energy of the thoroughly supervised.

Running away from a raided garden, out of breath and exhilarated, we would find a faucet by someone's house a few blocks away, rinse the dirt off the carrots, and then, happily chattering in whispers, walk toward our next conquest crunching the carrots down to their green-black crown, depositing the bushy green leaves in someone's mail box or under their windshield wipers and running away as fast as our giggles would allow. We ached to plant ourselves in the bushes in the morning so that we could see the expressions of some sleepy businessman discovering a bundle of carrot leaves pinned to his windshield, but we were never organized or brave enough to return to the scene of our crime. Clearly, as good as the carrots were, most of the reward was in annoying perfectly innocent people.

In the grade school years, when sleeping out was based in Rollie's back yard, our expeditions were small and usually just the two of us. In high school, before any of us had cars, we would sometimes learn that the girls from our neighborhood were having an outdoor slumber party and three or four guys would camp out in my back yard, waiting until it was dark enough to walk a few blocks over to where the girls were. I don't remember if they knew we were coming, but they didn't seem to mind. There was suppressed laughter as we all made a quick exit from their yard in search of late summer apples. Two or three boys could be quiet and stealthy, five or six boys and girls were not.

Once, when we had scaled a wall and all of us were up in the branches of a big apple tree munching apples and chattering, we were startled when a bright light swept across the alley side of the tree. In panic we jumped from the tree and clambered over a section of the wall farthest from the source of the light. By instinct we broke in different directions, but three of us had made hand steps for several of the girls and we were slow to get away. Tailed by a panting policeman who was not up to a long sprint we made good progress, his light making crazy but receding arcs on the street in front of us until he called out "Stop, stop or I'll shoot." Rollie remembered that as "Stop! Stop! In the name! of the law! or you'll taste! lead!", which always cracks me up when I imagine the headlines in the next mornings' *Daily Missoulian*: "Stalwart Guardian of Justice Shoots Dead Six High School Students Caught Stealing Apples from Mr. Hardenburgh's Wormy Apple Tree."

We stopped; we had apples in our hands and stuffed in our pockets.

"What the hell do you think you're doing?"

"Picking apples."

"Why in the goddamned hell were you climbing a tree at midnight to pick apples? They're on the ground all over the alley!"

He was in really bad shape and so out of breath that he could barely speak.

"I don't know," I said.

"Where did all those other kids go?"

My friend Lee was a year older and more articulate than I was: "Beats me!" he said.

"You know that's against the law, dontchu, you little shits!" He looked pissed.

We were silent. He took our names and our parents' names and I gave him my phone number, LIncoln 3-5722, and immediately regretted that I hadn't given him a phony number, although we were all confident that if we told a policeman a lie we would go to jail, which was far scarier than being grounded for a few days. He told us he was going to turn us in and that we would live to regret it.

Lee—who I was sure was headed for a career in either law or car theft—asked the cop how he had found us. The cop glared at him:

"The station got calls from three houses on this street saying that there were a bunch of kids out late making noise, and why didn't their parents pay any attention. It's midnight, you little turds should be in bed. And don't ever let me catchya doing this again."

I said we would never, ever do it again, knowing that we absolutely would do it again, and knowing that he knew that too.

He didn't call our parents.

We never let ourselves get caught stealing apples again.

This was my longest conversation ever with an enforcer of the law. It made me wonder what kind of kid grows up wanting to be a policeman.

CHAPTER

FOURTEEN

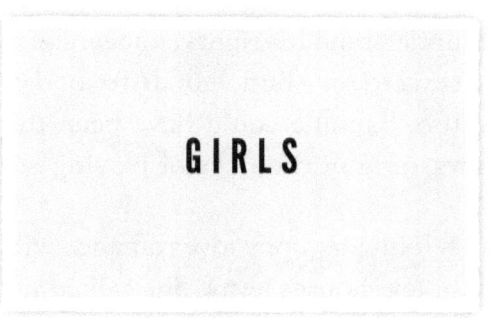

GIRLS

OUR LAST TIME together at Flathead Lake, when Sammie was a high school sophomore and I was about to start the seventh grade, new neighbors moved into the old Birmingham place a few houses down the road. The Loys had two teenage daughters, each of whom was quite lovely and neither of whom chose to acknowledge my existence. If we passed on the side of the road on the way to or from the Micken's store where either they or I had to yield to avoid stepping into the traffic, they didn't look at me, didn't smile, didn't talk, didn't get out of my way or thank me for letting them by. Sammie was doubly smitten and spent a lot of time courting them. I was an embarrassment to him and he banned me from being around when he was hanging out with them. One night he snuck down the fire escape and spent most of the night on their dock, creeping back into our bedroom as it was getting light. He got caught. Voices carry on the lake: at 2 AM Grandma and Grandpa had heard the girls laughing and recognized Sammie's voice. They were so agitated that they didn't sleep the rest of the night. Grandpa threw him out, sending him back to Missoula on the morning bus. My mind went wild imagining what he had been doing with the girls.

I have a picture of Sammie sitting on his suitcase beside the road, waiting to flag down the bus, complaining that Grandpa and Grandma didn't understand his rights as a teenager. An hour before the bus came he tried to set a bunch of driftwood on fire and I have a photo of that too: Sammie could have been the poster teen in advertisements warning of the risks of playing with matches and firecrackers.

After he left I fell into a puppy love romance with a girl who was visiting her aunt a few houses away. She talked me into being her boyfriend, which to her meant pricking her finger and mine with a sewing needle, mixing our blood, and swearing to be boyfriend and girlfriend the next summer. She uttered well practiced but inscrutable incantations while we solemnly wiped our bloody index fingers together and then licked the blood.

I was clearly not her first.

I did not get a fatal disease.

After that summer, I never saw her again.

That fall, Rollie's mom and mine got calls from Mary Anne Zimmerman's mother asking if we would be partners for her daughter and Mary Kraabel at Jean Campbell's School of Dance. Formal dances and proms were on the girls' distant horizon, but more immediate was the annual winter ritual of the seventh and eighth graders' two-year course in ballroom dancing in the meeting hall of the very dignified Episcopal Church of the Holy Spirit. Mary Anne's and Mary's mothers wanted their daughters not to be awkward when they began the dancing classes at the church. I think Rollie and I were chosen because we were the least intimidating of all the Paxson grade school boys: Rollie was quiet and shy, still smooth faced and boyish; he showed no interest in girls whatsoever. I was talkative and friendly with everyone and still a boy soprano. For me Mary Anne was way too pushy, but since I had a perpetual crush on Mary, it was as though a miracle had been bestowed upon me. Faking reluctance, I agreed as long as Mary was my partner.

And so for eight weeks, after dinner on Thursday nights we learned to fox trot and waltz to badly worn 78 RPM recordings of Glen Miller and Jimmy Dorsey in the big practice room next to Bill Campbell's Laundromat. Mary and I barely talked—we watched Jean dance with Bill, who was appropriated for the purpose between loads of commercial laundry, and then I put my arm around Mary's back, took her right hand in my left, and we executed, each whispering the rhythm—one-two-three, one-two-three, step-step-slide. Mary could not tell right from left without thinking about it and we often bumped into each other or headed off in opposite directions. She sweated, I apologized for stepping on her toes, she was gracious, and at the end of the lesson Mary and Mary Anne were driven home by a parent, and Rollie and I walked the twenty blocks home in the early winter cold talking about ham radios and Morse code and who had won the last Mickey McCullough-Johnny Butler fist fight on the playground. I kept from Rollie the secret that I was in heaven and agreed with his sour complaints about the lessons.

In January twenty girls and sixteen boys showed up for the beginners dancing classes at the Church of the Holy Spirit. We had been instructed to dress up. The boys failed to look different than usual; the girls, in pretty dresses, looked as though they were going to a birthday party.

The boys instinctively lined up against one wall, the girls against the other. We did not look at each other, or did so only furtively. First we were taught how to ask a girl to dance. The boys, we were told, always ask the girl, never the other way around. We were to walk up, bow slightly with our right arm in front of our waist, the left bent behind our back, and ask, "May I have this dance, please."

The boys didn't want to ask the girls, and stayed fixed against the wall. The girls shuffled their feet surveying the bunch of us, but when they saw the raw material that six-and-a-half years of barely civilizing grade school had delivered to them to work with, they too stayed flattened against their wall.

To break the deadlock, the veteran teachers had the boys stand in a line in the middle of the room facing away from the girls and had the girls line up facing the other way, back to back, no peeking. The girl's line was four bodies longer than the boy's. They were asked to side step to the left three times, so that if they had deliberately stood behind a boy they liked they were out of luck. Then the boys and girls were told to turn around and face each other. Sixteen boys looked at sixteen girls, several of whom immediately headed back to the wall, forfeiting their place to one of the girls not lined up with a boy. The girl in front of me did not run away, but neither did she look at me with an expression that suggested that I was the answer to her most feverish fantasies.

The boys, repeating after the teachers, asked, "May I have this dance?"

And without prompting, the girls repeated, "Yes you may. Thank you for asking." Mine gave a little curtsy, which unnerved me, having no previous experience with being curtsied to.

Sweaty hands were clasped and we were directed to spread out around the room. Invariably I was paired with a girl a foot taller than I was so that my eyes lined up with her collarbone. My partner would move my arm up her back to the appropriate height and place her right hand in my left. The needle was dropped and, with our arms stiffly keeping each other at the greatest possible distance in order to minimize the surface area of contact, we fox trotted or waltzed while the teachers roamed from couple to couple correcting posture or pushing us into turns once we had mastered the basic box step of the waltz or the straight forward and straight back shuffle step of the foxtrot. So intense was our focus on the steps and so uncomfortable the intimacy that there was no conversation between the partners. There was never eye contact, which would have been unbearable. We all sweated and from time to time I saw a boy sneaking a sniff at his left armpit to determine whether he had broken through his deodorant.

As the class advanced over the winter the teachers continued to try to get the boys to cross the room to choose a partner; most of the time we remained plastered to the wall, but sometimes a few of us would give in to the teachers' enthusiastic prompting and venture out, and then the teachers would grasp the other boys' hands and lead them to a random girl. No boy was allowed to dance twice with the same partner to insure that all the girls had some dances, since the girls without partners never danced with each other in the Church of the Holy Spirit.

On February 29th the girls were told that they could choose partners. I waited for Mary Kraabel, who chose someone else. I was requisitioned by Tinsel Teeth, the tallest girl in the class, who came equipped with full dental hardware. A snapshot of the room could have made the cover of *The Saturday Evening Post* or *Life Magazine*: a portrait of the forced, painful acculturation of a room full of socially and physically unskilled adolescents, mismatched in every respect except for age and an intense distaste for touching the person they were dancing with. TT was as thin and straight as a broom handle, an outspoken keeper of rules whose expression generally suggested that she found boys distasteful and me the worst of the lot, although her tightened lips may have been her way of hiding her braces. She also wore glasses shaped to resemble cat eyes, studded with fake jewels. I wore glasses and felt ugly, and accorded any boy or girl who wore glasses the same disrespect, especially someone who wore rhinestoned cat-eye glasses. As we danced she looked straight ahead over my shoulder and jerked me back into position if I failed to dance precisely as we were being instructed. My feeling was that she chose me only because she liked me less than any other boy in the class and knew that she had nothing to lose.

A year later in the eighth grade we actually looked forward to the dance classes—not because we wanted to dance, but because afterwards the Paxson students went just a few blocks away to Hansen's Ice Cream or we went to Katie Crutchfield's brick Tudor house—buried beneath out-sized cedars that made it seem like a Hansel and Gretel set—to play the earliest of courtship games: Post Office, Spin the Bottle, and Winkum.

Winkum was like tackle football, except that it involved chairs, there were no helmets, and only one person was in motion. All the boys or all the girls sat in chairs, with one extra chair. If the girls were sitting, a boy stood behind each chair. The boy with the empty chair winked at a girl and she was supposed to quickly leap out of the chair to run to his chair, and the boy behind her chair was to try to hold her in the chair. The girls were often faster or slipperier and would successfully cross to the empty chair. The boy with the newly empty chair would then wink at a girl—and keep trying until finally one broke free and filled it. Of course most of us wanted someone in a chair who we then got to hold—the sheer physicality of the game and the ensuing laughter added to the exhilaration of the body contact. In the tussle hands sometimes landed in places other than the shoulders. I always winked at Mary Kraabel; everyone knew I would; the boy standing behind her knew I would; she rarely broke away to sit in front of me. Mary winked at me once in a moment of pity or bad judgment, but the guy beside me thought she winked at him and beat me to her chair. My call for a replay was ignored.

GIRLS

The summer after the eighth grade my evenings were free and often my friends and I would meet on our bicycles and go to the Dairy Queen or someone's yard to play basketball or a street game like kick the can or hide and seek. Sometimes on Friday nights we went to the Bonner Park dances. Although we had learned to dance at the Church of the Holy Spirit, at Bonner we mostly watched high school boys who arrived in cars execute the sanctioned steps with strange girls from other grade schools who would become our freshman classmates in the fall.

The dances were held on the tennis courts with the nets removed. A record player recycled the pop dance music of that summer through loudspeakers hung from the court fences.

We bicycled over and hung around the edges feigning indifference—we were too self-conscious to fake coolness—but surreptitiously we watched the older boys' dance moves and the girls they were choosing as dance partners. There was a cooler full of pop packed in ice that we could buy for five cents and for another five cents we could get a bag of Gil Porter's Mt. Jumbo potato chips. Soda bottle and chips in hand we talked about the girls not already taken over by the older boys who were standing around a little self-consciously, pretending not to notice us Paxson boys.

"Who's the girl with all the petticoats?"

"That's Mary Zakos."

"Why haven't I seen her before?"

"She goes to Lowell."

"She's cute."

"Go on, ask her to dance?"

That generally ended the conversation, but as the summer wound down a few of us did ask girls to dance. My first was Mary Zakos, whose skirt stood out so far over many layers of crinoline petticoats that it was hard to reach my hand behind her shoulder. Dancing in the hot summer the boys all became rank, the combination of our sweat and Old Spice making us smell like bowls of Hormel chili.

Giving up on Mary Kraabel and all the other girls who knew me too well, I began to dream about the exotic girls from other schools I would meet in high school.

CHAPTER

FIFTEEN

THE HANDWRITING ON THE WALL

MUSIC WAS A big deal in Missoula, in part because of the well-respected school of music at the University, many of whose graduates stayed on in Missoula and wanted their children to have the experience of performing in larger ensembles. After high school every year a few students went on to schools of music and had successful professional careers.

By the sixth grade Rollie was playing the trumpet in the intermediate band, Stubby Wilcox the French horn, Bruce Sievers the drums. I wanted to play the trumpet, like Rollie. One evening Mom and I walked downtown to attend a meeting for new band and orchestra students so that we could find out what was expected. The star attraction was a piano performance by my classmate Judy Blegen's little sister Barbie, a fourth grader. She was so small that she couldn't touch the pedals and she had to sit on a huge dictionary. I had never heard classical music so what I heard seemed magical: for fifteen minutes she played a piano sonata without a score in front of her.

Mom paid for me to rent a trumpet and every week I had a short lesson at Paxson, and then spent another afternoon with the beginners' band. I had no natural talent. The band director, Mr. Miller, sent word to Mom that I would benefit from lessons, and for a year Mom hired Mr. Walton to coach me. He was a tuba player who had graduated from the University; the demand for tuba players in the Missoula music scene wasn't high and he supported his family by giving private lessons. In a fit of enthusiasm I had asked Mom to buy me a trumpet and promised that I would practice. Mr. Walton required that I play a book of exercises intended for advanced trumpet players and practice for an hour a day. The exercises were scales in different keys and with different tempos. There was nothing I recognized as music. I only practiced the night before. After a year he fired me: he said that he would rather that his family live a little closer to the bone than spend an agonizing hour with me every week.

I never got beyond the lowest seats in the trumpet section. As an eighth grader I was seated twenty-second out of thirty in the advanced band, which meant that there were at least eight people whose playing was more pathetic than mine. After recognizing that I had neither talent nor any interest in actually practicing, Mr. Miller suggested that I try the baritone, an instrument that might have been quite lovely if I had given it a try, but I stuck with the trumpet and mostly avoided entering offbeat. I mastered a few thirties pop tunes—"Over the Rainbow", "My Sweet Heaven", "Peg O'My Heart"—which I played with great verve and very loudly in my room until I left for college. If the neighbors got sick of hearing me they kept it to themselves. Mom gave my trumpet to a friend's boy when I moved away, which incensed me, although I hadn't expressed any interest in ever giving it a real try.

Taking on an evening paper route made after school athletics impossible, but music occurred during school hours. In the seventh grade we had mandatory weekly choral music practice. Among the boys the class quickly cleaved into athletes, musicians, and indifferents. Some of the big guys hated singing and gave the teacher Jim Cole a hard time. Jim taught choral music at ten grade schools, a half-day at each. He was big and imposing in the classic style of opera basses, and he was demanding. The non-singers fooled around: they made their changing voices crack, they sang nasally and exaggerated their bad pitch, they whispered wise cracks to each other.

After about a month Mr. Cole got tired of this. He picked out Rudy, the biggest boy among the rebels, who lettered in high school in all four years in track, wrestling, and football. He was the son of Mom's friend Rudy who was the shop foreman at Kraabel Chevrolet. He was officially Rudolph the Second but we referred to him as Rudy II.

Mr. Cole walked over to where he was sitting and grabbed him by the shoulder.

"Get up."

Rudy II didn't budge. "I said get up." This time Mr. Cole looked and sounded furious. With his huge hand he squeezed the muscle between Rudy's neck and his shoulder. Wincing, Rudy got up.

Mr. Cole dragged him by the shoulder to the front of the class, and turned him so that they were facing each other. They were about the same size.

"Hit me in the stomach."

Rudy just stood there. "I said hit me in the stomach." Rudy took a soft swing and poked his fist into Mr. Cole's substantial abdomen.

"Harder."

The class stared while this was going on. No one had ever seen a fight between a teacher and a student.

Rudy swung again, this time much harder. Mr. Cole didn't budge, and then suddenly his right fist flew toward Rudy's face in a huge arc, stopping just an inch short of Rudy's left eye. Everyone in the room let out a gasp. Rudy reflexively flinched and backed away.

Mr. Cole, standing sideways to where we were sitting, turned his head toward the back row, where the trouble-makers were. "Who's next?" Silence. "Come on, you guys always have a lot to say, come up here and say it to me".

More silence. Mr. Cole turned and looked at Rudy II silently, two feet between them; Rudy couldn't hold his gaze and looked away. Mr. Cole told him to go to the principal's office and wait for him there until the music hour was over. As he was opening the door, Mr. Cole called after him, "I only pull my punch the first time. The next time I won't give you that break. If you're still standing when I'm done, you can try to hit me back, but there won't be any more free shots. Now get out of here."

After that most of those boys would move their mouths but make no sound. Perhaps they really couldn't sing. That uneasy stalemate lasted until grade school graduation.

In the eighth grade Mr. Cole recruited a few of us to join the children's chorus in the University's opera program. By early spring I was bicycling to the School of Music auditorium three nights a week after my paper route for rehearsals and then dress rehearsals and then two performances of the famous double billing of "I Pagliacci" and "Cavalleria Rusticana" in full makeup (which I hated) and two changes of costume. I watched with unguarded fascination the real-life back-stage romance of the cast's handsome Canio and beautiful Nedda.

There were eight or ten of Mr. Cole's grade school students in the cast. Half went on to professional careers. Judy Blegen became the most famous and had a long career at the Metropolitan Opera.

Every quarter I had to take home my report card, give it to my mother for her to sign, and then return it to my homeroom teacher. The grading was simple: S and U, Satisfactory and Unsatisfactory. And the categories were also simple—reading, arithmetic, history, writing, art, physical education, and music. I always got satisfactory in those, and sometimes a few words in the teacher's comments box, like "Gordy is a good boy, but he talks too much." Almost every quarter I was given U's for penmanship, self-control, and cooperation.

This was embarrassing for Mom, who had to go talk to the teacher at least once a year and sometimes twice, because I was disruptive. I waved my hand hoping to be called on for every answer; when several other people gave wrong answers I would blurt it out. I answered questions before the teacher called on anyone and sometimes before she had even finished the question. I cracked jokes that were so full of private references to where my imagination lived that no one understood them; I made puns. I sometimes answered questions by giving a short lecture. Almost every day teachers would have students read out loud from the English or history lesson, giving each student a few paragraphs. When it was my turn often I kept going after the next student's name had been called out.

In the eighth grade, when nothing Mrs. Felker did suppressed my blurting out answers, our beloved giant janitor, Byron Price, put a desk outside the classroom door and when my teachers got tired of me taking over the class, I was sent out of the room to sit out the time until that subject had been finished and another was starting. I read whatever book I had brought along to school for such emergencies. I probably spent about a quarter of my time in the eighth grade sitting in the hall. For a while students passing would ask why I was in the hall, but everyone got used to it and stopped asking.

Early in the spring, a few months before graduation, Mrs. Felker told me that before I started high school I needed to learn "self control". She suggested that instead of answering questions or making

PART TWO

commentaries without being called on I make a check mark on a piece of graph paper every time I was about to talk but held my tongue. "As soon as you know the answer, you can write it down. See how high a score you can get and show me at the end of the day." I was pretty competitive and getting a chance to show her that I had known all the answers worked some of the time unless I was bursting with information about the subject or was bored. And when I did I was told to go sit in the hall.

One afternoon in May, after I returned from delivering papers and after we had cleared the dinner dishes, Mom said she wanted to talk with me. Mom was conflict averse. She had the awkward, nervous look that meant I was not going to like what I was about to hear.

She said that she again had been summoned to meet with Mrs. Felker.

"So, do you remember the tests you took in February?"

These were statewide exams to track students' progress at the end of elementary school. They went on for two days.

"I do. Didn't I do well?"

"Mrs. Felker said that you had tested into all the advanced freshman classes."

At first I was surprised. Then I was pleased. Then I was worried. "Does that mean they're making me skip a year?"

"No. She said you will be in the advanced freshman English and math classes and the next year also in the advanced biology class. She also said that your vocabulary and reading comprehension were at the level of a beginning college student. That's as high as the test goes."

At this she became a little emotional. Her eyes got misty and she stopped looking directly at me for a moment. She gazed toward the kitchen as though she was trying to remember if the oven was still on.

"Oh."

She continued to look away. "But . . . "

I had figured I was going to hear bad news, and now here it was.

"Mrs. Felker said, 'when he gets into high school classes with other bright students, maybe he will settle down and not talk so much. If he doesn't, I don't know who I am worried about more, him or his future teachers, God help them.'"

Mom looked at me with a little scowl for what seemed like a long time. She seemed to be considering what she was going to say next. "Then she said to me, 'I wish you good luck with him.'"

With that, not looking at me, she got up and went back into the kitchen. That was the end of the conversation, and she didn't return to either the good news or the bad news again. I don't think that Mom had ever told me directly that I needed to behave differently in school, any more than she told me that I needed to do better in school. She just gave me the information and left it up to me to figure out what to do about it. I suspect she didn't know how to make me different than I was. She also didn't congratulate me or say that she was proud of me.

In all of my time in grade school no one had ever said anything to make me feel that I was good at anything. It wasn't just me: I never heard that my friends had received overt praise except for Judy Blegen, who we all knew was some kind of gifted and beautiful alien. I only knew that I sang well because I had been asked to be in the University spring opera.

I'm sure that Mom actually was proud of me, and probably proud of herself, although she didn't say so. It was the first time she had ever come away from a teacher's meeting with anything but embarrassing news.

At the time I didn't have any way of putting what my scores meant into perspective. I knew that I had a lot of answers to classroom questions, most of them right, but more often than not volunteering information I hadn't been asked for only got me in trouble. I had no idea of what high school would be like, or how I would do in advanced classes, or where I was going in life. I had no idea how to be quiet. I more than half-believed that the fact that I read at the level of a Montana high school student about to start college proved that Montana high school students were crummy readers.

In the Montana of the mid-fifties, you didn't go around talking about your school marks with your friends. Given where they got into college, several of my classmates probably had similar scores. I never told anyone about my eighth grade reading score until I was in my thirties, living far away. People meeting me the first time were often surprised that I had grown up in Montana and wanted to know how I explained what had led me to my current life. My best guess was because I had spent so much of my time alone reading.

Our first home in Missoula, on Mount Avenue. We lived in the basement

Paxson School Fourth grade with Mrs. Metki. I am in the front row on the far left with a pheasant on my chest

Me before I started to wear glasses

The house on Beverly Avenue after one of many snowfalls.
This would have been a day for walking my paper route

Tenderfoot Boy Scout

At the Boy Scout Jamboree at Fort Missoula. I'm third from the right, the only scout whose belt was not tucked into his belt loops

Snow camping at Miller Creek. Hal Woods in front wrestling with his boot; I'm behind him and Rollie is behind me. Johnny Butler is striking a pose in the right corner

With Sammie and Mom on one of our rare times together at Flathead Lake

The Van Buren Street Bridge crossing the Clarks Fork
River above the island that Rollie and I claimed as our own

Sammie waiting for the bus the morning grandpa sent him
home for staying up all night with the Loy girls on their dock

Graduation from the Eighth Grade. I'm in the middle of the third row from the back, in front of Rollie, wearing a bow tie

PART THREE

CHAPTER

SIXTEEN

FRESHMEN

MY JOBS AFTER grade school graduation once again had kept me in Missoula almost the entire summer. Mom found out that the kitchen and dining room at the Lodge, the university's student union where she managed the information and registration desk and the scheduling of meeting rooms, would lose their college student busboys and dishwashers for the summer. She put me in line for one of those jobs and I went in to the kitchen manager's office to fill out the forms, admonished by Mom to use my best handwriting. Years of school completed—8; last school—Paxson grade school; previous experience—Missoula Sentinel paper route two years; lawn watering and mowing two years; shoveling snow, two years; shoveling sawdust, three years.

I got the job, eight hours a day, five days a week, starting at 6:30 AM. With a full-time summer job and a paycheck I had to apply for a social security number and file an income tax return. I started work

PART THREE

as soon as school was over. My job was to wipe tables clean when someone left, carry away glasses and tableware and plates and cups and trays for washing, clean up straw wrappers, napkins and ash trays and other junk left on or around the table, straighten chairs, sweep the floor, load baskets of glasses and dishes to run through the huge washing machine, fill bottles of catsup and mustard and sugar and salt and pepper and napkin holders, and pick up dishes coming off the washing machine and reload them into cabinets or counters to be used again. The pay was something like seventy-five cents an hour. I saved it all: with a paper route in the evening and a full time job in the morning I didn't have time to buy more than a twenty-cent movie ticket and ten cents worth of candy and soda once a week.

Without discussing it with me, Mom emancipated me from my monthly two-dollar allowance because I was earning my own money now.

Toward the end of the summer Mom's friend Marge asked her if I would be interested in the nightly cleaning job in her office, Bedard-Dickson: Insurance and Real Estate, and in the stock brokerage behind her office, the J.A. Hogle & Company. Mom said yes to Marge and let me know she had accepted the job for me. And so every afternoon when high school let us out I walked the mile north across the Higgins Bridge to Broadway. The brokerage kept New York City time and was already closed when I arrived at 4:15. The office was on the ground floor of the ancient Masonic Temple that dated back to the 1920's. The offices had cobwebby, cracked plaster walls painted a dull shade of olive green, a high, once-white stamped-metal ceiling with old-fashioned light fixtures dangling on cloth-wrapped electric wires that gave off a dim light, casting helpful shadows that easily covered any missed sweeping or dusting. The small trading floor reeked of chalk dust and cigars. Every night I dusted the counters and desks and chairs, swept the floors, and, holding my breath, I lugged the brass spittoon's porcelain pot to the toilet to dump the stringy spit and slimy cigar stumps and cigarette butts that floated in the stained water. I washed the pot and the spittoon, refilled the pot with water, set everything back in place, and cleaned the toilet and sink in the back. I felt filthy handling old men's collected excreta.

I was warned never to erase any of the hundreds of numbers chalked into little boxes beside stock exchange listings on the black board, and never to throw out the paper tape cascading down from the ticker printer that ran day and night, curling around its pedestal stand. There were baskets of older ticker tape and documents that I carried out and dumped in a beat-up bin behind the offices. Across the alley the kitchen vents at the Golden Pheasant Café gave off the only pleasant smell of my daily janitorial work.

By the time I had finished the brokerage, the insurance office staff had gone home and I dusted and swept and emptied baskets there. On Saturdays both offices were closed and I came in to mop the floors and wax all the wooden furniture and whisk out ceiling cobwebs with a brush on a long pole. The front windows had neon signs that buzzed and smelled of ozone. Working between their tubes and wires I washed and squeegeed the windows, cautious not to get electrocuted by the aged high voltage wires powering the tubes. Fried bugs by the hundred collected on the floor beneath the neon tubes and I swept them up, shuddering.

The Saturday cleaning took two hours. The mop water became dirty so fast that I had to dump it and refill the bucket with clean water three or four times; in winter, when everyone who entered was wearing heavy galoshes and walking through mushy snow, I had to change the bucket water every few minutes.

I was paid one dollar a day, plus a dollar tip once a month if I waxed the floors—thirty dollars a month, about what I had earned on my paper route. Thirty dollars could have bought 120 hamburgers, or tickets for sixty movies. In fact, in time it would pay for a lot of things that Mom did not have the money to finance—the money to go to school dances and to buy hotdogs and cokes at the Spartan football games on Friday nights; twenty-five cents toward gas money when we cruised around on a Friday night (at 15 cents a gallon, or sometimes during gas wars as little as 7 cents a gallon); fifty cents or a dollar for my share of a four-dollar case of beer.

I kept the job until I graduated from high school.

When we were misbehaving our eighth grade teachers, Mr. Ryan and Mrs. Felker, had never missed an opportunity to tell us that we were not ready to move up to high school: "Boys and girls! You are the worst class I have ever had. Ever!! This simply will never be tolerated in high school. The next person who I catch chewing gum I am going to send to the principal's office. Now stay in your seats and raise your hands and wait until you are called on."

At some level we knew that these teachers had been telling their eighth graders similar things for decades in the vain hope that they could reduce the chaos created by thirty hormonally disturbed children so that they could get a little work done at their desks.

But high school did loom large in our minds: we had older brothers and sisters whose maturity and freedoms we longed for; we would get to move from class to class instead of being with the same teacher and students hour after hour; there would be new subjects, like shop and drafting and home economics and business and science; and, mostly, there would be big kids to watch and to emulate and to become. There would be football and basketball games, and someday cars. Since the seventh grade, to the extent we thought of the future, the outer bounds of our horizons, our sole destination, had been high school.

I felt as though I had been lucky in getting "the better" of the two teachers every year in grade school, but in high school I could have had any of a dozen homeroom teachers: a typing or drafting teacher or one of the antique math teachers who wore the same suit and tie every day, or a geography teacher who never learned his student's names. Instead, I was assigned to Mr. Low, the head of the English Department.

Mr. Low changed my life.

We stayed with our homeroom teachers for all four year. Almost everyone in my homeroom was a stranger and in the first days we were awkward with each other as we tried to adapt to the rules and expected behaviors of high school. We were seated alphabetically. I was seated next to the stunningly beautiful Beda Lovitt, a smart, sophisticated, European-looking girl on whom I had a brief and futile crush, and who twenty years after graduation told me that after she graduated from college she "raped Russians for the CIA." I had no trouble believing that.

Ted Smith was also in Mr. Low's homeroom. Ted lived just a block over the line between Paxson and Washington grade schools and, although he played with my cousin Eddie and lived just two blocks from my Dad on Kent, I had never met him. Ted was quiet, distinguished, serious, bespectacled—the son of a University professor of Business Administration and one of our high school mathematics teachers. His life and mine were entwined for five decades, both as friends and as friendly rivals.

In the first few days, Mr. Low said we needed to elect a homeroom member to be on the student council. I was elected, I think because I was the most talkative and visible.

Mr. Low taught freshman honors English, sophomore English, and French. He was an angular, reserved, precise, mildly intense man with a tightly trimmed mustache and wire-rimmed spectacles, probably in his forties. He served in Europe during the War and returned, it was said, "shell-shocked." He had grown up in Boston and Salem in a prominent family famous for their jewelry store on Newbury Street, "Shreve, Crump, and Low", and he attended Amherst College. Every day he wore one of several well-kept suits with conservative neckties clipped to a crisp white shirt. I don't know how he became fluent in French, or what role that played in his military duties, but when I visited him after I graduated he told me that after the smoke settled and he returned to the United States he wanted to be as far as possible from Boston and the East Coast. He settled in as a beloved English teacher in Missoula, the kind of teacher about whom affectionate stories are written in novels and movies.

However much we discounted Mr. Ryan's and Mrs. Felker's warnings about our unique immaturity, we had taken them seriously. As though a curtain had dropped on our eighth grade behaviors, our classroom comportment was never much of an issue once we started high school. I was in both Mr. Low's honors English class and in Mr. Sugg's Honors Algebra class. The teachers were serious and their pace was fast. The students were all smart and they participated actively. There was no need and little opportunity for me to wave my hand wildly to speak, or to blurt out answers. In my Spanish class with Violet Boileau there were sophomore and junior students, as there were in drafting. Classes were quiet and orderly and a small freshman boy with a crew cut, big ears, and glasses who knew nothing did what he was told and stayed out of trouble.

Mr. Shepherd's drafting class was my first encounter with a subject that I had difficulty mastering (or maybe my second if you count penmanship as a subject, or third if you count Boy Scout knot tying, or fourth, if trumpet playing also needs to be included). While we had learned penmanship with straight pens and washable black ink, we learned drafting using ruling pens and permanent India ink, T-squares and triangles and French curves, laboring over a drafting board. Neatness wasn't optional: even an accidentally spilled drop of ink resulted in a returned drawing, anteing up five cents for a new piece of drafting paper, and starting over. We all perched tensely at our desks for a solid hour, everyone totally silent. Our first drawings were simple, but we quickly advanced to three dimensional and then curved and finally drawings in perspective.

I had taken drafting because I thought I wanted to be an architect. But no drawing I turned into Mr. Shepherd got better than a B-. What I thought was done well, he found deeply flawed: my arrowheads were not perfectly symmetrical, I could not eliminate slight line overlaps, and there were visible traces of the pencil drawing that were not completely erased when the lines were inked in; and my lettering was sloppy.

By the spring Mr. Shepherd had begun to smile and chat with a few boys, but he never graced my drafting desk with his presence. A few years later, when I passed him in the hall he didn't show any sign of recognition. I decided that he looked like Humphrey Bogart with a bad stomachache.

I finished my freshman courses with straight A's except for a C+ in drafting.

A career in architecture was delisted. I was disappointed: although I had no idea why I wanted straight A's, I clearly did. In grade school, along with everyone else I got a "satisfactory" in English and arithmetic and social studies; I had no way to differentiate myself other than by reading more than anyone else and answering questions I hadn't been asked and talking all the time—"talking out of turn," it was called. In high school I had a chance to stand out. Most subjects had frequent tests, all of our homework was graded, and the names of students who were on the honor or high honor roles were published every quarter. Since the other students in my advanced classes were also interested in learning, my performance was relevant and I was now visible as a good student. I found I liked to compete, and high grades gave me an identity that I could be a little proud of.

PART THREE

There had been warnings about freshman hazing from our older brothers and sisters and the occasional "wise" classmate. We were told that some boys were "pantsed," which meant that older boys held them down and pulled their pants around their ankles, pulled tight with the boy's belt, or sometimes they entirely stripped them in the midst of a crowd in the parking lot or streets around the school. If the grievance arose from a freshman talking with an upperclassman's girlfriend, the pantsing might be done in front of the girl, sometimes right in the hallways, with the girl cheering her boyfriend on, or so we were told.

While being pantsed was humiliating, it did not leave the lingering disfigurement that "scalping" a boy did. A bunch of older boys held the victim down while one clipped his hair with scissors or a straight razor, sometimes as a "Mohawk," but more often leaving behind a nearly denuded skull with randomly scattered uncut tufts. The boy was stared at for days, even after he tried to cure the damage by going to a barber, who had no alternative but to shave the boy's head nearly to the scalp as though he had lice. I heard that the barber a few blocks from the high school where I got my first baby haircut was a true humanist and would do these remedial haircuts the same day, for free if the boy did not have fifty cents.

Before the first home football game about three dozen freshmen showed up for the annual ritual of climbing Mount Jumbo to whitewash the huge letters made from rocks that spelled M C H S, carried up the mountain decades earlier. Although painting the MCHS on Mount Jumbo was shrouded with rumors of being a death march, it was nothing of the kind. Painting the MCHS was a "M Club" tradition and it was mostly boys that showed up. Two dozen boys carried five gallon buckets of whitewash up the hill, which involved frequent stops to change hands and a lot of sweating and panting, but no one was flogged or had whitewash dumped on them as had been rumored. For minor infractions of unspecified rules we were told to do pushups a few times, but that was the extent of the brutality. It was a warm, cloudless, early autumn morning, the dry grass on Mount Jumbo was fragrant, we all laughed a lot and in a way felt ourselves as somehow now a little more "in" than the rest of our classmates, perhaps what these kinds of rites were intended to do when the initiates are not abused. From Missoula's streets, when I looked at Mt. Jumbo I could see our work and feel that I belonged in Missoula in a way and at a level that had eluded me in Butte and during the grade school years in Missoula, no longer a scrawny kid chased home from school, nor the lonely, talkative chatterbox with irrepressible energy who competed too successfully with the teachers for stage time.

In mid-August I turned out for the freshman football team with some of the grade school friends with whom I played pickup football in Bonner Park. On the day of the turnout, we lined up outside the equipment room to be assigned worn-out cleated shoes, pants, jerseys, thigh and shoulder pads, and helmets. There was no fitting—the man handing out gear had been doing this for decades and guessed just by looking at us. I must have been given gear out of the "short, skinny kid" bin, but I felt authentic and powerful when I clomped onto the school bus in my cleats with forty other freshmen for the drive to the practice field where the new high school was being built.

The first workouts were nothing like football: I expected to have the ball snapped to me and to run through the line and make a few yards before being pulled down, or to be lined up in scrimmages as a fast defensive end. Instead, for two weeks we pushed blocking sleds up and down the field, practiced tackling dummies held up by one of the bored-looking equipment managers who would much rather have been spending time with the state champion varsity team, or we danced through rows of old truck tires, lifting our knees high trying not to trip and fall.

I contributed little to pushing around the blocking sled and I bounced off the tackling dummy without even the loud smack that rewarded heavier boys. But there was a bigger problem than the fact that I weighed 125 pounds and was only five feet and five inches tall. I couldn't see. Without glasses I was as blind as a bat. Mom said she couldn't afford to buy the kind of glasses that other nearsighted athletes wore with the shatterproof lenses and frames that were required by the school, and so I was practicing without glasses. Halfbacks needed to read the opposing team's backfield and had to be able to catch a pass. Without my glasses the backfield and my own quarterback and the ball were all a blur to me. To make the team I would have to try out to be a lineman—a guard or a tackle. The physics of football argued against my making the team as a lineman. And after a few weeks I slouched into the locker room after the other freshman had already left and turned in my gear. The equipment room man took the pants and jersey and pads in one big hand and threw them into a cloth-sided laundry basket without even looking up from the magazine he was reading.

In the spring I turned out for track. Like many little kids I could run faster than heavier boys and almost keep up with the long-legged tall boys. On our first practice day one of my friends suggested we run the two miles to the new high school where the practice track now was located. My running mileage the previous months was zero; my running mileage for the previous year was also zero. We ran in stiff leather shoes with spikes on concrete sidewalks and asphalt roads and we both had wall-to-wall blisters when we got there. Event by event we were evaluated by Don Delaney, the freshman track coach. Over the first week each freshman ran every distance—multiple heats of hundred and two-hundred-twenty yard dashes, the half mile, the mile. The only distances in which I made a showing were the mile and half mile runs. Through the long, cold Montana spring I suffered on the track, holding up for the first half and gradually fading in the final laps. My thighs aching and lungs burning, I dreamed of breaking my ankle or tripping against the inside curb so that I would have an honorable excuse for limping off the track. In the first meet against another high school I finished in the bottom half in both distances. A few days later I turned in my gear.

As high school began my voice changed, the premonitory signs of facial hair sprouted here and there, and I began to grow. Sammie was 5' 10" and I aspired to that. I stopped short, topping out at 5' 8" and about 135 lbs. But I had developed a reliable deep bass voice, the consolation prize of a pubertal growth spurt that started too soon.

Later I would sing in many of the high school music groups but athletics were never again a part of my high school life. I had never talked about trying out for a sport with Mom or Dad, or even Sammie, who, as a big-deal high school senior had zero interest in my high-school freshman life and tried not to make eye contact if we passed each other in the high school hallways. I never talked with anyone about how to train for a sport. And when I decided to quit, I had neither the problem nor the benefit of someone encouraging me to give it a longer trial or trying to coach me. And the truth is, at my size neither basketball nor football were realistic probabilities. The sports I might have been good at like soccer or cross-country running didn't arrive in Montana for decades.

CHAPTER

SEVENTEEN

THE LIGHTHOUSE KEEPER

IN THE AUTUMN of 1956 I began my sophomore year, still socially awkward but at least no longer a freshman. The new freshman stood out as strangely childish. Sophomores merely disappeared; we knew the conventions and the geography, but we were in no way important.

As sophomores we could sign up for the school-sponsored bus trips to watch the Spartan football and basketball teams play our closest opponents in Helena, Butte and Kalispell; the trips to Billings and Great Falls took as much as eight hours in each direction and only the players and cheerleaders went.

The sophomores were relegated to the front of the bus so that the junior and senior couples could hang out in privacy. On the trip back from a Kalispell basketball game I managed to snag a seat with the upperclassmen across from Bill Cadieux and Sharon Gordon and spent the first hour watching their silhouettes as they made out in the darkened bus. Both Bill and Sharon caught me looking more than once and Bill charitably asked Sharon if she would swap seats with whomever I was sitting next to and, apparently willingly, Sharon spent twenty amazing minutes teaching me how to kiss. She lay across the seat and in my lap and drew me close to her, her arms around my neck. When she pressed her open lips against my closed lips I was startled at their softness and the warmth her face gave off, the emboldening smell of her breath. I was astonished when she pushed her tongue between my lips and into my mouth. For twenty minutes she taught me how to French kiss—until then I neither knew that people kissed that way nor knew that there were words for it. For weeks I couldn't imagine what she thought of making out with me. Sometimes when we passed in the hall she smiled shyly. I practiced excuses for speaking to her, but always was tongue-tied. I have never forgotten her kindness.

My sophomore classes continued to be interesting and challenging: second year Spanish with Violet Boileau, advanced geometry with the formidable Virginia Speck, honors biology with Gus Hossack, geography with Agnes Brown, concert choir with Neil Dahlstrom, and advanced English with Ann Fowler. Homework now took at least two hours a night, with dinner squeezed in after I walked back from my janitor job downtown.

 The western slopes of the Rockies are cloudy in the winter, and the days are very short. By 4:30 in the evening in mid-December it is already dark. When you grow up in only one small part of the planet, you have no way of knowing that tulips bloom two months earlier in Maryland, that the flaming denouement of fall arrives in mid-November in Kyoto, not in September, that "really cold" in Oregon means ten above, not twenty below.

 At 7:00 most families had eaten dinner and washed, dried, and put away the dishes. Many would have been listening to radio shows. The few with TV sets were gathered in their living rooms in front of their small, black and white screens, watching *Dragnet* or *Gunsmoke*.

At 8:00 a few weeks before Christmas, Miss Fowler called me at home, something a teacher would almost never do. She would have had no trouble finding my mother's phone number—there were only four Noels listed, Robert E. Noel, my dad; Lloyd Noel, my uncle; Leah Noel; and a total stranger named Harry Noel who I never met. It was well known that I lived alone with my mother—a rarity in those days when most marriages lasted until death, and almost all phone numbers listed a man's name.

"Gordie? This is Miss Fowler."

"Hello Miss Fowler."

"Gordie, I want you to come to my room at eight tomorrow morning, before homeroom."

"Yes Miss Fowler."

Miss Fowler was rumored to have just graduated from an elite eastern college. We took this as an explanation for why she was demanding and humorless. Miss Fowler had two periods of sophomore advanced English. Everyone in those classes was a fast reader and bright, but we had never encountered expectations like Miss Fowler's. She required that we read a book every week from a long list of what she considered indispensable literature—that she pronounced "litter-ah-t'your", not "liter-ah-chure." We were to turn in a report that was analytic, not just a summary of the story: why was the book considered a classic? What were its major themes? How did the author use language in ways that were different than other authors? What major problems did the characters face? What did you learn from this story? She sprinkled her lectures with literary history and expected us to know what the Restoration was, how William Shakespeare earned a living, and why Emily Dickinson was an important poet.

PART THREE

To get an A, by the end of the first semester we were required to write a short story, good enough to be submitted to the school's literary journal, *The Kopee*. She encouraged us to write poems.

In November I had given her a story that I titled "The Lighthouse Keeper." She gave it back a few days later with a an unheard of "A+" at the top of the first page and a note in small neat script: "This is very nice, Gordie. Would you like me to submit this to the editor of the *Kopee*?" I said yes, and a few weeks later the editor also said it was a very good story; she congratulated me and said that it would appear in the spring edition.

Being called in to see a teacher before school seemed very unusual and must have meant that I was in trouble. After her call, as I was getting ready for bed, I had a vague sense of dread that continued the next morning as I walked to school alone and into the teachers' entrance. Miss Fowler's tone was always serious and without a trace of warmth, but her voice on the phone had been icey. I had a feeling that she had a problem with "The Lighthouse Keeper."

The manuscript has been lost, but I have told the story many times and know it well. It went like this:

Off the coast of the Carolinas, on a narrow strip of island perhaps a thousand feet long and a few hundred feet at its widest, there was a stone lighthouse. There was only the lighthouse—the island was otherwise barren of anything but rocks and sand and scrubby brush.

A new keeper had replaced the previous one in June. His lighthouse and the others like it along the Carolina coast warned ships of lethal shoals much further offshore than a captain might expect. There had been dozens of shipwrecks along that line of coast before the lighthouses were built, and even with the lighthouses, ships were sometimes driven onto the shoals by storms.

THE LIGHTHOUSE KEEPER

The lighthouse keeper lived in a small round room beneath the lantern, and on the lower levels were a kitchen and a storeroom.

He was no more than twenty, raised on a poor farm with too many brothers and sisters for the farm to feed. He had felt himself lucky to be hired for this job—he would have ample food, the work was far from hard, and he loved the beauty of the ocean.

One morning as he scanned the ocean with his spyglass he noted on the eastern horizon the tip of a mast. As was his duty, he noted it in the logbook kept beneath the glass windows of the lantern room. An hour later he checked again—the mast was only a little closer and lined up at the same axis as before, showing no sign of turning north or south. The winds were light and it did not seem unusual that the ship would be making such slow progress. By early afternoon he could make out three masts, but the sails were slack. In some places they were torn in strips and the lines that should have been taut were hanging loose, blowing about in the light breeze. As the wheel house and the deck became more distinct, he could see no crew.

An abandoned ship was rare he guessed. The ships that had come this close to his lighthouse had a crew but were off in their navigation. When they saw the lighthouse they invariably changed direction, north or south depending on their destination and the winds. But this ship kept coming. He figured that by late afternoon the ship would crash on the reefs surrounding his lighthouse, and if it missed them, would crash west of him on the mainland shore. He was indifferent. No lives were at stake, only the cargo.

As evening approached he scanned the ship from bow to stern for any sign of a crew. He was startled to discover a seething, writhing motion along the decks, atop the cabin, even on the abandoned wheel. He stared with puzzlement, and then, with a chill that ran up his neck and spread to his chest and back, he realized that the ship was overrun with rats and that the rats

PART THREE

probably had eaten the crew long before this, and then had eaten the sails and ropes. Whether the ship crashed on the shoals or the shore, the ravenous rats would look for food on the island. Until they starved to death on the barren island, he would be trapped inside the lighthouse.

In a panic, he raced from the deck down the spiral stairs, slamming shut the wooden shutters in the narrow windows that gave light to the stairs and air to his quarters. At the bottom he barred the door, never designed to withstand a siege.

The ship was now just a few hundred feet from the shore and he could see that the rats had not waited for it to crash. By the dozens they were swimming to the rocky beach. He watched them crawl from the ocean, he watched as they raced from one skimpy patch of foliage to the next, stripping everything bare as they went. As hundreds more landed some stood on their hind legs sniffing the air. First a few and then dozens raced to the base of the lighthouse and he could hear them scratching at the wooden door. Terrified, he cowered in the lantern room, alarmed that he could also now hear chewing on the window shutters below him. He had grown up a farmer: he knew that nothing made merely of wood could keep a pack of starving rats from food. In a few more minutes he was startled to see that the rats had climbed the rugged stones of the lighthouse and were clamoring on the glass surrounding the light, trying to scratch and gnaw their way through. He could see their flaming red eyes, their yellow-toothed, slobbering jaws, their ragged short fur a sickly patchwork of partially denuded skin.

Now, barely able to breathe, trembling, his heart pounding, staring at the starving rats on the other side of the glass, he heard the scraping of knife-sharp claws on the stone steps beneath him, first just a few, then more, racing up from where they had chewed through the door and shutters, the sounds coming closer fast . . .

he smelled their stink . . . then there was a rat on his leg, another on his hand, a sharp bite on his finger . . . something clawing, warm on his neck . . .

As I walked down the nearly empty hall to Miss Fowler's room, my heart began to race, my palms were damp, my stomach ached. I found her sitting at her desk writing in her lesson plan. She was dressed as always: a white shirt with an open collar, buttoned down the front; round horn-rimmed glasses; no jewelry. Her skin was pale, she wore no lipstick, and her long brown hair hung straight down to her shoulders. I cleared my throat to get her attention. She motioned me to sit down in a chair she had placed beside her desk.

She looked at me for a long time. "Gordie, the story you turned in about the lighthouse keeper . . . it was very good. Did you write that story?"

She paused and looked at me, waiting for a response. I said nothing, looking back, waiting for her to continue.

"You see, I just heard a story very much like it on the radio last night. Did you send your story to CBS?"

"No Miss Fowler."

"Did you copy that story, Gordie?"

I thought about how to answer. "I didn't copy it, I wrote it, but I got the idea for it from a book I read."

She looked at me steadily, paused, sighed. "I am very disappointed in you Gordie."

Miss Fowler studied my face. I did my best to meet her gaze but ultimately began inspecting my shoes.

"Do you know what plagiarism is? If you copied someone else's story and submitted it as your own, then you got credit for work that wasn't your own, and that's dishonest."

"But Miss Fowler, I didn't copy the story. I just got the idea for the story. All the writing is mine."

I scanned her face for a flicker of sympathy. Her face was a death mask.

"But it really wasn't your story Gordie. This is very, very serious. You stole someone else's story. I gave you an A for the quarter, but I will change that to an E. And I intend to tell the principal and Mr. Low what you have done. You'll be hearing more about this."

She turned away from me and went back to work on her lesson plan. I quietly got up and slowly walked down the hall to my homeroom. I didn't know what would happen to me, but I knew that I was over my head in very deep water—and once again there would be no rescuer.

In her first year of teaching, Miss Fowler would not have earned enough to buy a TV, which was still a luxury. She would be spending her evenings correcting our work or reading novels or listening to the networks' radio dramas and comedies. It was my bad luck that she had been listening to the weekly broadcast of *Suspense*. If she had been watching TV or reading a novel, the origin of my story might have gone unnoticed.

I rarely looked at the few books that Mom kept on a shelf next to the fireplace. One boring October Saturday I had picked up one, a collection of short stories called *The American Mercury Reader*. A decade later, when I knew more about literature and movies, I pulled that book off the shelf and discovered that the story Miss Fowler had heard had first been broadcast during the Depression by Orson Welles' *Mercury Theater of the Air*. I don't recall the story's title, but I read it, got the plot, and then I simply wrote the story scene by scene in my own words and turned it in. I didn't spend any time musing about morality, confident that this obscure story in an obscure book would be unfamiliar to my high school world.

The truth is, it *was* a good story, by far the best story I wrote in high school, good enough to fool Miss Fowler into giving me an A+. A few days later the *Kopee* editor called me at home and, with saintly tact, said that she had heard that I might want to withdraw the story, and was that true. That was a rhetorical question—she was going out of her way to be kind.

For a few days I was uncertain what was going to happen to me. Perhaps I could talk my way out of this. It was true that I had not actually copied it word for word. Perhaps this was less than plagiarism.

But I knew that matters were much worse than just rewriting a story in my own words. In the eighth grade I had bought my first phonograph with money from my paper route, a 45-RPM RCA machine that played the pop singles of the day, each side containing 3 or 4 minutes of music. As part of the enticement to buy the player, RCA included 25 free records, a random assortment of unsold recordings that no one would ever buy. "Korean Mud", the side B song on one of the records, caught my fancy, steeped as I was in the stories of the Korean War from my hours of reading old *Life Magazine* in Grandpa and Grandma's attic. Every time I listened to it I got teary, not something that happened to me very often. I took this as evidence of the song's deep poetic power. The song is about an American soldier, wounded in the Korean War, dying on a muddy battlefield. Because he was losing blood and there was no blood to give him, he died. The song goes on to urge people to go to a blood bank and give blood.

With Miss Fowler's encouragement of her students' attempts to write poetry, I had turned four stanzas of this dirge in to Miss Fowler a week after my fiction triumph, a word-for-word copy of the song, and it too she liked and forwarded to the *Kopee* editor who, when she called me about withdrawing my story, asked if there was anything she should know about my "really unusual" poem. There *was* something she should know, and although I did not explain why, she probably knew that it was not a sudden burst of good taste that led me to withdraw it as well.

PART THREE

Miss Fowler was so angry that she demanded that Mr. Berry, the high school principal, expel me and make me repeat the year. Mom was called in for a conference with Mr. Low and Mr. Hossack, Miss Fowler, and the boys' advisor, Mr. Whitmer. After Mom left, Mr. Low and Mr. Hossack and Mr. Whitmer persuaded Mr. Berry that I was a good student who had made a mistake and that I shouldn't be made to repeat the year.

When she left, Mom didn't know what decision the school would make. When I got home from my janitor's job that evening I didn't know either. Characteristically, she didn't scold me. I didn't say a word to Mom, not even to ask about the conference. I stared at my pile of homework, feeling sad and broken: I had trashed what little respect I had earned as a student. Soon every teacher would know that I had turned in a purloined story and a crappy song that I had stolen from a second-rate recording to get a better grade: I might never again be able to restore the trust that had automatically been extended to me and that I had thrown away.

When I came in the kitchen to help Mom get dinner served, she handed me a plate to take out to the TV trays in the living room.

Without looking at me she said: "I guess you won't do that again."

And I said: "No Ma'am." We ate in silence. She never mentioned it to me again.

The next day Mr. Low asked me to talk with him at the end of the day. He quietly laid out the conversations that had taken place, explained that Miss Fowler had agreed to let me remain in her class, and said that there would be no other punishment. Mr. Low had seen Mr. Hossack's evaluations of me and he had asked him to join the conference. They both had spoken strongly against Mr. Berry doing anything that would irretrievably tarnish my school record.

At the beginning of the second semester Mr. Hossack asked me to stop by after school. He told me that if I settled down and stayed out of trouble I would be able to get a scholarship that would pay for a very good college, that if I made up my mind I could do whatever I wanted. He didn't specify what that meant. Mr. Hossack was a big, exuberant, funny guy. He grew up the son of a park ranger in Glacier National Park and went to high school in Kalispell and to Carroll College in Helena. His taste in clothes was terrible and unvarying: black pants, a beige mohair sports jacket that had lost its shape many years ago, a plaid shirt, and a bolo tie. He loved teaching biology and was thrilled when he found students who were interested in his lectures and his labs. We dissected leaves and onions and looked at them under microscopes and learned the basic concepts of cell structure and function; we cut giant pickled worms to find their guts and hearts—and following that frogs and crayfish and perch gave up their organs to us. After every lab we were supposed to turn in a drawing with the parts of our dissection or microscopic inspection labeled.

Although I had failed to impress Mr. Shepherd with my potential as a draftsman, he had not failed to teach me. I carefully drafted my drawings in India ink, I shaded in the drawings with colored pencils, some life-like, some fantastic, and added extra details that I got from reference books and my encyclopedia, everything carefully labeled with near-perfect arrows. Gus returned them with high marks and wrote across one report, "you should consider going to medical school." By the end of the year his notes were simply "excellent Dr. Noel."

At the end of the first semester, Mr. Hossack had written on my report card, "An excellent student but must learn to control his tongue." For the second semester he wrote: "The best biology student I've ever had. GH."

My sophomore report card showed straight A's, except in English. For the first quarter I got an A, for the second an E, and for the semester a D. Mr. Low told me that Miss Fowler had strenuously objected to my partial reprieve, but for the second semester I did all of the extra work required to get an A, including the weekly book essay.

She treated me fairly and gave me straight A minuses on everything I turned in, and I finished the year on the high honor roll.

Miss Fowler stayed at the high school for another year, but then left. I thought about her and about the "Lighthouse Keeper" every day for many years. I have always thought that the spirits of Orson Welles and Elton Britt, the obscure-only-to-me country musician who recorded "Korean Mud", were lending me a hand, an awkward, lonely kid, raised by a working, single mother, who was trying hard to make some kind of positive impression wherever and whenever he could. Miss Fowler's harsh recommendation that I be expelled from school had the unintended effect of focusing the attention of several teachers on me. Mr. Low as my freshman English and homeroom teacher, and Mr. Hossack had seen something worth encouraging. As school went on having two of the men I most respected stand up for me changed both how I thought of myself and what I felt capable of as a student. Over the next few months I developed a future vision of where I might go and a sense that I could go there, all from having them give me simple praise and believing in me. They became cheerful advocates for my leaving Montana to attend college. They appeared to have recruited Mr. Whitmer to their campaign: he began dropping college catalogs for universities that I had never heard of on my desk in study hall every few weeks.

If Orson Welles hadn't written such a compelling story and if I hadn't loved Britt's maudlin song, I wonder what would have happened to me.

Although my crush on Mary Kraabel was never requited, even she noted that I was on a different path. In my sophomore yearbook she wrote:

"Gordy, known as blabbermouth, but you are getting quieter every year! Goody goody—Except with all your talking everyone still *likes* you. Geometry has really been hard & fun but you kept it lively. Honest Gordy I'm not really dumb in Geometry, it's just that you're a weeny bit smarter. Have lots of fun this summer & always. Mary Kraabel."

CHAPTER

EIGHTEEN

BIG WHEELS

MY VERY PUBLICLY stated goal during my years of delivering papers, mowing lawns, working as a busboy at the Lodge, and janitoring at J.A. Hogle, was to buy a car. In February of 1957, nearing the end of my sophomore year and approaching my sixteenth birthday, Mom got a call from Milo, the shop foreman at Kraabel Chevrolet. She had asked him to keep an eye out for a good used car for me to buy. The car Milo had found was a turtle-backed, two-door 1950 Chevy coupe with metallic green paint and a driver's side spotlight. It was in mechanically good shape, although it lacked a few critical ingredients to make it an acceptable car: white sidewall tires, fender skirts, full wheel covers, dual exhausts with Smitty mufflers, leather seat covers, and—most important of all—a radio. But mechanically sound, I was informed, was necessary for my Mom, who knew nothing about teen-aged boys or meets-basic-criteria Chevies. I bought the car for $350, all my own money, and Milo drove the car into our empty garage at 412 Beverly where I was told it should remain until May 5th, when I could get my driver's license.

I had gradually learned to drive before I had a learner's permit. When I was in the seventh and eighth grade Mom dated the owner of a successful furniture store, Red Matthews. Mom didn't leave me at home when they went out every few Saturday nights; when they had visited a roadhouse at the end of some deserted rural road Red used to let me drive his slush-box Chrysler station-wagon while he gave me instructions from the back seat. He was a tall guy and I had to pull the seat all the way forward to get my feet on the pedals. I drove at 10 miles an hour.

My Chevy had a manual transmission with the gearshift mounted on the steering wheel. That required me to figure out how to use the clutch while changing gears. I began to practice in my driveway when Mom wasn't home: happy hours of wild, random lurches, grinding gears, and stalling. The first time I put the key in the ignition and started the car I felt ecstatic, free, and delightfully bad.

The hardest part was a smooth transition into the first gear without too much or too little gas. To get better at that I had to extend my test track to the alley, and then the alley after that, figuring that an alley wasn't a street and therefore I wasn't really driving without a license. I always put the car away before Mom got home and no neighbor snitched on me.

When I got a learners' permit Sammie took me out a few times so that I could practice shifting, backing up, and parking. One wintery Sunday morning, while Mom was still asleep, Sam came by in his car and said he would teach me how to drive on the snow if I would make him waffles afterwards. I backed out into the alley, got going a little fast as I turned into the street, and fishtailed when I dropped the clutch too fast. The next ten corners I took sideways, but slowly I got the idea of turning into the direction of the skid, and pumping the brake. I did fine for ten minutes until Sam on short notice said, "turn left here." I jammed the wheel violently and we did a three-sixty on the ice and crashed into the curb. I did a hundred dollars worth of damage to my right front wheel and tie rod. We left the wounded car and trudged home silently in the glum slush. Sam didn't want to face Mom and left without his waffles. The next day Milo had someone from the garage tow the car in for repairs, and a week later I owned a $450 car.

I valued money more than thrill rides and that was my last accident in that car, although there were some narrow misses on icy roads during the next few years.

I drove to the county courthouse at eight in the morning on the fifth of May to be the first in line to take my driver's test. A weary looking highway patrolman in a drab brown uniform got into the passenger seat and told me to back out into the street, make left and right turns at busy intersections using hand signals, and parallel park. I passed on the first try. While I was terrified that he was going to arrest me for driving to my driver's test without a license, the trooper didn't comment: apparently he didn't think it was unusual that a sixteen-year old boy might already be driving by himself before he had his license. He scratched his signature on a form, told me to take it into the courthouse, and without congratulating me or saying goodbye, got out of my car. I felt as though there should have been champagne.

There was a tall, nervous-looking girl waiting for him at the curb: it was Tinsel Teeth. I waved at her gaily as I drove away. Nice girls didn't make obscene gestures in those years, although she would have been well within her rights. She settled for giving me a dirty look. I shuddered to think that we might have the same birthday.

Overnight I went from being a kid in a family with no car who had to tag along with other people, to one of the few boys who always had a car at his disposal and didn't have to ask parents for a key or gas money. After that, as soon as school let out at 3:45, I dropped off the two or three friends who I had driven to school and then drove downtown to my janitor job. After dinner sometimes I would drive back to school for an operetta or choir rehearsal. I could drive to football games, I could go out to restaurants and drive-in movies or to the Blackfoot river for an afternoon of tube floating and cliff diving. My world had expanded.

The car also made it much easier to go on dates. Dates were either a pass by a drive-in restaurant for a milkshake (25 cents) or a stop at the A & W Root Beer stand in the summer (5 cents for a small mug, 10 cents for large one), or a movie. That summer I double-dated a few times with some of the girls in my classes and Sandy Bouchard or Dick Ainsworth. The boys paid for everything, the girls—dosed with toxic levels of perfume and daubed with lipstick—were pleasant. No fires were ignited in anyone's heart.

Most Friday and Saturday nights my Paxson friends and I cruised the streets with no purpose other than killing time and seeing who else was out. In the fall we would be juniors and we felt too grown up to go the Bonner Park dances, but a few times in the summer we would squeeze six in a car and go to the double-feature drive-in movies. When someone didn't have the twenty cents for a ticket they hid in the trunk; we parked at the far edge of the last row where a few boys jumping out of a car trunk wouldn't be noticed.

In many small towns through the west there were band shells in a park where the local musicians would put on summer concerts. These were stodgy affairs, dominated by military marches and bad renditions of 1940's pop songs: "Stardust" performed by three tubas, or "Mule Train" with an authentic cowboy horsewhip-cracker. We rarely attended. One evening we agreed to meet at Courthouse Square because our high school band and orchestra members were playing. Hal, Dick, Tom and I drove to the park in our own cars and we planned to meet Scott Patterson there. We found each other, but it was halfway into the concert before we spotted Scott standing beside a pretty girl we didn't recognize. We headed toward him to scope her out. He clearly didn't want her to see him hanging out with us and in a louder-than-necessary voice, to be sure we heard, he invited her to leave the concert to get a root beer or milkshake with him. She said she had to tell her parents and they walked away toward the edge of the crowd. We all thought she was cute but it would not have crossed our minds to actually talk with her, let alone ask her to go driving or to a drive-in restaurant. I suggested that we put rocks in his hubcaps to spoil his fun. The four of us raced to his car, pried off his hubcaps, filled them with stones from the edge of the road, and hammered them back on before Scott and the girl got to the car.

We had not taken into consideration that his car was parked in front of the police station.

Dan Rice, the chief of police, was watching us the whole time from his office window and just as we got the hubcaps back on he came running across the street yelling at us. He alleged that we were stealing the hubcaps. We pointed out that, first of all, we all already owned hubcaps—would he like to see them?—and that, second, we were putting the hubcaps back on, not taking them off. At that point Scott showed up and Chief Rice told him that we were stealing his hubcaps. And we said, we weren't, we were putting rocks in them. And Scott asked why we were putting rocks in his hubcaps, for which we did not have an answer we cared to share in front of the girl. The girl took it all in, coldly thanked Scott, and said she would go home with her parents. Chief Rice herded us across the street to the police station and one by one made us call our parents to come to the station to get us. Chief Rice launched into a short sermon, holding up his boy, Dan Rice Junior, as the shining example of virtuous young manhood that we should aspire to. Dan was a senior, and at six-foot-four was the center and captain of the basketball team and an end on the football team. None of us had any possibility of being six-foot-four or a star athlete. We considered ourselves to be on the opposite end of the high school social spectrum, somewhere between very, very cool and hoods. Chief Rice suggested that we were not very, very cool nor were we very good hoods and that we all should be ashamed of ourselves—"and for God's sake, don't try to strip a car in front of a police station."

I was not clear what God had to do with it, but it is true that we probably weren't cut out for lives of crime and were no more likely to become criminals than anyone else in our high school. As far as I know, when we did something illegal after that, we did a better job of not being caught with apples or hubcaps in our hands.

In the Missoula of the fifties it was not hard for teen-agers to find a way to buy beer. It was practically regarded as a right to have a forged driver's license, although I didn't ever get one and didn't ask how my friends had obtained theirs. The way a beer purchase worked was to park outside of one of the four small grocery stores known to be pliable as they were getting ready to close: Olsen's, H & H, Worden's Market, or Morrie's Orchard Homes Market. We watched the front door; when we figured that there were no customers in the store, whoever looked oldest would volunteer. Hal Woods was our best bet—he was already five-ten, he sounded confident, and he had a credible ducktail haircut greased down with Brylcreem. He rolled his pack of cigarettes into his white-t-shirt sleeve, took a silver dollar from one of us, pulled open the screen door, and disappeared inside. Eighty percent of the time he reappeared with an uncool shit-eating grin on his face and a six-pack of Lucky Lager dangling from his left hand.

Sometimes I did the buying. Had I shown my license it would have confirmed that I looked two years younger than my actual age of sixteen and so it stayed in my wallet. Beer and tobacco were the high-profit items in these stores and were kept close to the front door. Our preferred varieties of beer were Highlander, made in Missoula, and Lucky Lager and Olympia and Rainer, made in Seattle. I would put the six-pack on the counter and slap down a silver dollar. On a good night the dollar was tossed in the till and I walked out holding the six-pack as casually as though I had just bought a banana. On a bad day the silver dollar was handed back:

"Come back when you are twenty-one."

"I am twenty-one."

"Ya-shore . . . So now . . . let's have a look-it your license then."

This was a hopeless situation. The license was not going to tell him anything he didn't already know. I was still short enough that I had to stand on the tips of my toes to get the beer if it was on the top shelf. Just leaving the dollar, grabbing the beer and running out the door was not a good option if I ever wanted to go back to the store. On these nights I shrugged my shoulders, pocketed my dollar, avoided eye contact, and wandered around the store as though looking for something I wanted more than beer. Then I would nonchalantly walk out. Six months later with the same clerk I might not be questioned and I would walk out the door with the prize.

To buy a case was much harder. For that we had to go to a bar, but not a high-class bar where the bartender would stop us at the front door or where one of our fathers might be inside having a drink with buddies. We needed to go to a cheap bar by the railroad tracks and we needed to find a middleman to be our agent: we had to find an actual adult, preferably a broke and thirsty one. For this we would head to Railroad Street, in the oldest part of Missoula, full of cheap hotels and boarding houses and saloon, where we could always find a drunk or a bum to buy us a case. The deal was that we would give

PART THREE

them four dollars and they would come out with a case; they could keep a six-pack. Within ten minutes we would spot one who looked like he could be trusted, but even so one of us covered the back door so he could not escape with all the beer. Drunks were less reliable than bums: they sometimes just sat down in the bar and started drinking with our four bucks, knowing that we probably weren't going to go in looking for them.

Spending the whole night drinking beer on downtown Higgins Avenue was risky. None of us wanted to get in underage-drinking trouble with the police, which would end up landing us in the high school principal's office and being grounded by our parents. In the summer we might go to a park and hope we would meet some girls, but most of the time we took long drives on the dozen country roads radiating out from Missoula—driving itself was a major thrill for us in the years after we had gotten our licenses. We could drive for two or three hours out Blue Mountain Road or Frenchtown Road, stopping from time to time to throw rocks at road signs or to pee or to walk out into the field, our collars turned up, our pants pulled low off our hips, a cigarette in one hand and a can of beer in the other, to watch the stars or the moon. We listened to the local DJs playing the pop music of the time—"Party Girl", "Singing the Blues", "Little Darlin'", "Bye Bye Love", "A White Sport Coat". We didn't take girls along on drinking nights. We acted more drunk than we were, which freed us up to name the girls we wished we were dating and to assess the probability of any of them going out with one of us. None of them did.

Sometimes two or three beers in we would go up Pattee Canyon Road to Farviews, high above the town lights, the most romantic—and public—place for couples to park. Above the last house at the end of the paved roads we crept up roughed-in dirt roads with our headlights turned off, to inventory who among the upperclassmen was parking with whom. When we spotted a car we would stop about a hundred feet away and sweep a spotlight across their windows. No heads could be seen at first, and then the driver would pop up—and if there was a couple in back, that guy too—to see what the hell was going on. With our searchlight in their faces they couldn't be sure we weren't cops. When we could see that they were riled up, we turned around and drove away as fast as we could, throwing up dust and rocks on the rough roads. Occasionally we would get chased if we had annoyed a football player, but mostly when we took off the couples just went back to making out.

Once we spotted Johnny Coffee's car parked. Johnny's family owned Missoula's most prosperous pharmacy and he lived in a gorgeous large house that was a city landmark. Johnny didn't have the standard used Chevy or Ford—he had his own new Ford Crown Victoria. He was dating one of the high school beauties, Bing Piccinini. Our emotions went far beyond envy and were closer to a sense of cosmic futility—parking with a girl as lovely as Bing Piccinini was never going to happen for any of us. Perhaps for revenge, three of us got out and noiselessly moved behind Johnny's car. There was silence inside. Neither of them were visible because they were lying flat along the front seat. We started rocking the back end of his car up and down as fast as we could for about ten cycles and then beat it back to our car and kicked up a lot of gravel getting away. Johnny was no athlete—small, not tough, and rich—the kind of kid who played golf. We had nothing to fear.

When we were seniors, at the Fox Theater at midnight on New Years Eve, everyone was kissing everyone amidst hand-thrown confetti and popcorn and a lot of hollering. I was happy and slightly drunk and doing my best at getting kissed. I was surprised to see Bing Piccinini's even more beautiful younger sister, Sandy, walking up the aisle toward me. She already worked as a model and dated college students. We made eye contact. She smiled. I wrapped my arms around her and kissed her on the mouth. She half responded. I am sure she had no idea who I was: we lived in different worlds.

CHAPTER NINETEEN

BUSHWHACKING

I HAD THREE jobs during the summer between my sophomore and junior years. Just for the summer I took over a morning *Missoulian* delivery route for someone who wanted the summer off. The route was in the older section of town just across the Clark Fork River from the University. Many of the deliveries were to apartments and row houses along three of the oldest streets—Broadway, Main, and Front. About half of the deliveries were to married students who had only to cross the Van Buren Street bridge to get to classes, much more convenient for them than the strip houses at the south end of town where many of the vets lived with their expanding families.

During the summer in Missoula I slept in the cool basement, awakened at 5 AM by birds and habit. Just past dawn I drove uptown and picked up my papers at the *Missoulian* printing plant near the Northern Pacific Depot with the dozen other boys who were also delivering papers to the north side of Missoula. Walking the leafy streets and closely packed houses where nearly everyone took the morning paper made this an easier job than my dispersed evening Sentinel route had been, and the early morning air and the nearly unbroken quiet were lovely.

By seven o'clock I was home eating breakfast before driving to the Safeway grocery store across the river on the west side of town. Working in the produce department at Safeway was the best job I had in high school—forty hours a week at something like a dollar an hour, unloading trucks, stocking the bins and shelves and chillers, picking through the vegetables and fruits twice a day to cull anything bruised or rotting, cleaning up the heads of lettuce and celery tops if leaves had wilted, misting the vegetables every hour with a hand-held spray.

When the potato trucks came in from Idaho we would unload forty or fifty of the hundred pound burlap bags that weighed just thirty pounds less than I did. I carried them on my shoulder to the walk-in cooler and stacked them four feet high. Onions came in fifty pound mesh bags, corn by the bushel, fruit in lugs weighing about thirty or forty pounds.

My boss was a kind and tolerant man in his 50's who was glad to have a diligent worker who saw carrying hundred-pound bags of potatoes as a good work out. When it was slow on rainy days or when we were both on in the evening Karl showed me how to wrap a packing box wire around a large Idaho potato and roast it in the incinerator in which we burned the hundreds of cardboard boxes that our stock was shipped in. He would go out to the dairy section and bring back a stick of butter and we would break the smoking potatoes open with our thumbs and stuff them with butter and salt and pepper and chew our way though the still steaming white fluffy potato and then its crisp skin. Or we roasted ears of corn in their husks, picked minutes earlier and delivered daily from Ben Hughes' truck farm that ran along the river ten minutes away.

Early in the summer Rollie began talking about our going to a place he had visited the previous summer with his parents. Like most of my friends, Rollie's family had a car and they could go on driving vacations, something my Mom and I never did. Although I had hiked in Boy Scouts, I had never backpacked as far or in as rugged country as Glacier Park, even though it was just about an hour from Grandpa and Grandma's house on Flathead Lake.

Rollie's plan was to hike to a chalet high above the tree line and then beyond that over the ridge above the chalet to a beautiful line of deep moraine lakes. He talked about the mountain goats they had seen and about how much the goats craved salt, since the melting of the ice age snows three times had leached all the soluble minerals from the soil. He wanted to haul in a block of rock salt as a gift to the goats.

The Trenouths had just one car that his father used to go to the Western Montana Clinic and to make house calls. But since I now had a car, the adventure seemed like an exciting way to finish the summer before starting our junior year.

I quit my Safeway job and paper route a few weeks before school resumed and got a friend to cover my janitor job. The next morning we drove the four hours from Missoula and parked at Lake McDonald Lodge in Glacier Park. We had all the gear we needed to be on our own in the wilderness for about a week, strapped to our backs on the wooden pack frames we had made in Boy Scouts, our gear and food wrapped in a canvas square and tied to the pack board with a diamond hitch. It was hot when we left Lake McDonald in the early afternoon and we were hiking in t-shirts and old sneakers: sixteen-year-old Montana boys didn't have the money for hiking boots. The main trail to the Sperry Chalet was seven miles with 4000 feet of climbing to the chalet, and then another 3 miles of trail high above the lakes a thousand feet below. The trail from Lake McDonald to the chalet was only used by hikers prepared for a steep, challenging ascent. Those not willing to attempt the climb on foot could join a wrangler-led horse and mule train that brought supplies and the less fit to the chalet. Beyond the chalet it was hikers only, everyone on their own threading narrow trails over cliffs and scrambling across avalanche chutes that plunged down to the lakes. Often in the rockslides there was no trail at all and we picked our way along the sheer slope in the scree and boulders until we could spot the trail on the other side. If you ran into a momma black bear with her cubs or a grizzly you figured out what to do and hoped you guessed right. Shy marmots stood on their hind legs as we approached, and then with a warning whistle to others disappeared into their rocky homes. Ground squirrels and grasshoppers chattered all around us, hawks and eagles circled above riding the winds, watching for the careless bird or squirrel.

We were heading to a shelter at the top Gunsight Pass another thousand feet above the lakes. Rollie planned to spend the night at the pass, leave the fifty-pound block of rock salt for the goats, then backtrack to Lake Ellen Wilson to camp for a few days. We passed Sperry Chalet about 7 PM, figuring that we could do the remaining three miles before it got dark, but not counting on the long scrambles bushwhacking through the boulders and high mountain shrubs where the trail had been wiped out by last winter's avalanches. Once we left the chalet and crossed the ridge above the moraines we saw no other hikers.

Summer days in the high Montana mountains are usually dry and hot, with temperatures that can cool off at night into the forties and thirties. Inexperienced, counting on the weather to remain warm and clear, we had not stopped at the Glacier Park ranger station to check the forecast. We had seen summer thunderstorms in Missoula and at Flathead Lake, but from the protection of our houses. In the high mountains there are frequent late-afternoon storms in August that suddenly blow up, towering black thunderheads that roll in over the high mountain ridges seemingly from nowhere, bristling with lightening and thunder.

Now I know that when the sky darkens and winds gust to 40 miles an hour and the temperature drops 20 or 30 degrees in a few minutes there will be hail or snow—but at sixteen I had not yet learned that. Two-thirds of the way around the trail skirting the lakes we were suddenly in a blizzard. We still had to climb the thousand feet up a switchback trail, in sneakers and t-shirts, to the shelter at the top of the pass, crossing a long perpendicular waterfall of snowpack runoff.

The temperature kept dropping to around 30 degrees. The marmots had disappeared underground. The low shrubs were flattened against the scrabbly mountainside, quickly collecting snow; the sketchy, rocky trail had disappeared beneath four inches of blowing snow. We started up the switchback trail that crossed left and right across the waterfall, the water-soaked rocks that we had to step on now coated with ice. We used our hands to steady ourselves against the mountain wall. We hadn't thought to carry gloves for an August hike. Our hands were white and aching, our feet soaking wet and numb. At times we were crawling back and forth across the waterfall on the tip of our toes, using our hands to maintain our balance. Suddenly a rock shifted under my feet and I lost my balance and slid backwards nearly straight down about 300 feet, clawing at whatever I could grab to slow my fall, another 500 feet of sheer cliffs still gaping beneath me. I finally stopped my tumbling fall by grabbing a stunted, prickly juniper tree. My packframe had split allowing the diamond hitch and canvas tarp to come undone. My gear and most of our food was spread another 20 or 30 feet down the snowy face of the steep slope below the trail.

Rollie took off his pack and scrambled down to check on me. He sat down beside me and we surveyed the long beard of food and equipment below us.

"You okay?"

"I think so."

"Should we try again to climb up to the shelter?"

"My pack frame is broken. I don't know how I could tie everything together again, or even find all my stuff in the dark. And it's pretty icy."

"Should we go back to Sperry Chalet?"

"Okay."

The hike back to the Chalet would be almost three miles. It was still snowing. With hands that were screaming in pain I pawed in the snow trying to find anything we could eat; I dug out my heavy sleeping bag and a long-sleeved shirt, a pound of hamburger and a pan.

We bushwhacked back. The trail was largely impassable or invisible and we made our way in the rapidly fading light and then darkness over rocks, around the slopes that were too steep to cross, and through hollows in which the wind had drifted in a half foot of new snow. At midnight we made camp at the chalet. We were shivering, wet, and miserable. Over a fire made from dry wood that we scavenged from under snow-umbrellaed trees we fried the hamburger in the aluminum Boy-Scout fry pan I had salvaged. We seasoned the hamburger, burnt on the outside and raw in the middle, with salt chipped off the fifty-pound block that made up much of Rollie's pack. It took a long time to get warm in our sleeping bags; I had no dry clothes, but Rollie lent me some socks to replace my soaking wet ones.

The next day we bought breakfast in the chalet and dried out our clothes a little. Then we made our way back to the falls and clawed our way down the slope to scavenge the rest of my gear and the food. We found the rope and canvas and made the best pack we could from my patched-together broken packframe.

The trip resumed. We didn't attempt to go up to the shelter at the top of the pass. Instead we hiked down to Lake Ellen Wilson, the largest of the lakes, and set up camp on its shore. There was no more rain, but now the weather was cool. We tried fishing all that day, but the lake was too cold to wade and we had trouble casting flies into the deeper parts of the lake. In two days we caught no fish and ended up consuming a week's worth of bacon and eggs. We attempted to make biscuits with the flour we had brought to dredge the fish, mixed with water and sugar and seasoned with the asthenic, tart huckleberries growing at the margins of the lakes. We baked the lumps of dough in the coals, wrapped in aluminum foil; without yeast or baking powder they were as hard and dry as chunks of wood.

When we ran out of food we decided to abandon our camp at Lake Ellen Wilson two days early and moved on to the next part of our trip. We hiked back to Sperry Chalet, dumped most of our gear on the porch, and hiked into the Sperry Glacier with the block of rock salt. There was no welcoming party of grateful goats to let us know that they appreciated our efforts: they must all have been still waiting for us at Gunsight Pass.

The trail from Sperry Chalet down to Lake McDonald is steep and invites hiking fast. On the loose rocks Rollie twisted his ankle with a pop that we could both hear. There were no ambulances or ranger rescues on backcountry trails. Rollie thought he could make it down if he didn't have his backpack. It was lighter by 50 pounds and I could carry both. He crafted a walking stick from a dead tree branch and we limped into the Lake McDonald parking lot by dusk.

That night we found an empty campsite in the Avalanche campground. We had replenished our supplies at the West Glacier Store and I fried potatoes in one pan while cooking hamburgers in another, relishing our first robust meal in three days. Almost immediately one of the black bears that hung out around the campground garbage cans was drawn to the smell of our cooking and walked into our campsite searching for food. I was so hungry that I grabbed the sizzling potato pan, dumped the potatoes into the hamburger pan and, yelling and waving the hot, empty pan, chased the bear out of the campground, taking a huge swing at his butt. Rollie watched the whole thing with his eyes bulging. He didn't say anything but I later learned that chasing a hungry bear with a hot frying pan might not have been a brilliant strategy.

In the morning we decamped and headed into the North Fork of the park, up a long dirt and rock road seldom used by park visitors. Our goal was to hike into Logging Lake, see some moose, and catch enough fish to survive. We drove to the trailhead and set about getting our gear together.

After an hour of loading our packs we silently slogged a few miles up the trail. This was low swampy country—attractive to moose, and very attractive to mosquitoes. Our mosquito repellant was ineffective and the prospect of two or three days of living with a nimbus of mosquitoes around our faces was discouraging and our confidence in our ability to catch fish had collapsed. We stopped and conferred. It took thirty seconds to decide to retreat to Grandpa and Grandma's house, where, although we were not expected, Grandma's worst dinner would be better than anything we could cook. Spending our last few days at Flathead Lake before school resumed was much more attractive than swatting mosquitoes.

Although we were not invited, I took our welcome to Grandpa and Grandma's house for granted. I don't remember how they reacted when we appeared at dinnertime, dirty and disheveled and without a clean pair of socks between us. We threw ourselves on their mercy. Grandma banished us to the basement to shower. She washed jeans and shirts and underwear for us, squeezed the water out with her hand-cranked wringer, and hung the damp clothes on the clothesline behind the house to dry while we went swimming.

The next day we hiked to Castle Rock high above the lake. We took a well-worn path there, but decided to bushwhack back. From Castle Rock we could see Flathead Lake, but once we got down into the heavy forests we were thoroughly lost. After hours of wandering—hot and parched because we had brought no water—we broke out of the woods onto the East Shore road, near a three-story high concrete tepee that operated as a soda fountain. We each ordered Flathead Lake Bing cherry ice-cream sodas, 25 cents each. Heaven. After that, cherry ice-cream sodas became a mandatory treat to cap off hot summer hikes at Flathead until finally the tepee went out of business. It became a cheap rental for itinerant hippies, and we moved on to beer at the end of hikes.

The next day, before heading back to Missoula, we sprawled on the beach baking in the sun. Rollie had a very early transistor radio the size of a pack of cards and we heard a song that became my anthem for that summer, Debbie Reynolds' version of "Tammy". I have no reason to think that Rollie was inclined toward sentimental pop ballads. But I had met Layne Westrum in my second year Spanish Class, and that aching love song seemed the perfect summer anthem for a romance that I hoped might develop.

The week I spent with Rollie in Glacier Park was my first excursion into a dangerous place without adult supervision. Our Boy Scout experiences gave us far more confidence that we knew what we were doing than was warranted. The newspapers in the West have frequent stories about kids in sneakers and t-shirts going out for a hike and being caught in a summer blizzard, but neither of us remembered those stories or thought they might apply to us. Our parents had no idea where we were going, nor themselves understood the risks of sudden bad weather at altitude.

On the other hand, ignoring the risks of jumping from cliffs into rivers, or hiking in backcountry without adequate preparation or gear was more or less what most of us did in those years, when there was nothing like the degree of warning and training we now encounter on entering a wilderness. In this, as in most things in my life, I learned more from my failures than my successes.

I never said a word about the blizzard and fall to Grandpa and Grandma or my mother.

CHAPTER

TWENTY

IN THE SPRING of our sophomore year Ted Smith was elected the junior class president; a half dozen students were chosen to be their homeroom representative to the class council, including Layne, Rollie, Hal Woods, Bruce Sievers and me. The student council gave each of the classes a concession to sell food at the games to earn money for class activities. The biggest concession was selling Coke and Seven-Up, which the seniors got. The sophomores sold peanuts. Ted asked me if I would be willing to run the junior hot dog concession at football and basketball games. My job was to round up students to carry baskets filled with hot dogs wrapped in napkins and hawk them through the stands that ran the full length of the University football field on both sides. Our Friday night games and the University's Grizzly games on Saturday afternoon filled the stadium. Few people cared about watching the weekly televised college Big Ten football game when they could spend a crisp autumn evening or afternoon watching the Missoula High Spartans or the University of Montana Grizzlies play.

A hot dog and a Coke were an essential part of the experience. I cooked hundreds of wieners in an electric frying pan in a primitive kitchen under the grandstands. We made huge amounts of money, all of which paid for the junior prom and for the smaller expenses of the Junior Assembly, the class talent show. I saw very little of the football games, but I met a lot of boys and girls with whom I had never had a class who volunteered to be vendors. A few weeks after the football season was done we transferred our sales to the gymnasium for the Friday night home basketball games.

It was hard work, the vendors also didn't get to see much of the games until the hot dogs ran out, and we all ended up with mustard and ketchup on our clothes, on our hands, in our hair. I had one friend tell me that the best thing about being a senior was that he didn't have to sell hot dogs at football and basketball games any more.

After every football and basketball game at home there was a dance with a band made up of the best members of the orchestra and marching band. Judy Blegen and Jo Jo Lester were the singers. The dances were held in the huge room where we ate lunch and had our study halls, cleared out by volunteers before the games and turned into a massive dance hall seething with students. I liked to dance and ended up dancing with girls who had no other interest in me than having a partner who could rock or waltz without crushing their toes.

As fall deepened into winter, Layne and I spent more time together. Layne had come to Missoula at the beginning of high school from Roswell, New Mexico, where her father had been an undertaker. Perhaps as a girl that I hadn't gone to grade school with she didn't have an archive of bad impressions of me. She was small, blonde, cute, friendly, energetic, and well organized. She went to St Paul's Lutheran Church. Montana was high Lutheran country: there was one Episcopal, one Catholic, one Presbyterian, one Methodist, one Baptist, and one Mormon church in Missoula, but there were five Lutheran churches. She sang in one of the choral groups I belonged to at the high school and I quickly discovered that she was a great dance partner. Every few weeks we went on movie dates or double dates with other couples—to a restaurant, or to a drive in movie. At some point Layne and I seemed to be going out regularly, although going steady was a serious step that neither of us was thinking about at the time.

Part way through the junior year our TV station, KGVO, wanted to start a local version of *American Bandstand* and invited students to the broadcast studio to dance. About twenty couples signed up each week. Layne and I danced on about half of the programs, learning to do the acrobatics of rock—hip flips, between-the-legs slides, underarm turns and double turns. The music came right out of the top twenty pop recordings of 1957, 1958, and 1959. The sponsor was the local Coca Cola bottler and we got a lot of free Coke. Our dancing became pretty good too. No one ever told me that they had watched the show.

In December Ted asked me if I would direct the Junior Assembly. I was pleased to be asked and I took it on, wrote a script, laid out the potential musical numbers and began asking classmates to participate.

Class assemblies were usually a loose assemblage of volunteer acts. There was no shortage of talent in the Class of '59. Often the same students appeared each year as they progressed through high school. In our class it was unimaginable that Judy and JoJo would not sing.

PART THREE

There were always a few other singers, sometimes a gifted clarinetist or pianist, someone telling Norwegian jokes in a good year, "knock-knock" jokes in a bad year, almost always a few skits of impenetrable satire, the humor understood only by the perpetrators. In most class assemblies the acts were strung together without any continuity or framing, introduced by the master of ceremonies: "And now Judy Blegen will sing 'The Breeze and I' with her sister Barbie Blegen accompanying her." "Now the sophomore girls will sing 'If I had my druthers' from 'Lil Abner.'"

I decided to write a musical that told a story, with songs and choreographed dances related to each other, based entirely on the pop music we danced to. I chose "Jailhouse Rock," which had hit number 1 in September of 1957, when rock and roll music and its performers were still regarded as morally corrupt by our parents and even more so by our high school teachers and administrators. Its choice as the opening song gave me the bright idea of building the assembly around a jailhouse theme. My conceit was that Missoula County High School would now be "Missoula County Reform School," that the teachers were our jailers, and that the vice-principal, Mr. Hunt, was the warden. I planned to have the dancers and singers wearing grey and black, and the students in the roles of teachers in navy blue with police caps. The sextet in which I sang bass would perform the sad ballad made famous by the Kingston Trio, "Tom Dooley", about a man captured by a sheriff named Grayson, about to be hung for stabbing the beautiful Laura Foster, with three dancers silhouetted behind a screen pantomiming the stabbing and then the sheriff hanging Dooley at the end.

My crowning idea was to have a classmate with a lugubrious voice intone periodic announcements from the warden between acts in the cadence and words of Mr. Hunt, our humorless vice-principal whose announcements always finished with the exhortation "God Speed!" In the script I named him Warden Godspeed. Toward the end of the assembly Mr. Godspeed would reveal his internal suffering from having to deal with the "prisoners" with a morbid solo rendition of "The Great Pretender" with a guitar accompaniment consisting of a single slashed chord, more or less in the key of the song.

The finale was to be the ringing of the end-of-the-day school bell and a jailbreak, choreographed to "Rock Around the Clock," with the students all escaping and Warden Godspeed wishing us all "God Speed," while fluttering a handkerchief at our disappearing bodies.

I was extremely proud of this concoction, a primitive version of a high school musical. We began rehearsals in January and lined up singers. Other than me, only the class sponsors had seen the whole script or knew the premise: through the first month of rehearsals the cast members were just working on their individual numbers.

Three weeks before the performance a senior student who was an office assistant knocked on Miss Fink's door during my fifth period English class and gave me a slip of paper asking me to come to Mr. Hunt's office. I was clueless about why I had been summoned. When I walked into his office he was pacing back and forth. I had heard of people purple with rage; Mr. Hunt's face was the color of a plum.

"I can't tell you how disgusted I am with this . . . garbage!" He waved the script in my face and then threw it on the floor. "I am very disappointed in you Mister Noel. We all expected better—much better—of you. I am cancelling the Junior Assembly. I have told Mr. Hightower and Miss George that this never should have gotten this far. Now get out of my office young man! Leave! Now!"

For once I was speechless. It seemed unwise to defend the script as original art that should be encouraged, or invoke my right to freedom of speech.

His clenched hands were shaking. He looked as though he wanted to strangle me. I turned around to leave, but he kept shouting after me: "And you better beware that nothing like this ever happens again. You are walking on thin ice, Mister!"

He pounded his desk with his hand, repeating, with his jaw clenched and lips pulled back in a snarl, "Thin! Ice!"

And with that Mr. Hunt stomped out the back door of his office, without wishing me God Speed.

I walked back to Miss Fink's class with the hopeless despair of a man condemned to be hung. The whole school would know that the Junior Assembly had been cancelled because of Gordie Noel. It had never crossed my mind that parodying the vice-principal and the teachers was breaking new ground that had been left unbroken for good reasons. The class sponsors, Mr. Hightower and Miss George, had looked at the script and had sent it on to Mr. Hunt without comment, but they were very much newly in love with each other and weren't paying attention. I had actually thought I could get away with this: it never occurred to me that anyone would object to what I had imagined to be funny.

A voice unknown to us did the morning intercom announcements for a while. In March Mr. Hunt came back on the air, but he closed with a sprinkling of "have a good day" or "good luck to our Spartans at the state track meet this weekend" or "it's icy so drive carefully." His eyes never again met mine with any warmth when our paths crossed as, unfortunately, they often did.

Once again I was in the middle of a debacle—so far a fairly private one. After school I met with Georgia George and Mr. Hightower. They were pretty sure that they could rescue the Junior Assembly, and equally sure that Mr. Hunt would not show up. They asked me to rewrite the script and drop the prison references and the allusions to teachers as jailers, but said they thought we could keep the opening and closing dance numbers—"Jailhouse Rock" and "Rock Around the Clock". The sextet performed Tom Dooley, but no one was hanged in pantomime. The soloists chose other music; we dropped "The Great Pretender". And in the end, it was a pretty good show with the acts loosely assembled and not linked to any theme, except in my mind. Nobody seemed to notice. We got a good review in the school newspaper, *The Konah*, that went so far as to pat me on the back for a good job.

In the summer Miss George and Mr. Hightower got married.

Layne broke up with me after Christmas. She had a crush on a senior boy, Jim McFarland, and she wanted to be available should he ask her to go to the Junior Prom with him. I was heartbroken. The Sunday services at St. Paul's were broadcast on a local radio station at 11 o'clock, and I took to doing my weekend deep cleaning at J.A. Hogle while listening to the broadcasts, wading through dirty mop water and feeling sorry for myself. St. Paul's had a good choir. I got used to the order of service and some of the ancient hymns based on baroque and classical music and sang and cried through them regularly, not because I was in touch with the Holy Spirit but because I missed Layne.

I went on a few dates and I ran around with my friends on weekends. Layne and I continued to be business-like partners in the assembly dance numbers that we rehearsed together each week. But there was no longer any fire in the relationship.

Since Layne and I were no longer a couple, I did duty as a dance and dinner partner with other girls. Some were boy-asks-girl events like the Demolay Sweetheart Ball, but others, like the Rainbow Formal, were arranged by the girls. I never knew what those organizations did. Our jobs as escorts were to rent tuxes—actually, in those days a white dinner jacket, black pants with a satin ribbon down the side, a cummerbund, a dress shirt that required studs, and a black clip-on bow tie. We bought our dates corsages. I always bought two cymbidium orchids fashioned together with baby's breath and forget-me-nots that I picked up from Garden City Floral, two orchids for five dollars, the same price as a steak dinner or 20 hamburgers. We would nervously pin the corsage on our dates' formal gown, someplace around the right breast, mom, dad, brothers and sisters looking on. And then our dates for the evening pinned a white carnation in our lapel buttonholes.

After the dances our group would arrange for dinner reservations at a supper club at 10:00, for which the boys paid. We got the girls home before their curfew. I wasn't looking for another girl friend and the events always seemed a little flat and pointless.

By our junior year most of us had learned how to be students. Only in physics and math was there overt competition, because exams were always scored and posted. In American History and English grading was less objective and our teachers didn't differentiate among us: an A was an A and we couldn't tell who may have done a little better or worse. Much of the grading was based on our participation in classes and no one was jostling to get called on. Mr. Low was kind enough to give me an A in first year French: I could write and I knew the vocabulary and he overlooked my pathetic pronunciation.

Once the assembly was done, prom preparations went into high gear. Mary Kraabel was in charge of decorations, and she and her decoration crew felt that the gymnasium would still look like a gymnasium. She and Mary Anne Zimmerman asked Rollie and me to see what we could do to screen out the two hundred feet of folded-back bleacher seats. We spent weeks making wood frames, stapling large sheets of cardboard to them, and painting the sheets blue. We ended up with something like a very long, very blue ocean liner with lit portholes screening out the bleachers on each side of the gym. Rollie and I spent forty hours creating these "sets," and yet neither of us would be going to the prom, Rollie because he was not interested in dating, and I because I wouldn't ask anyone other than Layne and she was waiting for Jim McFarland to ask her.

A communication chain of the "Katie asked me to find out if you like her" variety snaked in my direction three weeks before the prom. Layne had commissioned her best friend, Tinsel Teeth—who I imagined would have preferred that Layne never see me again—to ask another girl with whom I was friendly to give me the message that Layne needed a date for Junior Prom. It was not part of the message, but I later found out that Jim McFarland had asked someone else, and no one else had asked her because they assumed she was going with me. Layne did not want to miss her own Junior Prom and had resorted to asking me, indirectly, to invite her.

This was hardly the "I made a terrible mistake and I miss you and would you forgive me and I would understand if you never wanted to see me" message that would have signaled some kind of affection: it was a purely utilitarian proposition, in essence "You aren't going to prom, and neither am I, and we dance well together, and so would you mind asking me?"

I was smitten with Layne and had no pride and certainly no inclination to miss prom out of spite, and so the arrangements were made. I ordered orchids, planned with friends to go the Happy Bungalow for dinner after the prom, rented a tux, and the date was on.

There is something magical about a high school prom, and much of the magic is based on years of anticipating the moment and a willingness to suspend recognition that we were in our high school gym, where yesterday afternoon the wrestling team had been sweating out matches, not the Waldorf ballroom. Except for Rollie, my best friends were there with the girls they had been dating. There was a lot of suspense about which of his girlfriends Sandy Bouchard, the Key Club president-elect, would ask, Mary Anne Zimmerman or Joni Carpenter. Our gossip lines buzzed with the information that

PART THREE

Mary Anne had the edge, but I can't remember who he finally went with, or if the other girlfriend stayed home that evening.

On the night of the prom I drove to Layne's house in my freshly washed, waxed, and vacuumed Chevy. In her living room I pinned on her corsage while her father snapped pictures with her Brownie Hawkeye. I noticed that she had used two-sided Scotch tape to be sure that her strapless top stayed up. We picked up Ted and his date Judy Hirsh and arrived at the Prom, fashionably tardy. Ted was the president-elect of the student council, so our arrival had a tiny bit of drama and classiness. But the prom was dedicated to the seniors, and the real attention was on them—the sports stars and cheerleaders and beauty queens and the top students, some of whom already knew they were going to a military academy, or had a naval ROTC scholarship that would pay for their entire college education, or had been admitted to one or another prestigious college.

Layne and her friends had filled the dance cards that they hung from their wrists with their evening's dance partners, six before the refreshment break, and six after. As was customary she had reserved the first and last dance with me. I checked: Jim McFarland was not on her card. She also had filled my card—mostly with the girls who came to the prom with the boys she was dancing with. As I had feared, Tinsel Teeth was on mine. She and I had struggled since grade school to be civil with each other. We danced stiffly and silently. At the end I walked her back to her circle of friends, and thanked her, and she thanked me. I felt a glimmer of guilt for not even trying to make it more fun for her.

I don't remember a single thing about who else I danced with—we all were dancers, many of us in the television dance group and most on stage at the Junior Assembly. Dancing was fun, like playing non-competitive tennis, and except for slow dances, when conversation was possible, with rock and roll music it really didn't matter with whom we danced.

After the prom and the dinner, I took Judy, and then Ted home and drove Layne back to her house. I think we might have necked a little—probably nothing more than an arm around her shoulder and her head on mine. I was happy to be with her.

A few weeks later she asked me if I had noticed anything unusual when I picked her up for the prom. I told her that I had liked her formal, thinking that she was looking for a compliment. Without a smile she told me that three days before the prom she had gotten chicken pox. On the day of the prom she had taken aspirin to quell a raging headache and lower her temperature. She had covered up her spots with makeup so that in the darkness of the prom they would not be noticed. She had no appetite at all for the dinner she ordered. All of her girlfriends knew, but none of the guys she danced with. I suppose she didn't realize that she was infectious. As sick as she was, she didn't miss a dance. She was a tough Norwegian girl and in time she would prove more than a match for me.

About the same time that we started work on the Junior Prom, Ted Smith and Gus Hossack told me that MCHS was going to host the annual two-day meeting of the Montana Association of Student Councils and asked if I would organize the program. I said yes without a grasp of what was involved. This wasn't a glamorous task but I was pleased to be asked. It was a fateful decision.

None of us had ever been to a meeting of the Montana Association of Student Councils meeting, and most of those attending from high schools all over the state had never been to one either. I had no clue about how to create a meeting meant to bring people together from across a state to talk about what student councils did, or what they might do, or what problems student councils were likely to address.

I was free to create panel discussions about topics that I imagined would be relevant, create plenary sessions for keynote speakers to address the role of a student council in managing a high school student body. I organized workshops in which people learned how to write and publish minutes, or keep a budget, or deal with conflict. For several weeks before the meeting I wrote and typed dozens of pages of materials. Working with Miss George and her secretarial training students who retyped and formatted much of what I had written, we created a hundred page handbook for the meeting for which an epic mimeographing and collation effort taking hours was required. I had glossy covers printed and we bound the book.

For two days the visiting students carried around the book stuffed with the materials for their workshops, note pages, and documents useful to thinking about how to be a good student council president or secretary or treasurer. I was a glorified errand boy and master of ceremonies giving directions to meeting rooms, stocking workshop rooms with materials, and making announcements and introductions.

On the final day just before the noon lunch and farewell there was a business meeting. The location of the meeting next year and the hosts were introduced. The final piece of business was an election for the next association president. Ted announced that nominations could be made. There was silence. Then a voice called out, "I nominate Gordie Noel." Additional nominations were requested, but there were none. By acclaim or default I was elected even though I was not going to be my school's student council president.

I don't know what Ted thought—I never knew if he even aspired to this position. I certainly had not. And neither of us could have guessed what my being elected would lead to.

One thing that did not succeed was my run to be class president. Lee Yates, a varsity wrestler and the junior class vice-president, won in spite of my posters around the school featuring me as "Galloping Gordie, Supergoat." I drew a caricature of me with an elongated nose pressed to a grindstone that I turned with one hand, hot dogs under the other arm, a microphone in front of me, something that implied dancing, and a slogan in a balloon coming from my mouth: "gets things done." While that may have been true, apparently a proven record of getting things done and being a supergoat were not sufficient criteria for being the president of the senior class.

My year had begun with what was very nearly a disastrous summer blizzard. Rollie and I had found our way back to safety without being able to see the trail by bushwhacking in the dark for hours. For the rest of the year much of what I did outside of classes seemed a lot like bushwhacking through unfamiliar, sometimes murky territory, and recovering when something went wrong. High school was like that for most of my friends. We were learning how to date, shifting away from old friends as we made new ones, sorting out what we wanted to do after graduation, creating a community, mostly without the involvement of our parents, and under the engaged but not overly restrictive attention of our teachers.

At the end of the year I knew that I owed a lot to Mr. Low and Mr. Hossack, who saw in me something I hadn't seen in myself, and also to Ted Smith who, by asking me to manage the junior hot dog sales, the Junior Assembly, and the state student council meetings, had harnessed my diffuse energy and revealed to me how much I enjoyed organizing people for projects. After a decade of being an awkward and often irritating kid, in those visible roles I gradually became part of a coherent community. In high school this happened earliest and most prominently for athletes, musicians, and theater students, often in their first year. For students whose skills and interests were the less visible activities of scholarship and school service, the opportunities bloomed as school progressed.

We could already see that the future for some of us was going to take us away from Montana—in fact, many more of us than we

PART THREE

could have guessed. We were blissfully unaware that the French were losing the battle to re-establish themselves as the colonial masters of Vietnam and Cambodia and Lao and that the United States' decision to enter the Vietnam War would be a vortex that sucked many of us into military service.

CHAPTER

TWENTY-ONE

MOM

DURING MY GRADE school years I got home from school before Mom did. Even after I had a paper route, there were evenings when she wasn't home until nearly 7, just in time to make dinner. On these late nights she often had been driven home from the Chevrolet garage by Milo, the shop foreman. I didn't have the experience or imagination to wonder about the nature of their relationship; I only wondered whether she would ever be home. My loneliness was nearly overwhelming on these evenings and until she was in front of the house I feared that she had abandoned me, run away, been kidnapped. Mom kept the living room blinds shut so that we weren't sharing our lives with the neighbors. I kept the room dark and stood at the windows, pulling up one slat to see if Milo's car was there, impatient always, sometimes frantic. Even when she was at the curb they kept on talking for what seemed like an hour.

PART THREE

When high school started I had a full afternoon walking to my janitor's job, walking home, starting homework, and I cared less about where Mom was. By then she had moved from Kraabel Chevrolet to the University and could easily walk home. I was almost never home before she was.

Once I had a car I was more like a boarder and Mom saw much less of me. I left to pick up my friends when she was barely starting her day. I drove them home, then I drove downtown to work, and I got home just in time for dinner. After dinner I closeted myself in my room to do homework. I hung a sign on my door that announced I didn't want to be disturbed.

By the time I was a sophomore Mom had gotten a TV set. I asked her to keep the volume down: our house was tiny and my room only a dozen feet from the set. Without protest she went along with that. A year later she suggested having our house hooked up to the new cable TV that was being installed that would bring in all the national networks rather than just the ingle local TV station. I told her that having a lot of television options worried me: I didn't want to be distracted. She patiently went along with that too. Then, in March of my senior year, when it seemed likely that I would be leaving, Sammie and I bought Mom a cable subscription so that she would have more choices about how to spend her evenings after I had gone.

Since living alone with Mom was all I ever knew, I didn't think much about her loneliness or her needs for companionship, of how much more full her life would have been if she had a husband, perhaps another kid coming along behind me. We lived together like a couple: I did the chores that a husband would have done, fixing things, painting, taking care of the yard, and my share of the dusting and vacuuming and hanging out laundry. We sat down together for dinner every night.

There was one way in which being like a couple was growing increasingly uncomfortable for me. Mom had been upset when, in the sixth grade, I suddenly refused to undress in front of her and shut myself in the furnace room to change into my pajamas. But Mom had no modesty at all and as I grew up, her habits didn't. She hung her underwear to dry on the towel racks and cabinet handles in the bathroom for me to weave my way through, she walked around the house in her bra and panties, she walked in on me when I was using the toilet. When I was 15 I finally confronted her. I was lying in the bathtub, well beyond the years when bubble bath and a floating toy or two would have provided a little cover. Mom walked in the bathroom, pulled down her underpants, spread her legs, and peed. In the tiny bathroom my face was two feet away. I looked away. Later I told her not to use the toilet or come in the bathroom when I was using it, and to knock before barging in, even if she thought I was only brushing my teeth or shaving. She looked chagrined at first, then annoyed. She told me it was a tiny house with only one bathroom and it was inconvenient not to be able to use it whenever she needed it. But she didn't walk in on me again.

Mom had to cope with the development of an adolescent boy without the counterbalance of an older child or father in the house. She grew up with a sister and probably didn't know a lot about a boy's sexual maturation. There were no groups for single parents she could attend, and none of her many friends were raising children alone. With my discomfort out in the open I became progressively more guarded with her. I kept more of what I was doing to myself, rarely expressed any feeling or affection. If I felt like stopping by Dad's house, I did, and I didn't ask her permission or tell her about it.

My early sexual education consisted of stealing a few pinup magazines from the H & H market because I was too embarrassed to buy them, and listening to the anatomically inaccurate dirty jokes passed around among some of the boys in grade school. Like a little Puritan, I steadfastly refused to repeat a dirty joke, most of which seemed more stupid than funny. I refused to use any "swear words" now that I had given up peeing them onto the frozen streets of our neighborhood. I hid a few pictures of provocative but dressed movie stars torn out of the pinup magazines under my mattress.

In the eighth grade I had a long chest cold with a convulsive barking cough. I made it seem worse than it was so that Mom would keep me at home and I spent the days listening to soap operas (*One Man's Family* and *Just Plain Bill* were my favorites) and going through Mom's bureau and closet looking for adult "secrets". In the bottom drawer I found a business envelope postmarked 1936 containing a tattered *Montana State Department of Health Guide Book for Newly Married Couples*. The first half was devoted to line drawings of male and female anatomy and a totally de-sexed description of reproductive organ structure and functions. I learned that there was some kind of withering calamity awaiting women when they turned forty.

The second half was a bloodless narration of what the husband should do and what the wife should do and a discouragingly encyclopedic list of what could go wrong. Flapping window shades and crying babies were particularly likely to disturb the entire undertaking. The notion that there might be more than one position for either husband or wife was not introduced. Menstruation was treated like the arrival of the plague, requiring isolation of all the afflicted. Under what circumstances the wife might get pregnant was limited to suggesting that some times of the month were more likely to be fruitful than others. There was no mention of contraception.

All of this was news to me and I read it three times the day I discovered it, and I read it again a few times over the next two years, always being careful to put the torn envelope back carefully so that Mom wouldn't know that I had visited. Although the writing was at the level of an instruction book on how to make a dog house in your basement workshop with simple tools, it was hugely exciting, since at that time I still found reading the lingerie sections of the Monkey Wards catalogue arousing and their line drawings of bust size endlessly fascinating. Mom and Dad's 1930's guidebook was my entire sex education until dating entered my life.

Or almost all of it: when I was in the sixth grade Sammie told me that Marjorie was going to have a baby, and he asked if I wanted to know how that happened. I did. He said that Dad had told him that women had a hole like the tailpipe exhaust port on the back transom of a speedboat. And the man stuck something—Sammie didn't say what—in the tailpipe and stirred it around, and then the woman had a baby. Even at the time, and with no alternative information whatsoever, that didn't make sense to me: if girls had tailpipes I was pretty sure I would have heard about it before then.

When Mom noticed that my dates with Layne had gone beyond an occasional movie, she decided I needed a more complete education than she felt she could provide. About halfway into my junior year she told me she had made an appointment for me to see Dr. Svore, the general practitioner who had delivered me into the world and my tonsils into a jelly jar that I brought home with me after the operation.

I didn't know the purpose of the appointment. Mom said she thought I should have a check up because I was about to be seventeen. That sounded fishy to me.

I was ushered into Dr. Svore's office at 4 one afternoon. He sat behind a heavy oak desk wearing white pants, a white tunic with buttons across one shoulder, and a reflective mirror on his forehead, the perfect icon of an authoritative physician. There was a half-smoked cigarette smoldering on the edge of the full ashtray on his desk. He waved me toward an examination table at the side of the room, looked in my throat, felt my neck for glands, listened to my lungs and my heart, felt my crotch for hernias, and thumped on my knees to make my feet fly up. When he was done he told me to sit in the chair facing his desk.

"You seem to be healthy. Are you feeling okay?"

"Yes, I'm fine."

"Do you have any questions for me?"

"No."

"Okay, well tell Leah hello and that I said you were fine."

"Okay."

Guessing what Mom had had in mind, I beat it out of there.

After dinner, while Mom and I were washing dishes, she clearly was waiting for me to say something about my checkup. I kept silent.

Finally she asked, "How did your visit with Clem go?"

"He said hello and to tell you that I was fine."

"Is that all."

"Yes."

"Didn't he talk to you about anything else?"

"No, just asked if I had any questions."

Her eyes widened. "That's all?"

"That's all."

"Well I'll be Goddamned!"

And with that she left the room. Within a few minutes I heard her in a strident conversation on the phone with someone. I guessed she was working over Dr. Svore, who she had known for decades and whose wife Bernice was one of her Alpha Phi sorority sisters and best friends. I stayed out of her way for the rest of the evening.

She didn't send me back to see him, and the subject of sex didn't come up again, although occasionally she left notes on my pillow warning me of the hazards of girls who "melted down" too easily. She was impressively accurate.

Notes on my pillow required no eye contact and had become her chief way of dealing with difficult subjects. A few times she left a note asking that I try to throw up in my wastebasket if I was too drunk to make it to the bathroom.

When I was in the seventh and eighth grades Mom dated Russ Mathews, the owner of Missoula's Furniture Mart. I got some driving lessons and a lot of long Sunday afternoons in one or another roadhouse away from Missoula. I don't know if they chose those places so that she wouldn't be seen with Russ by her or Dad's Missoula friends, of if they just liked the idea of getting out in the country. We often made one or two stops at bars on the way to the restaurant, and they were in no hurry to get started eating after we got to the Nine Mile House or the Gold Creek Inn or the Sleepy Bungalow: they sat at the bar and drank one or two more cocktails while I played with glasses of Tom Collins mix and read novels and pumped Russ's nickels into the jukebox.

After I began high school Mom felt it was okay for me to be alone, and she and Russ would go out for the evening. Sometimes when I had gone to sleep before they returned, I woke up and heard them talking and suppressing laughs in the living room. This gave me the creeps: there was something about the laughter that made me jealous and I wanted Russ to go home. But I covered my head with a pillow and went back to sleep.

Russ disappeared in the winter of my freshman year. I asked Mom whether he had gone away. She told me that Russ had wanted to get married, but that she didn't think he would make a very good father: he had never wanted kids and he liked to party. I never knew which one of them broke off the relationship. Russ had money—not a lot, but much more than Mom would ever have from the kind of work that was available to her. She didn't tell me how she felt about breaking up, and I never would have asked.

PART THREE

At the end of that summer we took a trip to visit my Aunt Nonie who taught music at the state college in Bellingham, Washington. After that we visited Paul and Georgia Elliot, Glasgow friends of Mom's who lived in Seattle, and they introduced her to their friend George Velotta. He was an Air Force master sergeant, home on leave from a U.S. airbase in Thailand where he was a mechanic. In the next three days we saw a lot of George. He rented a boat and took us fishing on Puget Sound. We ate dinner in a nice seafood restaurant. He took us to a shooting range and taught me how to adjust the sight on a military rifle, bench fire it, and shoot standing up without the hard kick knocking me over.

We headed back to Missoula when school started up, but shortly after we got home George showed up in Missoula. After a day or two Mom said that she was going on a short trip with him and arranged for one of our neighbors to look in on me while I stayed at home alone.

They were gone over a weekend, and when she returned on Sunday night she told me that they had gotten married. He had returned to Thailand and wouldn't be back for a year, but when he came back he would retire. He planned to move us to Wisconsin and open his own garage.

She changed her name to Leah Velotta, which I thought far less melodious than Leah Noel. My name would stay the same and he wouldn't adopt me because she didn't want to lose Dad's child support payment. Mom hung his picture over the TV where she could look up and see it every night and as she walked out the door in the morning. For me, nothing else changed. I couldn't imagine moving to Wisconsin or living with a man who told me I was to address him as "Sir", but I didn't know what my options were to refuse and Mom didn't bring up the idea of moving again.

Late in my sophomore year, just a few months before I expected him to return, I noticed that Mom had hung a picture of Sammie with his girlfriend Pam where Sir George's picture had been. I looked around to see where she had moved his picture, but it wasn't to be found.

I didn't ask what that meant.

A month later I saw an envelope with Mom's monthly bank statements unopened on the top of the TV. It was addressed to Leah Noel, not to Leah Velotta. I waited a few days and then found the opened envelope in her desk drawer. I pulled out the cancelled checks. After the first half-dozen they were signed "Leah Noel."

I waited weeks for Mom to say something. I knew that when Mom was really upset her demeanor changed—I called that look "owly"— a form of squinty-eyed crankiness, often tinged with bitterness—as it was when I finally broached the question.

"I see that George's photograph is gone."

"It is."

I waited.

"I had the marriage annulled."

"Oh."

After a long pause, and without looking at me, she told me the story:

"He was in a big hurry to get married before he went back to Thailand. I didn't understand why but I went along with it. He said the reason was that once we were married he would notify the Air Force and I would start receiving a family payment. It was quite a lot of money. It didn't come and didn't come. I wrote to him and he wrote back that there was paperwork that the Air Force screwed up, but he had fixed it. But the money never came. Then he stopped answering my letters."

"Finally I wrote to the Air Force and they said that he had directed the supplement to be sent to him and had provided them with a form that I had signed agreeing to it. I had never seen that form and I told them so."

PART THREE

"So we won't be moving to Wisconsin?"

She looked at me for a few seconds with a sad, lonely expression. "Is that all you're worried about?"

"Yes"

"We won't be moving to Wisconsin."

She turned her back and rearranged something on the coffee table.

"I don't want to talk about it any more."

Perhaps it was normal for a sixteen-year old boy not to know how to comfort his mother, or to even feel that it would have been a kind thing to do.

Or perhaps it was our situation: I had never witnessed an adult comforting another adult, and while I was helpful around the house in many ways, emotional support for Mom wasn't one of them. I was only very relieved to know that they were not going to tear me out of Missoula and drag me to Wisconsin. I didn't really feel bad for Mom. I only felt relief.

Over time, and more from Sammie than her, I learned that she had filed a claim against George. The Air Force said that while he was overseas there was nothing they could do about it. She could take it up with him when he got back to the States. But there was no likelihood that he was coming back. She learned that this kind of fraud was common among soldiers, who found that they could supplement their salary with a marriage they didn't intend to ever return to. A friend speculated that George already had a Thai girlfriend and children and that he was using Mom as a way to get extra money to support them.

Mom had more reasons than being jilted again for being bitter. The day that Dad learned that Mom had remarried, he stopped his alimony payments to her, although the court required that he continue paying child support for me until I was 18. Sammie said that for years she had tried to get her alimony and child support payments increased as Dad's income rose from his entry-level cashier's salary to that of a bank vice-president. She had failed: both the alimony and child-support were pitifully small, and even at that Dad often failed to deliver his payments to the courthouse and she had to ask the court force him to pay.

George's name and Mom's short marriage never were mentioned again.

CHAPTER

TWENTY-TWO

THE WORLD BEYOND MONTANA

GUS HOSSACK HAD become the advisor to the Montana Association of Student Councils when I was elected president. Although neither of us had known about the National Association of Student Councils' annual convention, in late May we discovered that there was state funding for us to attend the meeting. Gus decided that he would drive Ted Smith and me to St. Louis in June.

Rollie Trenouth was planning to run for the position of treasurer of Key Club International in Chicago in July and he asked me to be his campaign manager. The student council trip to St. Louis would be cheap and reimbursed by the high school, but the Key Club trip entailed a cross-country train trip to Chicago followed by a sightseeing tour to Washington, DC, New York City, and Detroit. I had no money to pay for that but in an act of incredible generosity, Rollie's parents offered to pay for me. And as state student council president, I was invited to attend the National Youth Leadership Conference

PART THREE

in Estes Park, Colorado in August—a trip the National Association of Student Councils would pay for.

For the first time since I was twelve I didn't take any summer jobs because I would be away much of the summer. I lined up someone to take over my duties at JA Hogle when I was away.

The drive to St. Louis took us across Montana on US Highway 10, one lane in each direction. We saw five times as many antelope as cars. Five hundred miles from Missoula the highway headed south into Wyoming. From there we arced back up to North Dakota where we picked up their state student council president in Dickinson, and then we headed south toward Nebraska. We dined on the marginal food in truck stops, which, since I had never eaten in a truck stop, was exciting out of proportion to the quality of the meal. Breakfast came as a "stack of pancakes, hash brown potatoes, two eggs any style, and your choice of meat," fifty cents, fifty-five cents with a glass of milk or a cup of coffee. Dinner was meat that had been roasted, fried, steamed, or boiled into submission, with gravy, potatoes with gravy, dressing with more gravy, vegetables from a can and overcooked. Dessert was pie or a slice of chocolate cake. Dinner was one-dollar-fifteen tops, less if we had chicken or meatloaf or hamburger steak.

We slept in sleeping bags beside the car. The first night, in Wyoming, the only place that offered any protection from rain and wind was under a grove of trees in a cemetery. On the second night, in Kansas, on a rutted road that dead-ended in a cornfield and with rain still hanging around, the girl from North Dakota slept on the back seat and the rest of us slept under the car.

On the third day we checked into a cheap motel on the outskirts of St. Louis, close to the meeting at the Ferguson, Missouri high school. We hastily scrubbed up and presented ourselves at the registration table. We were not warmly welcomed. My election as the Montana state president had come late in the school year, and Gus's decision to attend came even later. When he called the association's headquarters he had been told that we were too late to register. Gus was clearly operating on the principle that it is better to ask forgiveness than permission when he decided that we would go anyhow. The Executive Director was at the registration table when we arrived and Gus presented the obvious fact that we had just driven 1500 miles to get there, that we were dressed in suits and ties and that we were expecting to participate. The director muttered, "I had an idea that you folks were just going to show up." He had the weary look of a school principal beaten down by decades of trying to manage adolescents. Although I was to see him twice more that year and I was a nice kid most of the time, I never became his cup of tea.

Gus paid and we were handed packets and badges and meal tickets and we were official. We sat in a large auditorium part of the time, and in small rooms the rest. I listened to speeches and participated in discussions, but mostly I watched and listened to the other students, my first exposure to my generation outside of Montana.

One of Gus's dreams was to see a major league baseball game while we were in Missouri. To his disappointment the Cardinals were not playing in St. Louis while we were there, but to the west the Kansas City Athletics were playing an evening game against the Washington Senators on Friday. When the meeting finished on Thursday evening, we headed north along the Mississippi River, spending a steamy night in thick woods outside of Hannibal Missouri serenaded by frogs and screaming critters in the underbrush. The next day we took our time wandering through Mark Twain country on our way to Kansas City.

The stadium was stunning. It held more people than the entire population of Missoula and the lighting probably used as much electricity as Missoula used. We did baseball park things, rooting for the home team, eating hot dogs and soda and peanuts. Fortunately, to avoid paying for parking Gus found a city park not far from the stadium where we left the car and walked to the game. We spent the night on fresh-mown grass under huge hickory and ash trees, the first fire-flies I had ever seen dancing among the leaves and stars, heat lightening and thunder in the distance. The temperature never dropped below eighty degrees.

It took us two more days to drive back to Missoula, visiting Mt. Rushmore and the Badlands along the way. We washed up wherever we stopped for breakfast. We must have been pretty rank by the time we rolled into Missoula. Before the summer of 1958 I had only been out of Montana three times, once to California when I was 7, and twice to Bellingham, Washington. I saw a huge chunk of Middle America—and that, not the convention, was what I got out of the trip. I saw big league baseball for the first time in Kansas; heard frogs croaking as I had imagined Tom and Huck would have heard them; slept in a cemetery in a thunder and lightening storm; felt the hair on my neck rise when I heard growling and scuffling in the woods along the Mississippi in the middle of the night; and saw a bit of trucker life. The Badlands and Mt. Rushmore were no longer words under grainy pictures in a worn-out geography book. I saw just how big Montana and Wyoming and the Dakotas were, how vast the Great Plains with their boundless wheat and cornfields.

The night before we left St Louis, Gus had treated us to a steak dinner in a smoky barbecue house that had a blues band, in a part of the city where we were almost the only white people. The music, the smell of the sizzling meat, the throngs of people so different than I was used to in Montana astonished me; I felt like we had travelled to another country.

In July Mr. Thomas, the Key Club advisor, and about a dozen members boarded the Northern Pacific North Coast Limited, destination Chicago. The North Coast Limited was one of the legendary streamliners—as glamorous as the California Zephyr, the Broadway

Limited, the Sunset Limited—famous for its white linen and silver service dining, the Traveler's Rest club car and it's "Vista Dome" views of the mountains and plains that sped by at 70 miles an hour. There were dozens of small towns with passenger train service along the NP tracks between Seattle and Chicago, but the Limited skipped most of them and made the 1700 mile Missoula to Chicago trip in 29 hours, stopping only at Butte, Billings, Bismarck, Fargo, and Minneapolis. Being kids with limited bankrolls and no trouble sleeping, our seats were in the coach. The wide, comfortable seats tipped back, there was a footrest, and for 25 cents we could rent a big fluffy pillow for the night. With the first class sleeping car passengers, we answered the dining steward's call to lunch hurtling toward Billings, and his call to dinner somewhere in the arid prairies east of Billings.

Union Station in Chicago was far enough from where the Key Club convention was getting started at the Conrad Hilton Hotel that we had to crowd into taxis with our luggage—another first for me. The Conrad Hilton was the flagship hotel for the Hilton chain with three thousand guest rooms and a nightclub that featured elaborate stage shows and an ice rink. During the week of the convention the Hilton was infested with more than a thousand 16 and 17 year-old boys, each straining to be grown up but with overflowing, testosterone-driven high spirits and marginal judgment. It took us only a few hours to locate a place to buy balloons, fill them with water, take an elevator to the top floor, and break into a stairway to the roof marked "no public access" from which we dropped water bombs on the cars on Michigan Avenue twenty-nine floors below. We never knew whether we succeeded in getting the balloons far enough away from the building to avoid hitting the people walking on the sidewalk in front of the hotel. When we walked to our rooms after the opening night banquet we discovered wheeled trays with silver domes covering plates that had viable food left over. We helped ourselves to untouched hard rolls, cheese plates, and a few desserts. Over the next few days not a few silver-plated cream pitchers and sugar bowls, china teacups, and silver plated spoons found their way into our luggage. I kept loose change in a Hilton silver-plate cream pitcher on my bureau at home for years.

My job as Rollie's campaign manager was to visit the suites in which each state's delegation were caucusing. Outside of the doors boys in dark suits sat with clip boards and I would ask if they could give a time slot to Roland Trenouth from Montana, who was running for the office of Key Club treasurer. Mostly I was turned away without a time slot and without an explanation. I thought perhaps I needed to give a little pitch on what Rollie would do for Key Club's finances. I must have made something up because Rollie was running on character, not policy, which amounted to saying that he was a good guy who would do a good job. It soon was obvious that I knew absolutely nothing about Key Club finances or running a forty-eight state campaign. It didn't occur to me that I was turned away because New York wanted to meet the candidates from "important" states like California and Illinois with a lot of chapters and a lot of votes, who would reciprocate by providing time and votes to New York's candidates. Montana was of little interest to them in this bargaining. In the end I got Rollie into a handful of caucuses, but he lost. He later sent me a thank you note saying that he didn't think it was my fault that he wasn't elected. I am pretty sure that his parents hadn't invested in my trip with the expectation that my management skills would pay off in launching Rollie into a political career, but I still felt responsible for his loss.

We saw a little of Chicago when we played hooky from some of the meetings to walk as far north on Michigan Avenue as the recently constructed Prudential Center Tower and took the elevator to the 42nd floor to look out over the vast flat prairie across which the second largest city in the United States had sprawled out, restrained only by Lake Michigan. We could see far out on Lake Michigan, where freighters coming through the St. Lawrence Seaway were steaming toward the docks near the Chicago River. To the south and west switching yards, livestock yards, thousands of warehouses and small factories and meatpacking factories seemed to be held together by a vast tangle of railroad tracks. On the far southeastern horizon we could see the billowing smoke of the blast furnaces in Gary, Indiana.

On a free evening Mr. Thomas took us to the famous George Diamond Steakhouse tucked under the elevated train loop on Wabash Street in an historic Sullivan and Adler building. We sat at long tables, the air strongly scented of smoke and burning beef, the room brightening occasionally as flames raged when fat cuts of meat were thrown on the grills. The crowd around us grew noisier as the evening lengthened and alcohol levels rose. There was no easy way to characterize the clients—there were tie-wearing businessmen, tourists in shorts, large families dressed up for an evening out, a corner table with five shifty-looking men wearing dark pinstriped suits and hats pulled low over their eyes who didn't look like businessmen. The room could have held twice as many customers as all the supper clubs in Missoula combined.

The centerpiece of the convention for many of us was not a deep insight into how organizations like Key Club and the Kiwanis Club served as vehicles through which responsible citizens could fulfill their societal obligations to serve those needing help. The centerpiece was the closing luncheon enthronement of the (very) famous actress Kim Novak (*Picnic, The Man with the Golden Arm, Vertigo*) as the Key Club International's Woman of the Year. The scene was mayhem—several thousand young men in a ballroom jammed with round tables seating twelve, set with Hilton linens and silver, and piled with food. Kim Novak was a tiny figure far across the room from the Montana table, seated at an elevated dais with a wing of dark-suited men to her left, and a wing of dark-suited boys, the incoming and outgoing officers, to her right. After dessert there was a very short and totally unnecessary speech explaining why Miss Novak had been chosen as the Planet's One and Only Woman. To receive the proffered plaque she stood in a very, very tight black dress—white hair swept back—glamorously waving. No Missoula girl could look like that. When she descended from the dais there was pandemonium as she came within touching range of hundreds of boys who quickly became a thousand boys, all trying to take a pictures or get her signature on their luncheon menu. The Montana tables were too remote to be able to get closer than a hundred feet. I stood on my toes and took pictures with my new Argus C_3 camera, bought to document the summer but suited only for close ups and panoramic views of distant objects. I came away with a dozen pictures of the backs of other boys' heads and the moment was lost to history. I caught a glimpse of her when her escorts took her toward a door near to us where press photographers were waiting with their Graflex press cameras. She was only twenty-five, but, in spite of her heavy makeup, I thought she looked hard and tired. I felt sorry for her.

I was surprised that there was no Key Club International Man of the Year. Alfred Hitchcock might have been a good choice.

After the luncheon we headed for Union Station to catch the Pennsylvania Railway's overnight train to Washington, DC. Compared to the North Coast Limited, the train was notably shabby and worn. The tracks jerked us sharply from side to side, the wheel noise was louder, the windowsills and toilets grittier. The air conditioning was no match for the subtropical heat. After a night of fitful sleeping, around eight in the morning we pulled into Washington's Union Station and emerged into the steam oven of an east coast July. The air was as stale and worn out as the train had been. Carrying our luggage we all were sweating just getting to the taxi stand. The acrid stench of car exhaust poured in through the taxi's open windows.

We were staying in one of Washington's most famous hotels, the Willard, often called the social and political center of the Capitol. The furnishings of the public rooms were ancient, florid, and solid, the spaces vast. We had no business being there, a bunch of hyperactive teenage boys who had just been throwing water balloons off the thirtieth story of the Conrad Hilton and nearly rioting over Kim Novak. Affairs of state were settled in this place, treaties and political alliances and billion dollar business deals were hammered out in its private meeting rooms, nearly every president had lived at the Willard at one time or another, and so many movie, theater, music and sports celebrities had eaten or slept there that the walls of the men's bar and the less formal dining rooms were a tapestry of signed photographs floor to ceiling, corner to corner.

Dressed in very little—light chino pants and short-sleeved shirts—we were nonetheless nearly knocked back through the massive front doors of the air-conditioned Willard by a wall of swampy air that poured in from Pennsylvania Avenue. In the course of a day we climbed the Washington Monument, reverently read the inscriptions at the Lincoln Memorial, passed by the Jefferson memorial, and prowled through a half dozen of the rooms at the Smithsonian.

At 2:00 PM we arrived at the Capitol to meet our Montana State Senator, Mike Mansfield. Mansfield was a graying, slender, charming man who seemed to have nothing else to do but meet us. He had arranged for us to sit in the Senate gallery to watch a session and, after talking with us for ten minutes about what we would be seeing, walked us over to the Senators' private elevator. Just as the door opened a younger and even taller and more handsome man began to exit. Mansfield introduced us as future voters from Montana and the other senator shook our hands. The tall, handsome man said he would be happy to run us up. He closed the door of the manual elevator and pulled the controller to ascend—bidding us farewell at the entrance to the gallery. Senator Mansfield escorted us to our seats and then got on about his business. As we took our seats, Rollie leaned over and asked in a hushed voice "Do you know who the elevator operator was?" I did not. He said, "That was John Kennedy, the senator from Massachusetts." This was the summer of 1958 and by the next summer Senator Kennedy was running for President of the United States. Senator Mansfield had a long and distinguished career in the House of Representatives and Senate; after Lyndon Johnson became Kennedy's vice-president, Mansfield became the longest serving Senate Majority leader, and after that he was the Ambassador to Japan, somebody a Montana boy could brag about in any company.

The next day we went to Mount Vernon and then to Arlington Cemetery. Soaked with sweat, we silently walked through the rows of grave markers, studied the statues, took pictures of each other at the Iwo Jima Memorial. We had no way of processing so many men dying, most of them barely older than we were. We knew that as soon as we turned 18 we would have to register for the draft and that we would be at risk of being inducted into one of the military services. We walked through silently and if we had questions about why the United States had fought so many wars, about whether someday some of us would be buried here or in some other military graveyard, we kept them to ourselves.

In the afternoon we were back at Union Station and on our way to New York City. We stayed at the Taft Hotel. By now we were veterans at settling into hotels and exploring cities and we ticked off the top ten things that high school boys did when they visited New York City: Grand Central Station, the Empire State Building, Rockefeller Center, St. Patrick's Cathedral, Central Park, the Staten Island ferry, Wall Street, a long sight-seeing trip through Times Square, a Broadway musical, a Saturday afternoon baseball game at Yankee Stadium, the Yankees against the Boston Red Sox. We saw many of the legends of baseball on the field that afternoon: the Yankees' Casey Stengel, Yogi Berra, Whitey Ford, Don Larsen, and Mickey Mantel, and Boston's Ted Williams. The Yankees won; they were 92-62 by the end of the season and went on to win the World Series, which for the first time I was interested in.

In another few days we had visited the Ford Motor factories in Detroit and were on the trains back to Missoula. We were worn out and mostly we slept or stared out the window or played cards to pass the two days. We arrived at the Northern Pacific Depot on a hot Missoula afternoon. When we got off the train a wave of heat hit us, but it was dry and the air smelled of pine and fir. We could walk without soaking our clothes with sweat.

My next commitment as the state student council president was to attend the National Youth Leadership Council in Colorado. To get there, I had to take a Northern Pacific local train from Missoula to Butte and switch to a very short train that went south to Wyoming through the beautiful Wind River Valley to Rock Springs and Cheyenne and finally Denver. An exhaust-blackened diesel switch engine pulled a few mismatched freight and mail cars and two passenger cars. Its crew was the engineer, a fireman-switchman, and a conductor. There were about twenty passengers dressed in plain clothes spread through two ancient cars with deep red velvet seats and yellowing, dusty gauze curtains. There was no food on the train, one cold-water bathroom, and no pillow service. During the day we opened the windows to let in fresh air, and during the chilly night we pulled them shut. In the late afternoon the train pulled into the Rock Springs depot and everyone—engineer, fireman, conductor, all the passengers—trooped down Main Street two blocks to a restaurant that had set a table for about twenty-five people. We each ordered dinner and something to drink and ate quietly. When we had cleaned our plates and used the bathroom we walked back to the train, each of us carrying a paper bag with a sandwich to eat before we went to sleep. The train started up and wound its way through the river valleys and mountains and parched prairies of Wyoming. We went for hours without seeing anything living; even along the riverbanks there was practically nothing green. The colors of the wind-sculpted riverbanks and gorges were spectacular browns and reds, the light at sunset turning the eastern cliffs into vast screens of intense orange.

In the morning other students who had arrived by train and I were met at the Denver Union Station by a bus that carried us through the flat plains around Denver high into the Front Range of the Colorado Rockies to Camp Cheley in Estes Park. The other students were extraordinary—accomplished leaders in their high schools and states, sophisticated, and knowledgeable about national affairs. Some were in elite public high schools like Boston Latin and New Trier, many had traveled outside of the United States. Without their being rude, none seemed interested in getting to know me. I did the best I could not to feel out of their league: all I had done was to put on a well-organized and useful meeting in a state the total population of which, six hundred and sixty thousand, was smaller than the cities many of them came from.

Much of our time was spent in outdoor amphitheaters or around large picnic tables discussing the issues we thought we would be facing as we left for college and entered adulthood: the Cold war and the ever-present risk of another world-wide war; atomic bombs; the suppression of freedom around the world; teen-age drinking. There were about sixty of us, half girls, half boys. At the time I didn't notice that everyone looked more or less alike, all but two or three of us Caucasian: that was what I was used to.

There were active civil rights movements in the United States and other countries, but we didn't talk about them, or about poverty, or migrant workers, or the paucity of women in many of the professions. We did not discuss the unequal treatment of women or question why many of the private colleges that many of us were considering were still all-male. There was no talk of religious discrimination: the prayers at our meals were unapologetically Christian and their inclusion as natural and unquestioned as the pledge of allegiance. I had absolutely no insight into the movements that would rock the United States over the next two decades, and I had no understanding of the wretched treatment of laborers, of immigrants, of American Indians, of women around the world who were battling for a stable, safe home, the right to vote, higher education, and self-determination.

On the train trip back to Missoula I didn't ponder anything that had come up during the meeting. No righteous fire had been ignited in me, no sense of a mission larger than beginning my senior year. I thought about the year ahead with untroubled excitement. I was not worried about anything and the worst I had to look forward to was cleaning out the stock exchange and insurance offices every night for another nine months. The J.A. Hogle spittoon and the dead flies under the hissing neon lights were the only thorns in my crown.

CHAPTER

TWENTY-THREE

IN MY JUNIOR yearbook, Sandy Bouchard had written:

"Gordie, well in such a short year you've come one hell of a long way. Last fall I or anybody else wouldn't have thought that you would have swept all honors as you did. Must have been that P.W. that did it because you didn't go out with the boys very much."

A handful of the other boys I had been running around with for the past few years made the same allusion in their year book notes, often in the same language. Being "PW" implied that I had a girlfriend who kept me on a tight leash, or that I enjoyed being with her more than with the guys.

Sandy and I were friends in part because his brother Mike and my brother Sammie had been friends. Sandy was fair, blonde, good looking. He was friendly and effortlessly put other people at ease. He also loved to have a good time and, though a good student, he was not nearly as serious or intense as I was.

PART THREE

My outings with Sandy usually didn't involve my Paxson friends. Sandy had a gang from Bonner and Milltown, where their fathers worked in the giant lumber mills. The Paxson boys hung around Missoula, but the Bonner boys were inclined to head to the woods and rivers.

In the summer before we started our senior year we went on two weekend camping trips in the thick forests off the lower Blackfoot River, where Norman Maclean set his wonderful autobiographical novel, *A River Runs Through It*. Much of the area was roadless wilderness, but nearest the river there had been heavy logging to supply the lumber mills in Missoula and Milltown. The old logging roads provided us with access to dozens of creeks and meadows and mountain peaks. The Bonner boys had even better sources for beer and whiskey than we town boys; in the preparation for our camping trips they stockpiled more beer and liquor than food. We spent the evenings telling stories and drinking and kicking at the campfire to knock the dead branches we used as firewood into the center of the fire pit to keep the flames going.

Sandy claimed that he could set his urine on fire: "If I get my alcohol level high enough it gets into my piss." He had been drinking beer on the drive in and now was drinking whiskey. His speech was a little slurred and he was laughing at things that weren't funny: I figured his alcohol level was high enough to put his claim to a test.

"No way," I said.

"I've done it."

"Got witnesses?"

"Okay, No-Hole! I'll betcha."

"How much?"

"My Mom wants me to take her friend's daughter Mildred to a drive in movie. If I win, you have to sit in the back seat with her."

"And if I win, which I will, what do I get?"

288

Sandy pondered. He was on his third whiskey now. "You get to take whoever you want and I'll sit with Mildred."

"But that's what I'll get if we don't have a bet. No way."

"Okay. I'll ask any girl in our class to go out with you, just once, as a favor to me."

"Dina Adams."

At this point, Don Labbe, who had spent most of the evening staring at the fire and stirring the coals, spoke up: "I think she's Bud Lake's girlfriend."

"So? Sandy said anyone."

"He'll kill you!" Don stated this as a fact obvious to anyone. Don had a point. Bud was a tackle on the football team and had a reputation for picking fights with anyone who messed with his girlfriends.

"Ill just tell him that it was Sandy Bouchard who asked her out."

"Okay, I'll do it. You're on," Sandy said.

And at that he unzipped his fly, stepped to the edge of the fire, thrust his pelvis forward to improve the trajectory, and let go. The promised flame-thrower failed to ignite. The part of the fire he was peeing on began to dim as he wet down the coals. The camp was filled with a great stink, like those places under bleachers where thousands of men and boys have peed for decades and the smell has become ineradicable.

We spent much of the rest of that evening gossiping about our school friends, telling bad jokes, and pretending to be more drunk than we were. In the morning, under Don's tutelage, I made cowboy coffee in a huge tin can, boiling it for five minutes and then settling the grounds by throwing eggshells into it. It tasted awful and it was several years before I tried drinking coffee again. The eggs and bacon came out okay but the greasy sliced fried potatoes were mostly raw and the oatmeal was scorched on the bottom. So much for my Boy Scouts' cooking merit badge.

PART THREE

A few weeks later, at the beginning of our junior year, Sandy and a girl who was not Mildred picked me up and we drove to Dina Adams' house. I think Dina agreed to the date because she liked Sandy and figured I was harmless. At the moment she and Bud were not on good terms and so I asked her out a few more times, but Bud got worked up and told her to stop dating me. No one got beat up. I wasn't surprised that Bud didn't find me to be a credible threat.

I can't remember a single movie of the dozens I saw on dates at drive-in theaters. That probably wasn't the point of going to them.

On another trip in the middle of winter, we hiked into a Forest Service supply cabin used in the summer by trail crews and broke open the latch on the front door. We spent a couple of nights there. The place had an outhouse and a stove that could be used both for heating and cooking, better than the snow camping we had planned, but certainly this was listed by the Forest Service as an act of vandalism, although we left the place in good shape.

In the summers we rustled up inner tubes and floated down the Blackfoot. One inner tube was outfitted with a net full of beer that dangled through the center to keep it cool. The rapids weren't powerful at this low-water season and we could bask in the sun, drink beer, and occasionally jump in the river and swim behind our tubes. None of us cared that our skin got burned in the three or four hours on the water: bad sunburns were evidence of a successful summer.

We finished near a thirty- foot cliff where the river took a sharp turn and the water was twelve feet deep at the base. We took turns jumping from a ledge half way up and goading each other to jump from the top. Ultimately we all did make the leap from the top, feet first, our hearts in our mouth during the long free fall. The only safety check we had done was that none of us had ever heard of anyone getting killed jumping from that cliff. We bragged about our jumps to our friends but never mentioned it to our parents.

Once we had cars we began to drive ourselves to the away games. One night coming back from a basketball game in Kalispell in a blizzard we were unable to see either edge of Highway 93 along the west shore of Flathead Lake. The snow limited the use of our headlights, not very bright on a six-volt car battery to begin with, and dimmer still with the heater running full blast. The driving snow turned the road, the shoulders, and the ditches into a uniform white strip with no center and no edge and no high or low. For a long stretch between Kalispell and Polson I walked in front of the car along the right edge of the road so that the driver would not drift off into a ditch. I was wearing penny loafers and cotton socks, my feet soaking wet, toes freezing and hands tucked down the front of my pants to keep my fingers from freezing. When I was so stiff that I couldn't talk, someone else took my place, and then I took his. A two-hour trip turned into a five-hour trip.

Often our determination was not tempered by any sense of risk. Other people died in blizzards, even people who had cars, but it never crossed our minds to turn around and find a motel for the night. We hadn't refilled our gas tank to make sure that we wouldn't run out of gas if we got stuck. We hadn't brought a shovel, or adequate clothes to do a middle-of-the-night hike with the temperature hovering just above zero in a driving snowstorm. We never checked weather forecasts or cancelled plans. Schools were never closed; if there were two feet of new snow, we walked to school instead of driving. Winter was winter, and we dealt with it as it came. We didn't brag about it to our friends, not because we were embarrassed, but because it was just ordinary, what they probably would have done too.

CHAPTER

TWENTY-FOUR

SENIORS

ON OCTOBER 5TH, 1957 our advanced algebra teacher Gertrude Clark walked into our first period class, put down her lesson book, and announced that if we were in that class we owed it to our country to become nuclear physicists or aeronautical engineers. "Boys and girls, the survival of the United States and the free world depends on you".

The previous day, the Soviet Union had launched Sputnik. It was the first space satellite to orbit the earth, and with it the future of hundreds of thousands of teenagers and college students took a dive deep into the murky waters of the cold war. Since 1949, when the Soviet Union exploded its first atomic bomb, children all over the United States had been doing atomic bomb drills in schools, although we joked that Missoula and most of Montana were not important enough to blow up. With the launching of Sputnik, panic that the Soviets might be able to defeat the western countries in a

PART THREE

missile-based nuclear war soared. Still nearly two years from graduation, neither my friends nor I had definite ideas of where we would go to college or what we would study. Through the previous twelve years of prosperity and peace the world had begun to recover from the devastating Great Depression and two world wars. For our warbaby generation opportunities seemed to be limited only by our imaginations and determination. Now, global social forces were threatening to kidnap our futures.

In the 1950's, about half of the senior class went to college after high school. Many of us in the Class of 1959 were conscious of where our grades were in comparison to other students. Math and science exam scores were posted with our names; the school newspaper and the *Daily Missoulian* published the names of the students on the high honor roll every quarter. Bruce Sievers and I had subtly jockeyed to be first on physics examinations during the junior year, and now during our senior year we ran nose to nose in chemistry. There were several of us clustered near the top, including Myra Shults and David Bowman, each of us quietly pushing to get a 100% on every test. Most of the college bound students had taken the SAT examinations at the end of the junior year. No one reviewed or practiced for the tests—we just walked in to the study hall on two Saturday mornings, our only preparation being eleven years of Montana public schools. Several of us got pretty good scores on the SAT exams: David, Myra, and I were chosen as National Merit finalists; I qualified for advanced placement in college biology, chemistry, and Spanish.

I don't remember being especially anxious about getting into college, even though Mom had no way to pay for it. Going to college had arrived as a foregone conclusion on a blazing hot summer afternoon when I was twelve. Grandpa had dispatched me to weed his vicious raspberry patch. It was hot, sweaty work and the thorns gouged my arms and face.

An hour later Grandpa came up to check on my progress and found me buried deep in the brambles reading a book. I had cleared only four or five feet. In his exasperation he began to shout at me: "Who do you think is going to pay to send you to college? Why won't you do a little work for me?"

He began to sputter and pace up and down the row, yanking at the grass himself. He told me to get out of his garden.

I had never seen him angry before. He probably said more, but those words stuck with me. I hadn't even thought about college until then, and I wasn't focused on it until Miss Fowler tried but failed to get me thrown out of high school and Mr. Hossack had told me that if I didn't mess up again I could probably get a scholarship to a good college.

After Sputnik, when Mr. Whitmer, the boys' advisor, dropped college catalogues on my study hall table, they weren't for liberal arts colleges, but science and engineering schools. He suggested that I go to Rose Polytechnic or perhaps to Rensselaer Polytechnic, where Mickey Gonsor had gone a few years before. I kept the Rose Poly Tech catalogue in my bedroom, but I had no interest in moving to Terre Haute, Indiana or Troy, New York and had little knowledge of what engineers did to save the world from the evils of Communism.

I chose colleges to apply to more by whim than research. There were catalogues from most of the private colleges and the prominent state universities in the advisors' office. Respecting Miss Clark's exhortation that those who could, *should* become engineers and nuclear physicists, I applied to the Massachusetts Institute of Technology and the California Institute of Technology. The wastebasket in my bedroom had college pennants on it and that served as my "best universities in the US" list. A few of them ended up on my list—Harvard, where Tommy Boone had gone the previous year and Don Albright a few years before that—and Cornell and Dartmouth. Mr. Low had not joined the recruitment wave sweeping tens of thousands high school students into the technologic forces fighting the Soviets with slide

PART THREE

rules. He gently encouraged me to consider his college, Amherst; he thought it was the best of the small private colleges, and it had fine humanities and science programs.

Since I knew nothing about colleges besides their names, there was no logic behind my decision not to apply to Princeton, Yale, Columbia, Stanford, the University of Pennsylvania, Notre Dame, or NYU, whose pennants were also on the wastebasket.

Mr. Hossack said that since I was applying to places that were hard to get into I should apply to six. My sixth application was to Mr. Low's Amherst.

The annual Christmas Cantata each year was the school's biggest musical event attended by hundreds of adults, many of whom did not have children in school. There was no separation of Christianity from school, and no one questioned the appropriateness of either the Christmas Cantata or caroling in the halls or Christmas trees in the lobby.

The concert choir and soloists sat in the balcony while a series of tableaux were presented on stage behind a scrim, which allowed full black outs for scene changes, as well as the use of focused spotlights to highlight the abundant angels who were elevated on a black platform, hovering over Mary, Joseph, and Jesus in a stable.

Freshman didn't sing in the concert choir. I signed up to be a shepherd after I was beaten out for the role of Baby Jesus by a pudgy Baby Jesus doll with attached halo. After the cast members were made up and dressed we waited for our scenes in the large theater classroom next to the auditorium, sitting on the floor or doing homework at one of the desks. While waiting for the shepherds to be called for their first appearance, I was showing someone how flexible I was by hooking both of my feet behind my neck. Before the few people who were watching could tell me how cool I was we were called to the stage for the next scene. The room quickly emptied of the shepherds in robes with crooked staffs, angels fully winged out, kings leaning on their scepters and chomping on their beards. Except for me: I was in a tight ball on the floor and could not get either foot from behind my neck. I rolled around as I struggled, banging one elbow and then the other before tipping forward with my face pressed against the floor. With a super effort I shoved my left heel with my right hand and I sprang open like a jack-in-the-box. I scampered down the hall, through the stage door and into the scene very late, evoking a laugh from the audience in front and the angels behind. The Virgin Mary gave me a dirty look, not the last time that happened.

After my freshman debut as a shepherd the theater department didn't recruit me for a return performance in the cantata. That year my voice plunged from tenor to bass. I could sing a low B, I had good relative pitch and a resonant sound, and I could follow Mr. Dahlstrom's conducting: I had no other musical credentials. The next two years I sang with the choir in the balcony where I was not a risk for spoiling any sacred moments until I was a senior, when I was asked to sing the role of the king bringing myrrh to the infant Jesus. It was a low bass line and I could usually hit those notes in rehearsals, although not with complete reliability. I was always nervous singing a solo, and this was the cantata's most reverential moment in a sold-out auditorium. The tenor nailed the gift of gold, and then the baritone produced a smooth offering of frankincense. After the choir led everyone to the perfect light they held their breath as I launched my solo with an epic rumble that wobbled through an astonishing number of off-key notes, probably the shakiest delivery of myrrh in the history of Christianity.

Until Christmas break I pretended to be reading a book when walking between classes so that I didn't have to look anyone in the eyes.

PART THREE

That spring at the Easter service in my church I sang an antiphonal solo from high above and behind the congregation with the same humiliating results. That was the last time I let anyone talk me into performing as a soloist.

Late in February I travelled for the second time to the East Coast, not by train, but by airplane. I was invited with about 50 other state student council presidents and thirty-five foreign students to the annual Williamsburg Student Burgesses, paid for by the New York Herald Tribune. The title of the meeting was something like "Democratic Leadership in the World—A Challenge to Youth." The Student Burgesses Meeting had been going on for a number of years in Williamsburg, an early capitol of Virginia, where an important part of the evolution of our government from a republic to a democracy had occurred. Many of the houses and public buildings had been faithfully preserved or recreated by the Rockefeller family.

Because Mom could not drive my manual-transmission Chevy, Dad was taking me to the airport for a late morning flight to Great Falls. He had gotten up early and saw that a heavy snow had fallen, making the streets in Missoula hard to drive. He called the airport, where the agent told him that the Missoula airport was shut down because of the storm. I was still packing when he rang up the house. He sounded tense.

"The airport is closed. There's no way for you to get the flight to Great Falls for at least two days. I'll be goddamned if you're going to miss that conference. I'm going to drive you over the pass to Great Falls. Your flight doesn't leave from there until 2:30."

"Geez Dad, is the pass open?"

"It is for now. I called the highway patrol and they said I might need chains, so I'm taking them."

"Is Great Falls open?"

"I called the weather station at the Great Falls airport. They expect most of the snow to be dumped on our side of the divide."

"Okay."

"I'll pick you up in fifteen minutes. I gotta get gas."

I raced to finish packing, put on my suit and tie and pulled on a pair of heavy overshoes. Dad showed up in his new green Edsel station wagon, dressed in his hunting clothes. He had thrown a heavy scoop shovel and a bag of sand in the back. He tossed in my suitcase and we fishtailed away from unplowed Beverly Avenue, sliding around corners. The highway was in better shape than the city streets because of plow trucks going up the pass every hour, followed by trucks scattering salt.

In the summer we would have gotten to Great Falls an hour before my flight to Detroit was scheduled to take off. Dad was in his race car driver mode; he kept both hands clenched to the steering wheel and pushed the speed as high as he could go and still stay on the road. The only time he spoke was to swear when the Edsel skidded on the windy back road over the continental divide that, on a good day, was two hours faster than going on the main highways. He had only owned the car for a few months but it already reeked of cigarettes and he chain-smoked for the entire trip, leaving a rear window cracked to serve as a chimney. The snow flakes were thick and heavy, limiting our vision to a few hundred feet ahead; half a dozen times we had to get out and sweep off the headlights and windshield. We didn't eat; we didn't drink.

We stopped once to pee deep yellow craters in the snow at the side of the road. I hadn't peed side by side with Dad since I was ten: on a fishing trip he challenged me to see who could pee further. I won by a yard.

The Great Falls airport was on the edge of town and as we came down from the pass we could see a plane landing from the west. Dad drove right to the airport door, ran around the car, handed me my suitcase, and I gave him my overshoes to take back.

"Well, sir. We made it," he said.

"You are going to stay in Great Falls, right, not drive back?"

"You damn betcha I'll stay here. Doing that drive once in a day is enough. Good luck."

"Thank you for bringing me, Dad."

"I sure as hell didn't wanchu to miss that meeting." He reached for his wallet. "You got any money?" He handed me a ten-dollar bill.

I turned to walk into the airport, where the plane had already started to board eastbound passengers. I had no language to say more to Dad about what he had just done for me. I didn't understand my feelings—a mixture of relief, excitement about my first plane flight, anxiety about getting on the plane before they closed the door, and confusion about Dad. At the airport door I looked back at him: he was watching me, a thin, small man in hunting jacket, cap, and gloves. He waved. I waved back, and turned away. It occurred to me that my Student Burgesses meeting in Virginia and all that had happened to me in the past year and a half were important to him. I hadn't known that he ever thought about me or cared about what I was doing. I hardly knew him.

Ten minutes after I boarded and found a seat near the back of the plane we were taxiing. I was on my way.

The Detroit airport was the most magnificent I had ever seen; it was also only the second one I had ever seen. I bedded down on a couple of airport chairs over night and at six AM boarded my flight to Washington DC, a huge Boeing Stratocruiser, the first passenger airplane with a pressurized cabin that could fly high above the clouds; it famously had a lower deck which was used as a lounge, similar to the club car on a train. Plane travel was luxurious then, like the higher classes of ocean liner travel. All the men were in suits; the women boarded in lovely winter dresses and suits, with pillbox hats and high-heeled shoes. I was traveling with the state student council president from Michigan who had written me to ask if we might fly together from Detroit since she was afraid of being in an airplane. Except for one piper club flight during which I threw up all over the plane, I had no more experience than she did, but we sat together and as the sun rose over the curved horizon we saw out the window glorious puffy pink clouds from an altitude at which most people had never flown. We drank the free champagne that Northwest gave out on all of its Stratocruiser flights, no ID's requested, and no seat belts either.

As interesting as the Key Club trip to Chicago, Washington DC, New York City, and Detroit had been, and as stimulating as the National Youth Leadership Conference in Estes Park was, the February trip to Virginia had the greater impact on what happened to me in the final months of high school.

We changed airplanes at National airport and in less than an hour we were at the Norfolk airport. For the next five days we lived in a luxurious hotel outside the boundaries of historic Colonial Williamsburg, with photographers from the New York Herald Tribune taking our pictures and reporters writing articles about what high school seniors selected from all over the world thought about the future of democracy and the possibility of world peace. We spent several days on guided visits to the buildings of Colonial Williamsburg with history professors who described the nature of the earliest settlements and their governance under colonial rule. We conducted debates in the Capitol and Courthouse, acting out 18th century practices, ate dinner in the Raleigh Tavern which served as the center of Williamsburg's political life, and listened to speeches from now-forgotten politicians and professors and journalists about the roots and problems of our democracy in the face of the post-war global ideological conflicts and the perils of fracturing western colonialism in African, Asia, and middle eastern countries.

PART THREE

The morning of our departure I was in the Norfolk airport about to fly through Washington D.C. back to Montana. I noticed on the departure board a flight continuing from National Airport to Boston. It occurred to me that instead of flying back to Montana I might fly to Boston, where MIT and Harvard were considering my college applications. I found a pay phone and with a handful of dimes and nickels ready to deposit in the phone, asked the operator to put me through to Harvard and from the Harvard switchboard to Tommy Boone in his freshman room in the Old Harvard Yard. His roommate answered the phone. Although the odds against connecting with him were diminishingly small, the roommate grabbed Tommy as he was about to leave for a class. He said sure I could come, and I could sleep overnight in his room; he would take me to the Harvard Union for meals and I could join him in classes. Airplane tickets were totally changeable then. I cancelled my Montana flights, contacted the admissions offices at Harvard and MIT to ask if I could visit with them, and a few hours later I was at Logan Airport, trying to figure out the Boston subway system.

We had covered the popular Kingston Trio song "Charlie and the MTA" in one of our Boys Senior Sextet performances and as I rode the crowded and smelly ancient streetcars and subways from the airport to Scollay Square to Park Street to Harvard Square, trying to chart my progress by glimpses of station signs through the grimy windows, the words kept cycling in my mind: in the 1940's a mayoral candidate promised to improve the subway and trolley system if elected, and a pair of songwriters described his endless and roundabout journey so complicated that he never found his way back home. I was in awe that twelve months after performing that song, and without any fore-planning at all, I was actually riding the MTA in what then had seemed far, far away Boston.

In the late afternoon I found Tommy's room and walked with him and his roommates across the Harvard Yard to the Harvard Union.

I was impressed: About 800 of Harvard's 1200 freshmen were seated at tables with loaded dinner trays in front of them, all in coats and ties, all in conversation, all seemingly cheerful since the first semester exams were now a few weeks behind them and spring exams were months away. Tommy signed me in and I paid for dinner and went through the line impressed with the variety of what was being served. Tommy introduced me to his friends as an applicant from his high school; they were friendly but uninterested. After dinner we spent the evening in the Lamont Library while Tommy studied and I fell asleep three pages into a copy of *Finnegan's Wake* that I had pulled off a shelf.

The next morning I went to Tommy's lecture in Emerson Hall and then walked a short distance for an interview with the Director of Admissions, Fred Glimp, a friendly man in his early forties who I had learned from Tommy had grown up in Boise, Idaho. We talked about the Student Burgesses' meeting, the Estes Park Youth Leadership Camp, the Key Club Trip, and what my favorite subjects were. I told him that I loved literature and thought I wanted to be a doctor. It was about as unstressful as the conversations I had with my barber.

In the afternoon I took the subway a few stops back toward downtown Boston and toured MIT. I talked for a while to a Missoula student who had graduated from MCHS the previous year. He and everyone else I saw were wearing grey sweatshirts. His said "Tech is Hell." Everyone looked pallid, grim, tired, and—perhaps—not clean, or at least not well groomed. My MIT interview was quite different, focusing on my interest in science, possibly engineering or nuclear physics. The enthusiasm of the man talking with me seemed to flag when I asked if there were literature courses. He made the case for MIT's general education requirement, but I concluded that one did not go to MIT to study the humanities or to become a physician.

At the end of the day my impression was that MIT and the students I saw were grungy, and that Harvard and the students I met were comparatively elegant, happy, and self-confident. Harvard's campus had been there since 1636. I loved the dozens of 19th century buildings, cared for with the expectation that they would be used for another 320 years. Although the oaks and maples and elms were bare, they were centuries old, huge and rugged and inspiring.

Until the trip to Boston, the six colleges to which I had applied all seemed equally attractive, although they were very different. On the plane I closed my eyes and tried to sort out my excitement and my sudden longing to go to Harvard. Some of the reasons were tangible—I liked the idea of being in Boston with its historic buildings, the literary home of much of the American fiction I had read, and the seat of the American Revolution. I loved that there were two-dozen universities and colleges in Boston and that there were great museums and a famous symphony. Harvard was the implicit American model of a great university, what Oxford was to Britain.

But the intangible was even more powerful for me: that Harvard was Harvard and no other university had its long history of academic excellence, a place where great books had been written, great scholars had worked, great politicians and lawyers had been trained. In the Harvard Union twelve hundred freshman wore Harvard's exclusiveness as casually as they wore their tweed jackets and blazers, regimental striped ties, and oxford-cloth button down shirts. I knew that few came from places as provincial as Montana, that many had illustrious parents and families and educational backgrounds. I knew that I was not them, but I wanted to be among them even though I could not imagine becoming like them. For some reason it wasn't scary to be a total outsider—it was exhilarating.

And although I was ashamed of it, I recognized a selfish desire to acquire an identity that I could respect, even if others didn't.

When I got back from the East Coast I made the bad decision of going over Rogers Pass to a basketball game in Helena with Sandy and his friends, easy enough in the afternoon when there was still light, but much harder coming back at midnight in a howling snow storm. We could see the road well enough, but another car full of Missoula High boys had lost its headlights. Sandy, who was a little wild both before and after he became an Air Force pilot, drove beside the lightless car in the oncoming traffic lane to light its way, pulling in behind at the last second—or less—when a car bound for Helena came toward us, hurtling up the slick, twisting, narrow highway. I sat silently and stiffly the whole way, sure we were going to be a headline in the next morning's *Missoulian*: "No Future for Five Missoula County High School Students Killed in a Head-on Collision on Rogers Pass Returning from Spartans Basketball Game."

Both cars made it back.

I had left my car outside Sandy's house in Bonner. At 3 AM I drove home through windless empty streets, large flakes fluttering in my headlights, Missoula transfigured by untracked snow, every branch frosted. Total silence.

Our college applications had been put in the mail, we were coasting through classes no longer hard or critical. I was aware that I had passed through a door that night, curtained only by the translucent snow, but a door through which I could not go back. I knew that I would not again drive in deep winter snow in Montana. I knew that I would never again take a road trip with Sandy or camp with the Bonner and Milltown boys, never again go to a high school football or basketball game, never again spend a night walking in a blinding blizzard to keep a car from driving off the road.

I could not know that in the next few years many of us would put on a uniform and go off to war, that Sandy's brother Mike Bouchard, the donor of my first dating car, would be shot down over North Vietnam and never be found, that Sandy would be flying transports

PART THREE

and helicopters in Vietnam, and that Rollie would survive a helicopter crash there. I had no sense at all of the future, but I was expectant and optimistic. Had I bothered to guess what the future would hold I would not have gotten a single thing right.

After returning from Williamsburg I was asked to give a speech about the Student Burgesses. I gave an assembly to my 400 classmates in the auditorium, with slides that I had taken in Williamsburg, wearing the three-cornered hat that each of us had been given. I talked about the earliest unsuccessful settlements at Jamestown, and then how colonists gradually learned to live in a land very different than England, with a continuous threat from the native communities that had lived in prosperity along the lush shores of the James River; about the early pre-revolutionary government, and how the ideas that Jefferson and other Southerners brought to the writing of the Constitution and Bill of Rights conflicted with New England values and goals. And I talked about what the students from Europe and the United States saw as the threats to democracy around the world and what responsibilities those of us born at the beginning of the Second World War had toward our own citizens and those of other countries.

The assembly was successful enough that I was asked to give it to the juniors as well, and then to businessmen at a Rotary Club luncheon. The presentation was my president's report at the spring Montana State Student Council convention.

When I came home from my office-cleaning job on April 22nd, I saw that Mom had placed an airmail letter from Amherst College on the living room coffee table, propped up against a vase holding a single purple tulip. It was a rather fat letter. The hair on the back of my neck stood up, a quick shiver went down my spine. I wished that Mom hadn't seen the envelope. I didn't want her to be around when I read it, and without talking to her I went into my room and closed the door. I was sure that what was inside was going to be momentous and that the envelope needed to be opened as though it was already an historical document—the letter that set the direction of my future. I found my scapel-sharp hunting knife and like a surgeon opening an abdomen, I slit the envelope cleanly, being careful not to cut any of the pages inside. One by one I unfolded them, forcing myself not to see a single word, drawing out the most important moment in my life to fully savor it. The first page was typed on heavy, watermarked paper.

> "Dear Mr. Noel: I am happy to inform you that you have been accepted by the Committee on Admissions and Scholarships as a member of the Class of 1963 and that you have been awarded a scholarship of $1400 for the coming year. With this award you will have to provide about $482 from your own funds to meet the comprehensive charge of $1882 for tuition, room, board, and college fees. I must ask you to make a firm decision about Amherst by May 1. If you want a place held for you, please send by May 1 a check or money order for $100. This sum is not refundable. Theodore Bacon Jr. Associate Dean."

I was stunned, more numb than excited. I felt not a flicker of triumph. No other college would be notifying me of acceptance before I had to notify Amherst of my decision. Amherst had backed me and the other boys who were waiting for letters from other colleges into a corner. How could I keep my options open if any of the other colleges accepted me and still not give up Amherst if theirs was my best offer?

I was angry with myself for not being excited that Amherst accepted me: a great moment had arrived, I should have been elated, but instead I was disappointed and apprehensive. I didn't talk to Mom. I went outside and wandered around Bonner Park, turning over the Amherst acceptance in my mind. I had been offered admission and a scholarship to an outstanding college on a beautiful campus with strong humanities and science departments. I had no idea if any other offers would be coming in the next two weeks. Mr. Low had always wanted one of his students to attend his college. He had stood up for me in one difficult situation after another—something my brother and father hadn't done—and given the respect I felt for him, turning Amherst down would be betraying him.

I thought about accepting Amherst's invitation, sending the hundred dollars, and then backing out. But this would only compound my betrayal with dishonesty: a yes was a yes, and a hundred dollars was a vast sum, more than three months of work at J.A. Hogle and Company, enough to buy a hamburger deluxe with fries every day for a year.

And yet, since coming back from Boston, I fiercely wanted to go to Harvard; being an Amherst student in rural Massachusetts was not my dream.

When I returned home I told Mom about the letter. She seemed unsurprised: from the weight of the envelope she had guessed that Amherst had offered to take me. When I told her about the scholarship she didn't light up with pleasure. For her a full scholarship was simply what had to be, because there was no other way I could attend an expensive private university three thousand miles from Montana. She asked if I was going to accept it. I told her I wasn't sure. She didn't ask why and she didn't offer any advice. Perhaps she too was waiting for Harvard, which would have been as much of a triumph for her years of sacrifice as it would have been for me, although she never said that and neither did I.

I wasn't interested in telling Dad. I was grateful that he had driven me to Great Falls when I couldn't get the flight out of Missoula, and I knew that if I hadn't made it to the East Coast for the Student Burgesses I never would have gone to Boston and wouldn't have visited Harvard. But he had never been part of what it had taken for me to apply to highly competitive colleges. I felt that I owed him cool politeness but I didn't think any advice he might give me would be useful. I decided to wait until I had heard from the other colleges and hoped that I would have the satisfaction of telling him that I was going to Harvard. I dreaded having to tell him that I would be going to Amherst because I thought he would not hesitate to point out that I wasn't good enough for Harvard.

The next day I drove home from high school at lunch and asked the Missoula operator to put me through to the switchboard at Harvard College. A woman with a broad South Boston accent answered.

"May I have the Dean of Admissions, please, Mr. Glimp?"

"Of course Dearie."

A woman answered. "Hello, this is the Admissions Office. How may I help you?"

"Hello, my name is Gordie Noel and I am calling from Missoula Montana to speak with Mr. Glimp. Is he available?"

"Yes, I think he can take a call . . . ."

I could hear her muffle the phone, and then a familiar voice came on the line. "Hello, this is Fred Glimp."

"Mr. Glimp, it's Gordie Noel, from Missoula, Montana."

"Yes, Gordie, I was told you were calling. What can I do for you?"

"Mr. Glimp, yesterday I received a letter from Amherst admitting me. I know that you have not sent out letters yet, but I'm afraid that their deadline arrives before I will hear your decision."

There was a pause; I thought I heard the faint sound of papers being shuffled.

"Well I'm unable to tell you what decisions the Committee on Admissions has made about the entering class. The letters will go out in another week." A pause, and then: "But I wouldn't worry about it."

"Oh. . . . Oh. . . . Um. . . . Jeepers!"

I thought that this probably meant that I would be admitted, but I wasn't ready to believe it. I was shaky, my palms sweating, my voice slightly tremulous.

"Well, Amherst also offered me a full scholarship."

"Ahh, I also won't be able to tell you the decisions of our Committee on Finances and Scholarships." He paused, as though weighing what he would say next. "But . . I wouldn't worry about that either."

My mind went blank; I was unable to speak for what seemed to me like a long time. I didn't have a script in mind that included having to deal with the delivery of a dream on the phone from the man who was responsible for it.

Finally, in a slightly husky voice I managed, "Okay . . . That's . . . that's astounding, amazing . . . Wow! Thank you . . . Thank you very much."

"You're welcome. Have a nice day. By the way, how is the weather in Missoula? Still snowing?"

Mr. Glimp grew up a few hundred miles from where I was standing talking to him and I knew that he was only half joking about snow in late April.

Back at school my mind was far from my classes as excitement began to sweep away my disbelief and euphoria swept in. At the end of the day I went to talk with Gus Hossack in his office, and then with Mr. Low. Gus was exuberant, but offered no advice other than to point out that I had two great choices, with possibly more to come.

Mr. Low looked tired; he was somber and, in detail, made the case that a smaller college would be better for a Missoula boy, that I was less likely to get swallowed up at Amherst. He was not strident, just more reserved than usual. He delivered most of his comments standing at his window looking out at Mount Sentinel, his back turned toward me, his hands clasping and unclasping behind his back. I saw that his shirtsleeve cuffs were a little worn. I had never noticed that before.

I think he had had this conversation a few times in the past. He asked me to take my time before turning Amherst down.

In the end I betrayed Dan Low and chose Harvard. For days I kept to myself that I had been admitted to Harvard: to volunteer it would be bragging, but I was practically vibrating with the desire to shout it out. As more students received college acceptances and asked me what I was going to do, I joked that I chose Harvard because it had the third biggest library in the world, with six million volumes. I couldn't tell anyone that being accepted to Harvard was a validation that made up for years and years of feeling that I was not likable or competent or interesting. In Montana in 1959, a state heavily settled by northern European immigrants where nothing was taken for granted, if you wanted something you had to work hard to earn it and even then you probably weren't going to get it. Nothing was given to you. I felt that I had earned it, but even more I felt incredibly lucky because I knew that there were a thousand other boys who had also earned it but would not be admitted.

At the same time I felt sad that my decision had deprived Mr. Low of the satisfaction of knowing that his thoughtful advice had been accepted, and for a few weeks I felt awkward when I greeted him every morning in homeroom.

Over the years I have met many men from Amherst and never failed to like them. I have often wondered what my life would have been like if I had gone there. There were several women's college close to Amherst and certainly I would have met someone there and married and had a family. But then, had I followed Mr. Low's path, the three talented, warm, intelligent, beautiful young women whom I treasure would never have been born. Nor would any of the rest of what followed college have happened in the same way or at all.

Life is mostly like that. Robert Frost got it right. Although, in my case, perhaps I took the path that, when offered, was the one more, not less often, chosen.

PART THREE

A day after my conversation with Dan Low, and a week before letters from the other colleges were due, Harvard sent me a telegram confirming my conversation with Mr. Glimp: "Glad to inform you of admission and financial aid of $1600 scholarships and assured $400 term-time job if wanted."

Early in May I received letters from the California Institute of Technology and Dartmouth College turning me down. Cal Tech knew that I was no nuclear physicist and I had been put off by the Dartmouth graduate who interviewed me—a Bitterroot Valley farmer wearing overalls and barn boots—who had correctly determined that he and I were not made for each other and that Dartmouth could get along without me. Cornell University in Ithaca, New York offered me a full scholarship in their College of Engineering. The Massachusetts Institute of Technology offered me admission, but no scholarship. And the University of Montana offered a full scholarship covering all expenses at either of their universities, although I had not applied. So did Wesleyan in Ohio, which until their offer letter arrived I didn't know existed. I think my minister gave them my name.

By mid-May we knew that Ted Smith would be going to Oberlin College; Bruce Sievers would be going to Stanford; Byron Johnston accepted MIT's offer and the next fall I met him, pallid and wearing a "Tech is Hell" sweatshirt; Rollie Trenouth would be going to Columbia University; and Sandy Bouchard would be going to the Air Force Academy, following in the footsteps of his three older brothers, all of whom had been in the Navy or Air Force. Layne had chosen Iowa State College in Ames to study interior design; Mary Kraabel would be going to the University of Washington. Many of the guys who I had been running around with since grade school were going to either the University of Montana in Missoula, or Montana State College in Bozeman. Others were going to the Lutheran and Methodist colleges in Minnesota and the Midwest or near Seattle. A few guys were heading for military service. Several of the girls who had been class leaders were marrying their older boyfriends as soon as school was over. Of my good friends, only Rollie would be close enough to visit.

As the seniors saw each other in the hallways or classrooms we exchanged plans. We promised each other that we would see each other in the summers at least, but those of us that were leaving the state felt in our bones that the community we had belonged to was both irreplaceable and dissolving—like Brigadoon, about to subside in the mists, not to return in our lifetimes.

Academically the seniors were through after the third quarter: the grades from the fourth quarter did not get used to calculate class rank or for college applications. We drifted through our exams, turned in our homework, but for the most part everyone knew how to be a high school student and we were trotting without breaking a sweat. Bruce and I continued to vie for perfect scores on Chemistry exams; now it was beyond personal, Harvard vs. Stanford.

A few weeks before graduation Mr. Miller had us do our last chemistry experiment—determining the melting point of lead and copper and tin. We used small high-fired ceramic pots that could withstand very high temperatures and measured the temperature it took to soften the metal enough to make it malleable, and then the temperature at which it became liquid.

I was fascinated. I asked Mr. Miller if he would mind if I created a little blast furnace in the lab to try to melt iron. He agreed to it, although in retrospect it was a very, very bad idea. At home I read about blast furnaces in the World Book to find out the melting temperatures of metals and how mixing oxygen with burning fuels would raise furnace temperatures. I read about the construction of blast furnaces, knowing that they had to be able to resist higher temperatures than it took to melt iron ore.

PART THREE

I went to the Missoula Mercantile and bought several gas jets and pipes and valves for high flow natural gas furnaces. I bought cement used to make furnace blocks and molded them inside a steel bucket and then cut holes into the buckets on opposite sides. On one warm, quiet, peaceful May afternoon during our chemistry lab period I attached gas lines and compressed air lines to two y-shaped pipes screwed into the two gas jets. I placed a chunk of iron inside and covered the bucket with the firebrick cap I had made. With the gas turned on low and pointed through the holes in the side of the bucket, I lit the flame and turned the gas up high. Then I turned on the compressed air and a foot long flame blasted into the holes. I turned the gas and compressed air to the highest setting. There was a roar that exceeded 130 decibels and the lab table began to shake. Mr. Miller, who was correcting lab reports at his desk, dismissed the other students and turned off his hearing aid; without it he was stone deaf. After about ten minutes the teachers whose classrooms were above the science wing descended on Mr. Miller to say they couldn't be heard in their classrooms and they wanted to know what was going on. Neither Mr. Miller nor I could hear them and they gave up and soon there were hundreds of students milling around the lawns. A half-dozen neighbors called the fire department telling them that the school was about to blow up or launch into orbit. In ten minutes two pumpers and a hook and ladder truck roared into the parking lot.

I turned the furnace burners off when I saw the fire trucks outside the windows. I was disappointed because the entire bucket was glowing a promising orange-red. Of course I had no way of getting the top off and so couldn't see if the iron had melted. Six firemen poured into the lab with fire hoses they had attached to the school's hydrant system aimed right at me and the glowing bucket.

A guy in a chief's helmet looked around the room and came toward me; Mr. Miller was still bent over his desk grading.

"What the hell is going on in here?"

"Just a blast furnace," I said.

The chief looked at the bucket and then at the cloud of acrid smoke hovering just below the ceiling.

"We got calls that there was a fighter jet taking off behind the high school. You got folks very riled up."

I was pretty proud that I had made enough noise to sound like a fighter jet. The chief walked over to Mr. Miller and passed a hand between his nose and the papers. Mr. Miller looked up with a sweet smile and a puzzled look on his face. He put his hearing aide back in, wished them a good afternoon, and asked what they were doing there. The firemen made me leave, determining that both the school and I were unsafe, not deterred by my protestations that scientific studies of great importance were being disrupted.

I stopped by the next morning before classes. My construction was a triumph: everything had cooled off and the iron was a blob in the bottom—I had gotten above 1400 degrees Fahrenheit. The bucket and the ceramic I had molded inside were charred but intact. The room smelled like a blacksmith's shop.

I had another—and my last—chat with Mr. Hunt that afternoon, accompanied by my usual body guards, Mr. Low and Mr. Hossack. It was agreed that I would be allowed to graduate but that I was not to darken the doors of Missoula County High School as long as Mr. Hunt was vice-principal. I had to pay for some flasks and beakers that broke during the violent shaking. Mr. Miller was told that he could not turn his hearing aid off during school hours. Several classmates thanked me for giving them a nice May afternoon off.

A few weeks later I was climbing Mt. Sentinel and encountered Mr. Miller, who was an avid hiker. I was in a t-shirt and jeans. He looked at me with the same puzzled look that he had given the fire chief, as though vaguely recognizing me but unable to remember why. I began to reintroduce myself but saw that he wasn't wearing his hearing aid, and so I just waved at him and kept going. He was a wonderful teacher who had simply seen so many thousands of students that he had stopped trying to keep us straight.

Graduation events filled the final days of the school year. Three hundred and fifty of us in suits and dresses and all of our teachers attended the senior banquet a few nights before we graduated. A string quartet of junior musicians played during dinner, a minister gave an invocation, anticipation and nostalgia filled the room. Suddenly, none of us were eager for the year to end.

A few days before graduation we received our final Yearbook. The teachers had given up jamming any more facts into us and let us write valedictory notes to each other. Tinsel Teeth and I were both in Miss Fink's English class and as my yearbook passed around between several people who wanted to write in it, I was surprised to see her writing me a note:

"You were really lucky when you lost the senior class election last year. Look at what you got—all the wonderful trips as our State Student Council President. Whatever you do, it is always successful. Best of luck to you always in whatever field you enter—science, politics, religion. I know you will be good in your chosen field. I hear we won't be seeing you much this summer but I'll be looking forward to seeing you at Christmas. Best of luck again. TT"

I was humbled. I had thought that she disliked me since grade school. It hadn't occurred to me that perhaps she was just as awkward as I was, that when she chose me as her partner in the dancing classes it wasn't because she didn't want to embarrass herself with a boy she actually liked, but because she felt more comfortable with me than with some of the other boys. I was ashamed that, because she wasn't attractive to me, because she was straight and serious, I had so dismissed her that I hadn't realized that perhaps she wished we were friends.

At the beginning of the class her yearbook had passed through my hands and, having nothing to say to her, I simply passed it on. The next day I thanked her for her nice note and asked if I could write in her yearbook. But it never happened.

Miss Clark also asked if she could write in my yearbook. She had warned me repeatedly to focus on school, cut down on my other activities, and become a rocket scientist to fight world domination by Communism. She took a prominent front-page location where everyone else would be sure to see it:

> "I burn my candle at both ends,
> It gives a lovely light!
> But oh, my foes and ah, my friends
> It will not last the night."—Gertrude Clark

When she handed it back without a smile, she told me that I should have gone to MIT.

On the afternoon of the final day we posed for homeroom pictures in our caps and gowns and then 400 of us marched into the front rows of the gymnasium, which was packed with more than a thousand people. Both Dad and Mom were there. Dad sat discretely in the bleachers to the side and Mom sat in the center of the auditorium with my grandparents. The symphony orchestra played countless rounds of Elgar's *Pomp and Circumstance March* as we filed in. There was a prayer by Lutheran minister who called down God's mercy on our immortal souls, and then speeches by the principal, Mr. Berry, by

PART THREE

the school board president, and by an illustrious graduate, Clinton Hester, who graduated from MCHS in 1915, became rich, and wanted to talk about himself. A few awards were given out to teachers and the graduating captains of the boys' sports teams.

And then one by one we were called on stage by Mr. Berry. As a student's name was called and admissions to colleges, scholarships, and awards announced he or she walked the short distance to the stage, climbed a few stairs, and crossed the stage to receive the diploma. Everyone received applause and some students' families whooped and hollered.

Initially the ceremony ran like clockwork.

When my turn came, I didn't know what Mr. Berry would announce. He began with "University of Montana all-expenses scholarship, Lions' Club Scholarship, National Merit Scholar Finalist." By then I was going up the stairs. Then he added "Montana State Student Council President, delegate to National Youth Leadership Conference." I stopped and turned around and went back to the top of the steps to wait, since if he was going to read all that stuff I was way too early. There was laughter. "Represented Montana at the New York Herald Tribune Student Burgesses in Williamsburg, Virginia, Montana Boys State." I started out again. "Admitted Harvard College and awarded the John Harvard Scholarship." I stopped again and folded my arms, tilting my body to one side as though waiting impatiently. Now there was steady laughing. "Massachusetts Institute of Technology, Amherst College with full scholarship, Cornell University with full scholarship." I was bright red. The whole auditorium was laughing. I got off the stage as quickly as I could, avoided eye contact with everyone, missed the first step, stumbled down the rest of the stairs and my cap fell off, which provoked another round of laughing.

Mr. Berry kindly overlooked the E and the disenrollment Miss Fowler had recommended, my censored satirical class musical, and my near-bombing of the chemistry lab just a few days earlier.

Myra Shults, Bruce Sievers and Ted Smith followed me a few minutes later. Their introductions went on for a long time as well, but forewarned, their timing was better and exits more graceful.

After the graduation, after meeting our families and friends, after saying good by to classmates and promising summer reunions, for the last time the group of us that dated and danced and took classes together went out for dinner, and then we went to a student's house for a party that lasted past midnight. Apparently curfews were now a thing of the past. Well after midnight I drove Layne home, and the two of us and a few other students who followed us there danced in her basement rumpus room until about 2 AM when her dad yelled down the stairs that we were making too much noise and that I should go home. He was an undertaker and appreciated quiet.

It was a night of euphoric happiness. I was in love with Layne and thought I would marry her. We had finished high school. Almost all of our friends were going to college, many out of state, our futures were exciting.

A few days later I left for a summer job with the Forest Service.

CHAPTER

TWENTY-FIVE

OUT OF MONTANA

SUMMER JOBS FOR most college kids in Montana were in seasonal industries. In the eastern plains the greatest number of jobs were on ranches—cutting, baling, and stacking hay, moving irrigation pipes, applying pesticides, branding spring calves, or running harvesters or plows or fertilizer spreaders. Some men and women found work in the National Parks, resorts, and dude ranches waiting tables, cooking, serving, cleaning cabins, or building trails. Girls more often than boys worked in drive-in restaurants like A & W Root Beer, whose business rose with the tulips and fell with the September leaves.

In the mountainous areas of the western states most of the jobs were related to the vast forests and the Forest Service was the best employer. Maintaining millions of acres of forest required the Forest Service to double or triple the staff in hundreds of ranger stations during the few months in which the woods were accessible and tinder-dry. The ranger stations needed energetic, strong laborers to build fences, survey log sale plots, clear areas of dead trees where there had been fires in the past, build trail, re-roof and re-paint and re-plumb ranger station buildings, and clear weeds that spread diseases to the trees planted after virgin forests were clear-cut.

Even more, the Forest Service needed the crews to fight the hundreds of lightening-strike fires that bloomed after every late-afternoon thunderstorm. One of the jokes I grew up with was that there were only two seasons in Montana, winter and fire season. It was the forest fires that made Forest Service work so lucrative for college kids: we could not take permanent jobs, but we had the whole summer free and we met their need for the huge expansion of workers during the summer.

Rollie, Ted, Bruce, and I got Forest Service jobs in the spring of our senior year. Bruce's dad was a senior forester at the Region One headquarters in Missoula; he found a close-by ranger station for Bruce to work in. My uncle Lloyd was also a senior forester. He had set up the "remount" stations all through the west, modeled after the Army's system for supplying troops during the Indian wars and then the First World War, using horse-led mules to pack enormous loads into areas where trucks could not travel. Lloyd developed dozens of Forest Service ranches where hundreds of mules and horses were kept, ready to be used to supply lookout towers in the spring and early summer, and to haul supplies for fires that were beyond passable roads.

Lloyd found me a job "pulling ribes" in northern Idaho. Heavy logging in northwestern Montana and northern Idaho at the beginning of the 20th century gradually cleared most of the stands of huge cedars, pines, firs, and spruce. Much of that land was left to reforest itself as the timber exploiters moved on, pushing new roads into the seemingly endless untouched forested valleys and mountains. But natural reforestation was slow and the demand for timber kept increasing as the old growth trees were toppled and hauled away. In Idaho huge areas of cut forest were thought to be suitable for a new kind of tree-farming, monoculture—the planting of just one kind of tree. Monoculture allowed reforestation of faster-growing varieties of trees that could all be harvested at the same time, increasing the profits of the logging industry and keeping lumber prices down. The consequences of monoculture and clear-cutting—reduced forest diversity and the healthy regrowth of trees that depended on other kinds of trees to stand above them when they were young—weren't recognized for decades. One of the tree species chosen for monoculture was the western white pine: it grew fast, was suited to the climate, and when mature produced cheap wood for framing. What was not anticipated was that the barren forest floor left after the big trees that had shaded out low growing plants were cut down rapidly filled with gooseberry and currant plants, a species called ribes, and that these plants were the intermediate host for white pine blister rust. In a healthy, diverse forest, this wouldn't have been a big problem, but when every tree is a white pine, and every wild gooseberry and currant plant has the fungus that causes blister rust, the vast plantings that were expected to produce large profits for timber companies and salaries for workers were at risk of becoming worthless. And so the Forest Service hired summer crews to work in the woods destroying all the ribes plants. That was the job that Uncle Lloyd found for me and that Ted Smith was doing in southern Idaho.

A few days after graduation I had to report to my blister rust camp. I had never set up a room for myself: my haphazard bedroom on Beverly Avenue evolved, without the intervention of planning, choice, or taste, from furniture from Grandpa Orvis's store and my accumulation of gear and souvenirs and books and records and comic books. In Idaho I would be living in one quarter of a large tent with three other boys, barren except for four cots and a wood-burning stove. I loaded my car with everything—everything—I

PART THREE

thought I would want to be comfortable: a coffee table I had made as an eighth grade shop project, a dozen books I thought I should read before college, a pipe rack with six pipes and a humidor of Walnut Blend tobacco, an immersion heater and a box of Lipton tea bags and cups and sugar, clothes to relax in and working clothes of jeans and work shirts and wool socks and the incredibly expensive handmade leather White's logging boots with spikes in the soles needed for walking across slippery logs that cost two-weeks' wages.

I stopped by Layne's house to say goodbye on the Sunday before I was to begin work at the camp, the two-door car stuffed with my homemaking and work gear. It was a sad goodbye. The camp was more than five hours away. I had no plans to come back until after she left for college.

US Highway 10 between Missoula and Coeur d'Alene was one lane in each direction; passing a car by pulling into the oncoming lane was at your own risk. If I got stuck behind a logging truck or hay bailer or transport truck on the steep ascent to lookout pass or on any of the twisty roads along the way I had to either pull into the oncoming lane and pass them or add hours to the drive. My Chevy labored over the mountain passes, threatening to overheat. I drove with the windows open to keep the car cool and me awake and sang along with whatever song I could find on my radio. From Coeur d'Alene I turned north past Spirit Lake, and then Lake Pend Oreille, and the little town of Sandpoint. In the late afternoon I got to the Priest Lake Ranger Station and found the Lamb Creek Forest Service road and drove twenty slow, bumpy, dusty miles through heavy forest to a wide meadow with a dozen white tents lined up on both sides of a two-track wagon road that ended in a mess tent billowing smoke. This was "home," where I expected to be for the next three months.

A federal worker doing entry-level labor was classified as a GS 3. My hourly salary was $1.56 an hour before taxes and social security. That penciled out to about $62 a week, or $750 for twelve forty-hour weeks. My room and board at Harvard would be $400 each, so I would just about cover that. However, what we all hoped for was a good fire season. If I worked more than forty hours in a week I would get "time and a half", so a single week of working 16 hours a day for 7 days would earn about $200. A couple of weeks on the fire line would get me up to around a thousand dollars, almost enough to cover room, board, and two round-trip train tickets to Boston.

Forest Service crews working at blister rust camps were organized loosely along military lines. We were awakened at about six AM by the loud clanging on a huge iron triangle by Cookie, the nearly toothless, scrawny, fabulously profane cook who smoked as much as his wood-burning stoves. I slept solidly in those days, but we all knew that Cookie's activities started two hours earlier than our wake-up time because he wasn't quiet when he split logs and heaved the quarters into the ancient, iron boiler that heated water. We washed our faces and hands at a twelve foot long wooden trough that leaked water its whole length and then dumped what was left into a makeshift stream that rose and fell with the cycles of our morning wash-up and evening showers. Peeing was also at a wooden trough, but there were a handful of outhouses for those who needed to sit for while. Getting all thirty of us through there in the morning before breakfast was tight, especially if someone felt some urgency about his morning ablutions and eliminations.

We got out of bed and directly into our work clothes that we hung to dry on hooks along the inside poles of our tents. There were no laundry facilities—we took care of that by driving into Priest River or Sandpoint on the weekend—and unless we fell into a mud hole, we wore the same clothes for a week. Cookie forbade corked boots in his dining tent, so we walked through in sneakers and filed by a long table piled with more or less the same food every day: loaves of squishy soft store-bought white or wheat bread, cold toast that Cookie had made an hour before, cheap strawberry jam without detectible strawberries, grape jelly, hot and cold cereal, bacon, scrambled or fried eggs, cold apple pie made from canned apples, cold leftover steak, black coffee, and thin, acrid orange juice made from dry powder. We worked our way along the table, filling a plate with our breakfast and then sat silently eating. There was almost no conversation beyond what was needed to round up our food and eat.

After we ate we scraped our plates and dumped them in a tub of hot water, then went back to the food table to make our lunches. Most of the guys were big and made two or three meat sandwiches or took a couple of the cold, tough steaks and stuffed them and vegetables and fruit and cookies and a few cans of juice into the five pound cloth flour bags we carried our lunch in. A single sandwich and some fruit and cookies did for me. When we climbed out of the stake-body trucks in which we were driven to the starting point of our work we tied the bags to our belts and carried them and a canteen on a strap with us as we moved through the woods.

Washing up, eating, and the long drive to where we started were all on our time, as was a half-hour lunch break. The clock usually started around 7:30 or 7:45 in the morning and we toiled—there is no better word for it—until 5 at night, when the trucks picked us up and hauled us back. In between we thrashed through twenty-yard-wide lanes of evenly planted fifteen-year-old white pines. The lanes had been marked with flags by a veteran of the blister rust camps whose job it was to lay out 25 lanes long enough to keep us busy until the end of the day. The lanes went straight through whatever was on the ground: fallen logs, rocks, creeks, cliffs. We zigzagged from side to side dragging "ribe ropes" behind us—thin green woven nylon parachute cords, incredibly tough, that we dropped at the far side of our lane so we could tell the lower boundary of our sweep back. Our job was to spot and pull out every gooseberry or currant plant in the lane, cleaning the forest of the intermediate host for the blister rust fungus to stop the spread of the tree-killing epidemic. We each covered about a mile or more of white pines in our lane, stripping off our shirts as the day heated up. We were scored each week on the number of square feet of forest we had cleared of ribes plants and the number of plants we had missed by a checker who came through the next day. Our scores were posted. Some guys worked fast and covered more ground to be at the top of the list. I merely plodded, suffered, and daydreamed through the Sisyphean work.

In every way, I was an outsider. Of the four of us sharing a tent, I was the only one who had furnished his quarter, the only one with a stack of classic books on a coffee table loaded with pipes and a typewriter. Lance was the tent-mate I remember best. He had finished a year of agriculture studies at a college in Arkansas. Every night he stood on his hands doing fifty pushups with his feet high over his head. He was built like a fullback. Because of his very thick southern drawl it was hard for me to follow him in our conversations, not because he didn't have interesting things to say, but because I couldn't decipher most of his words.

One guy left our tent on the third day and went back to New Jersey. He had mistaken a blister rust camp for an outdoor woodsmanship camp and had expected to be rolling logs, canoeing, and learning how to speed chop and throw axes.

The fourth guy, George, had bad skin, the face of a bird, weighed no more than I did and was four inches taller. He was too quiet for me to tell if he was weird.

Dinner was more lively and relaxed than breakfast. When we got into camp we could usually guess what Cookie was making by the smells drifting downwind. Chicken and steaks and pork chops were always fried and always served with "spuds," boiled potatoes that we lathered with butter and salt and pepper. Spaghetti was served with pork and beef meatballs boiled in red sauce that came in large cans. Salad was always chopped lettuce and carrots and celery and more pallid tomatoes dosed with Thousand Island dressing, no other choices offered. If Cookie was hung over after his weekend off he served us pork and beans and brown bread. Four days out of five dessert was glutinous apple pie, and once a week after a grocery run we had ice cream.

After we filed past the serving table, we took up seats based on what we did or did not want to hear other people talking about. Much of the conversation had to do with sports, and what didn't have to do with sports focused on cars, girls, and personal fitness, in that order. There were not literature or contemporary affairs tables.

Lance wasn't the only guy who maintained a substantial warehouse of muscles. Poles had been tied between trees for pull-ups, and an area had been cleared for weights made from gallon buckets filled with concrete with a slender peeled tree trunk running between them as a bar. In the woods behind the cook-tent, basketball and volleyball courts had been scraped clear of weeds and one or another was in use until dusk made it impossible to see the ball.

I had always had an "only child's" life in which I didn't have to share space and time with brothers or sisters. At school I was surrounded by people very different than I was but we coexisted with defined rules and roles. Now I was with twenty-five guys about my age, from different cultures, each of whom was free to operate by his own rules, and the only place I could escape to was my corner of the tent. I was aware that I was distancing myself from everyone, that confronted with twenty-five men from very diverse backgrounds I made no effort to become friends with most of them. When asked what I was doing in the fall I disingenuously said that I was going to a small college in the east. I knew that I had built a barrier by acting like a snob and wasn't distraught when several of the guys referred to me as "professor".

A summer job in the Forest Service was probably the best way for young people without skills to make money over the summer and many of the guys were hoping that if they did well they could get on a fire crew in one of the ranger stations the next summer, or even get into the smoke jumpers. We all labored, but with very different levels of motivation and contentment: for some of them this was an aspirational job, for me, a utilitarian one.

Toward the end of June we heard that our camp had been chosen for a trial of a new method of fighting blister rust—spraying the bottom four feet of the white pines with a chemical called Acti-dione, an antibiotic that in the laboratory was able to kill the fungi. If pulling ribe ropes through the constant tangles and hang-ups of the forest floor was mind-killing work, spraying trees was mind- and body-killing. We were each fitted with a five-gallon tank that we filled with the oily chemical diluted in water. We hoisted the fifty-pound tanks on our backs and with a hand pump connected to the tanks by a rubber hose we trudged back and forth in the lanes, spraying the trunk of each tree. Because the tree trunk was wet we didn't need to pull ropes to mark our progress, but hauling the heavy tanks up and down hills for eight hours a day was grueling; we all sweated profusely because the tanks kept our backs covered. When we ran out of spray, we refilled the tank from two five-gallon jerry cans that we lugged up from the road, about a hundred pounds in our hands and another fifty on our backs, in total a bit more than I weighed. By mid-day our pants and shirts were soaked by the stinking wind-blown spray.

At the beginning, the summer of 1959 was not looking like a great fire season for those of us hoping for the overtime and high pay that came with working around the clock day after day. It was a rainy year, and in the valleys the streams were running higher than normal, when usually they would have been down to a trickle. All of the small ponds were soggy and their resident mosquitoes, frantic for fresh blood, swarmed around us. We frequently had to cross ancient slippery fallen logs across ravines and crevices, hoping that the spikes on the bottoms of our boots would not tear loose from the rotting bark and wood, sending us plummeting with our tank five or ten or fifteen feet. It happened to a few people. I was lucky.

Occasionally we discovered artifacts remaining from the cutting of the virgin forest. In the early part of the 20th century when the huge logs were felled there were no bulldozers to skid them out and no roads or trucks capable of hauling the logs away to mills. We came across aged cedar sluices still standing on high trestles—huge troughs that sent logs careening down a mountain. Water was pumped up the mountain to fill a reservoir. A twenty-foot cedar log six or seven feet in diameter was dragged by mules or oxen and hoisted into the chute. When the gate at the head of the chute was opened the log was washed down the mountain. From the foot of the mountain the logs then were dragged by cogwheel steam locomotives down the valley to a road head where a cart pulled by oxen would take the logs away to a river or railroad siding. A few times we came across the thick cedar plank "corduroy" roads laid down in the swampy ground on which the cog engines trundled.

Since these forests were logged far from any roads, few people had visited. There were no hiking trails, no waterways. Deer and elk were plentiful near the Forest Service roads and there was no need for hunters to hike deep into the forests where we were working. Every week or two I would stumble on some small, hard to reach canyon so rugged that the loggers had passed it by and I would stand in awe, lost in time beneath a grove of cedar or fir or hemlock half a millennium old and a hundred feet tall, the sky shut out, leaving the fern and moss covered forest floor in dim twilight with cathedral-like rays piercing here and there through the sparse windows in the canopy, the place as calm and reverent as a monastery, a silent vestige of the once great forests that had covered northern Idaho and Montana after the last Ice Age. I relished the idea that I may have been the first human ever to be in the presence of that magnificence.

It was late in July before we were called out of the woods for our first fire. We were trucked to the camp where we loaded our fire gear and clothing and toiletries into old war surplus backpacks and then climbed up into the open bed of the trucks. The fire was a few hundred miles to the south, ignited with dozens of others by a lightening storm, now burning out of control, driven by hot, dry winds coming up from California and Nevada.

Our butts were battered by rutted dirt roads on our ride from our worksite to the camp and then from the camp to the paved highway, our bodies thrown against each other at sharp corners. Everyone was excited but grumpy after a full day of work with a long drive and hike ahead of us.

We arrived at the fire about eight at night, with a good two hours of workable daylight left to hike the six miles into the fire line. In addition to our packs and canteen, each of us tied the two sack lunches that Cookie had made to our belts. We picked up a shovel in one hand and a Pulaski in the other. The wind was blowing away from us toward the fire. As we got within a mile we could smell the fragrant smoke and see the charred, naked tree trunks outlined against the glowing night sky streaked with ribbons of orange where the fire was exploding into the dry, resinous crowns of the trees. We unloaded our gear at the edge of the fire where fallen logs and branches that had burned several days before were still smoldering, the sounds of crews that had arrived earlier distant above us.

We spent the night working with headlamps attached to our helmets, scraping out of the shallow, rocky earth a two-foot wide trail at the edge of what was still burning. We used the five-man bump-up method: our crew was divided into five teams and strung out over a few hundred feet. Each of us hacked at the ground with the hoe end of the Pulaskis to get the burnable duff loose and then shoveled it out of the trail so that fire had nothing to creep through. We used the axe end to chop out roots and logs to clear them from the fire line. If anything inside the fire line flared up, we threw dirt with our shovels to smother the flame. When I caught up to the guy ahead of me, I yelled "bump" and took over his part of the line, and he bumped up the guy ahead of him. In decent conditions we could build about a half-mile of fire line an hour.

We worked all night and all through the next day. At five PM we were pulled back to a fire camp that had been created and a crew from another blister rust camp took over our line. At its peak, there were probably two hundred of us building fire line.

A packer from one of Uncle Lloyd's remount stations had brought in food and drinking water and chain saw gas on the backs of mules. There was no other way to fight back-woods fires: six miles was a long way for a huge D-8 Caterpillar tractor to bulldoze a road into the fire. We could not suppress this fire with water: there was no source of water close by, and man-hauling in hose and pumps over that distance was close to impossible.

The crews worked from late evening when the fire had cooled down, through the night until about noon, and then slept through the hottest part of the day, making a rough bed of fresh fir branches, sleeping in the same clothes and boots we worked in. A rough wash area was made by lashing skinny poles to each side of two trees and propping tin washbasins between them. We washed our hands and faces before eating and after using the makeshift latrines, but we were never clean. Everyone stank of sweat and smoke.

When the fire had been circled and the edges were burnt out we were pulled off the fire and our places were taken by a mop-up crew that would fell still-burning tree trunks into the burned area using two-man crosscut saws or chain saws. At the end of the hike out, a nearby town's yellow school bus had been commandeered to take us back to our blister rust camp. We stormed the first roadside restaurant we came to, washing up in its bathroom, changing to any clean clothes we still had in our backpacks, then devouring white-china-plate-loads of pot roast and mashed potatoes and gravy, with white bread to soak up the gravy, and canned green beans and huge quantities of milk. We quickly chewed through their entire day's supply of pies. Lance ate two orders of everything, and so did a dozen other big guys.

Heaven—in Idaho of all places! A ten-cent tip was typical for lunch. We left quarters.

Summer passed agonizingly slowly. I had always wanted summers to go slowly, but I couldn't wait for this one to end. On weekends some of the guys drove to bars in Sandpoint or Priest Lake. Apparently age was not carefully checked, and although some of them were no older than I was, they were big and scruffy and looked older and got served. The foremen, who were seasoned Forest Service summer employees, came back with bawdy stories of girls they claimed to have scored with, but for all the raunchy details, they couldn't be verified and some of us were either skeptical or disinterested. I was both. I had no desire to join them. I read Homer and Melville, Steinbeck, Sarte, and Camus, felt sorry for myself, and typed long, lonely letters to Layne.

One of her letters backcame to me with the address: "Postman, Postman, do your duty; give this to my blister rust cutie." Cookie, who did the mail runs when he went to Sandpoint to restock groceries, delivered it to me on one of our white china dinner plates with an exaggerated bow and a snaggletoothed, lecherous leer.

We got called out twice more in August—once traveling by a chartered Greyhound bus to a huge fire in Southern Idaho that Ted Smith also worked, though we never met.

PART THREE

The other was just over the Idaho border in Montana, near Thompson Falls, about a hundred miles from Flathead Lake. We were on the fire for nearly a week and were sooty from hardhat-to-boots, bearded and exhausted when we were finally trucked out to Thompson Falls to meet a bus that would take us back to Priest Lake. We had a few hours to kill. In a bar with all of the crew I ordered a roast beef sandwich and a beer and got both without anyone checking my drivers' license. Down the street the Thompson Falls General Store was having a clothing sale. I took a fancy to a bold plaid grey, white, and light red Woolrich jacket with four patch pockets. Its price had been knocked down to ten dollars, about half price. I didn't have enough cash. The owner said I could write a check, but I didn't have my checkbook with me. He handed me a pencil and one of the small white paper sacks that he used for selling the gum drops and licorice and a dozen other kinds of penny candy that were ranked in jars at kids-eye level on his front counter. I was amazed that he would take a check from me—who he didn't know and who looked like a tramp that had fallen in an ash bin—written in pencil on a paper sack, without an account number. He told me I could use anything to ask the bank to pay someone, a check was just a convenience. I wrote:

> 14 August, 1959
> From First National Bank, Missoula Montana
> Pay to Thompson Falls General Store
> $10.00
> Ten and no/100's dollars.
> Gordie Noel

I was too dirty and the weather was too hot to wear the coat, so I packed it out in a grocery bag. The candy sack cleared the First National Bank a few days later and with my other cancelled checks was returned to me in the mail. I have owned the coat for more than fifty years. It hangs in a closet with other clothing relics, a little worn at the button holes and cuffs, but still warm and functional.

A few days after coming back from Thompson Falls the camp boss hiked up the mountain on which I was spraying and told me I should drive to the Priest Lake Ranger station and use the pay phone there to call home. He must have known the message I was going to get, because he said to take along whatever I would need if I decided to go back home. During his afternoon nap, in the quiet, upstairs bedroom I slept in every summer at the Flathead Lake house, Grandpa had died.

No one who had loved me had ever died before. I was too numb driving home to cry or to lay down any memory of the five-hour trip.

Perhaps we should have seen this coming; possibly Grandma knew more that I did not hear. In the spring Grandpa had called Mom to tell her that he had gotten into a car accident while driving from Phoenix back to Montana. He felt too shaken to continue the drive and wanted Sammie to fly south and drive them back to Flathead Lake. That afternoon I drove Sammie to Butte to catch a flight south and two days later Sammie brought them home. Grandpa had driven down to Missoula for my graduation a few months after the accident and I thought nothing more about it. But after his death Mom and others said that Grandpa, always a slow and cautious driver, was no longer confident of his driving and he must have wondered how he would continue his annual migrations south into the much heavier traffic of Phoenix or Long Beach during the winter, or even how he and Grandma could safely continue their summers in Montana with their weekly drives to shop in Kalispell.

By the time I arrived home from Idaho Sammie had gotten Grandma from the Lake and brought her to Mom's house. My aunt Nonie was on her way by plane from Bellingham, Washington, with my cousin Diane. Grandpa's body had been brought to an undertaker in Missoula.

The next morning Grandma asked if I could talk with my minister at the Methodist Church, Rev. Herbert, to arrange a funeral service. He was available, and my choir director Neil Dahlstrom agreed to sing. The funeral was arranged for the next afternoon. Beyond Grandma, Nonie, Diane, Mom, and Sammie there were no other family members and no reason for postponing the funeral. Grandma met with Rev. Herbert and explained without detail that Grandpa believed in God but was not religious. Mr. Dahlstrom drove by and Grandma told him a couple of hymns and bible passages Grandpa had liked. The small service the next day lasted only twenty minutes; an hour later we buried Grandpa in the Missoula cemetery seventy-six years and ten thousand miles from where he was born in Lithuania.

When I got back to the blister rust camp I had lost the endurance I would need to drag myself through three more weeks of lugging and spraying and climbing in the hot and itchy forest. After another week, about five or six days before Layne was going to leave for Ames, Iowa, I got a severe pain in my lower back as I twisted and lifted my full tank onto my shoulders. I took off my tank and lay on the ground. When one of the foremen walked up the lane checking to see that all the trees had been properly sprayed I told him I had injured my back. It was premature to suggest that I wouldn't be able to work. I could have rested for a few days and then decided, but I wanted to stop. The decision that I had had enough and wanted to go home crystallized in an instant, and, although feeling guilty and a little embarrassed, I took the opportunity to leave.

That evening the crew boss had me fill out a termination paper that explained my reason for leaving, and by seven PM I had loaded

Chez Noel Idaho into my Chevy and I drove away from the camp, my spirits soaring for the first time in weeks.

I had the bright idea that if I took back roads through Thompson Falls to Ravalli, and then south down US 93, I would have an easier time staying awake because the twisty and narrow road would require my complete attention. Too late I also discovered that the woods came right down to the edges of the constantly curving road. It was a moonless night and I turned my spotlight to the left edge and used the bright lights, but still deer from time to time stood at the edge with blazing eyes and at the last moment jumped across the road just ahead of me. With hours to go and well past the time I usually slept, I kept snapping back to alertness from an early stage of sleep in spite of operating the windshield wipers and the radio full blast and keeping all the windows open. Descending from the top of a hill I got going fast and hit a corner at about 70 miles an hour and found myself a few hundred feet from fifty steers lying in the middle of the road and grazing on both sides. The next hundred yards I braked, skidded, and swerved violently through the cattle, missing a dozen of them by inches. I was still at sixty when I came out the other side of the herd. I pulled off the road, set the parking brake, and walked back with a flashlight in my shaking hand. I had left black skid marks on both sides of the road. From the center of the road the cattle looked at me unperturbed, still chewing.

I got home at 3 AM. Mom didn't know I was coming. My blister rust camp was over two weeks early, but I was not too much shorter in cash than I had hoped for because of the firefighting overtime pay.

In hindsight, my first long stint away from home, the awkward community of the blister rust camp guys, and Grandpa's death were more than enough reason for me to have depleted my resilience and to want to leave earlier than I had planned. I had never heard about grieving or attending to personal emotional needs. I had no language for "I need time to mourn," and no precedent.

PART THREE

It was wonderful to be home again, in a comfortable bed, with Mom's dinners and an icebox in which I could graze far from Cookie's menacing glare: complaints were not welcome in his cook tent, and he threatened to quit anytime someone asked for anything out of his routine or complained about the food. Our foremen let us know that Cookie was more valuable than any of us.

Layne and I were able to spend her last few days together as she packed up and we had a full-blown teary and emotional farewell that was a satisfying confirmation that she was still my girlfriend in spite of the long separation, and that she would remain my girlfriend even though she would be in Iowa and I would be in Massachusetts.

For a graduation present, Layne's parents had given me their fifty-one volume set of the *Harvard Classics*, the pages of which were uncut: they had not read a single page, saying that the books were destined to go to Harvard to be read. Although I would be in a university with millions of books, I still packed several boxes of my own books and included a dozen volumes of the *Harvard Classics*. A few days before leaving I drove to the Greyhound bus depot to ship two boxes of books to Cambridge.

Mom had a vintage canvas covered wood and brass steamer trunk that she had taken to college. In the drawers that took up one side of it I packed my pipes and tobacco and knickknacks and a few paintings and my underwear and socks. On the other side, meant for gowns and tuxedos, I hung my grey suit, my black suit, a few neckties, and a heavy Harris Tweed overcoat I had bought from Mr. Dragstedt, whose lawn I had been mowing and watering since I was 12. Mr. Dragstedt gave me a good deal on that coat, which also lasted more than a half-century.

Mom and Grandma and Nonie insisted that Grandpa's Haggar slacks be altered to fit: "they are top quality and too good to just give away—your Grandpa always bought the best." They also pushed me to take an ill-fitting bold plaid sport coat that they regarded as up to date and appropriate for an Ivy League wardrobe. I resisted: although they knew nothing about the dress standards of college boys at places like Harvard, and I didn't know much, I had eaten dinner with the freshmen at the Harvard Union, and I had seen the flannels and tweeds and regimental striped ties in the windows of the men's shops on Harvard Square. I loved my grandfather, but I hated being sent to college with the altered and worn clothes of an old man. Montanans were practical, then as now, but it made me feel poorer, more provincial than I wanted to be.

The afternoon before I left I drove to the Northern Pacific Depot and checked Mom's steamer trunk on the next morning's North Coast Limited, along with the two Samsonite suitcases that Grandpa and Grandma had given me for graduation, full of socks and underwear, shirts and chino pants and sweaters, and warm clothes I would need to get me through the cold days of winter.

A week after Layne left for Iowa, I left for Boston. I needed to be at the Northern Pacific depot by 5:10 AM. I slept restlessly, waking up repeatedly to check the clock. I was impatient to move out of Missoula, out of my life with Mom, and I dreaded missing the train and forever being stuck there. I woke up early and hustled Mom out of the house well before it was necessary. The ten-minute drive up Higgins Avenue seemed endless, the long wait on the platform with her even more endless.

The engineer always sounded the train's whistle about three miles from the station so that anyone sitting in the waiting room could walk out to the long platform. A few station workers told us where to stand, I saw my other suitcases and steamer trunk towed by on a string of huge baggage carts, which heightened my sense that I was really leaving, not just going on another trip. A few people recognized Mom and came close to say hello to her or goodbye to me. There were some classmates going to the Lutheran colleges in Minnesota who stuck with their brothers and sisters and parents but gave me a little wave.

PART THREE

The streamliner roared in with the prominence of an ocean liner being docked: a ride on the North Coast Limited was a ride to destiny, not to be taken lightly. Blowing steam from its squealing brakes the train slowed, stopping precisely where we had been told to stand. At each open door a porter lowered a metal stool and passengers began to descend, friends and family shouting to them in the pre-sunrise brightness. The porter brought down a few suitcases that he thought were too much for their owners to manage.

And then the door stood open, ready for us to board. Luggage was being unloaded fast onto empty baggage carts, mailbags were thrown out of the mail car. Our baggage and outgoing mailbags were loaded and people began to climb into the coaches with the porters' help.

I turned to say good-bye. Mom looked sad and tiny. I moved away a little, as though to escape into the waiting coach.

"Well, goodbye. I'll see you at Christmas."

Mom said, "Can't I have a kiss?"

I spoke without thinking. "Mush!"

My face was burning. I offered my cheek, she kissed it, squeezed my arm. I could smell her lipstick, feel her kiss like a sticker on my skin.

"Love you," she said and looked at me expectantly.

I said nothing.

I backed away. "So long. Take care of Jet. Good luck getting the car back home."

I was embarrassed by Mom for being emotional and ashamed of myself for being distant. She had sacrificed much of her life for twelve years to raise me by herself. I knew that what was an exciting adventure for me was a momentous loss for Mom, but I could not bring myself to express affection or acknowledge that she would be living alone for the first time in her life, or to even thank her for all that she had done for me.

I waved goodbye, and climbed out of her sight. In less than a minute I had made my way to the reserved seat, hoisted my suitcase to the luggage rack above it, and stooped down to wave—at a safe distance. Mom was crying softly. The train was at the depot no more than ten minutes. The engineer blew a short blast on the whistle to indicate that the train was starting up, the coach shuddered and then we started rolling east; Mom slowly receded.

Fifty feet down the platform I was surprised to see Dad, standing alone, in khaki pants and shirt, hands in pockets, just staring at the windows flicking by. I didn't have time to wave to him; I doubt that he saw me. He must have been watching when I was saying goodbye to Mom, perhaps afraid that she would see him, keeping his distance so that he wouldn't interfere in Mom's letting me go.

And then we were beyond the station and passing the Highlander brewery, the Van Buren Street bridge, Ben Hugh's truck gardens along the Clark Fork banks.

I sat on the edge of my seat as the train gathered speed, passed through Hell's Gate Canyon, East Missoula, Milltown. Mom's kiss was burning on my cheek. I could smell her lipstick. I didn't want any part of Mom going east with me. I walked to the end of the car and in the toilet room mirror saw the faint traces of her lips. I scrubbed at my cheek with a wad of coarse paper towel, soap and hot water—two, three, four times, until my skin felt abraded but purified.

Back in my seat I pulled out a copy of *The Stranger* that I had bought a few days earlier and held it tightly in my right hand. But for nearly two hours I watched out the window as the remnants of my old life in Montana passed behind me. We were following the highway that at the age of six had taken me, alone on a bus, from Butte to Missoula and from there to Flathead Lake. The bus had stopped at each of the little towns and crossroad service stations, but the train raced through them heading through the mountains and prairies to Chicago.

PART THREE

The train had left Missoula at 5:35 AM. Nine hours later, someplace far to the east, during the long crossing of the empty Great Plains, just as we were leaving Montana, the dining car steward came through the car to take reservations for dinner. He stopped at my seat and asked me which seating I preferred. I said I planned to eat in the less expensive café car, which required no reservations. He said, "you have the best steak dinner in the United States of America waiting for you in the dining car. I know your Dad. He got on the train in Missoula, paid for it, and told me to be sure you knew about it. Which seating do you want?"

That evening, with an hour left of daylight, I was seated across from a silent old man wearing a spotless white cowboy hat. He was facing forward, his deeply lined face tanned and blank, chewing without expression or eye contact. The dining steward, resplendent in his navy blue coat with gold piping and sharply pressed navy blue trousers, pulled back my chair, unfolded my napkin and handed it to me, watching while I placed it in my lap. I sat looking at Montana receding behind the train through the wide window that ran the length of the table that was set with linen, silver, crystal, tiny salt and pepper shakers, and a fresh rose. My mind was a thousand miles ahead, thinking about the station transfer in Chicago, two thousand miles ahead, thinking about arriving at Boston's South Station with my suitcases and steamer trunk and boxes, my taxi ride to Harvard Square, meeting my roommates.

The dining car attendant served me a thick T-bone steak with baked potato, fresh green beans, and, finally, fresh apple pie a la mode. He told me that the steward had personally selected the steak for me and told the chef that Dad said to serve it medium rare.

When he seated me and handed me my napkin, the dining car steward had said: "You have something special to look forward to."

He meant the dinner, but I took it a different way. I was out of Montana and deeply happy.

The Missoula County High School Cantata: shepherds to the left, kings to the right, angels everywhere

My sophomore English report card from Miss Fowler

Mr. Hossack   Mr. Low

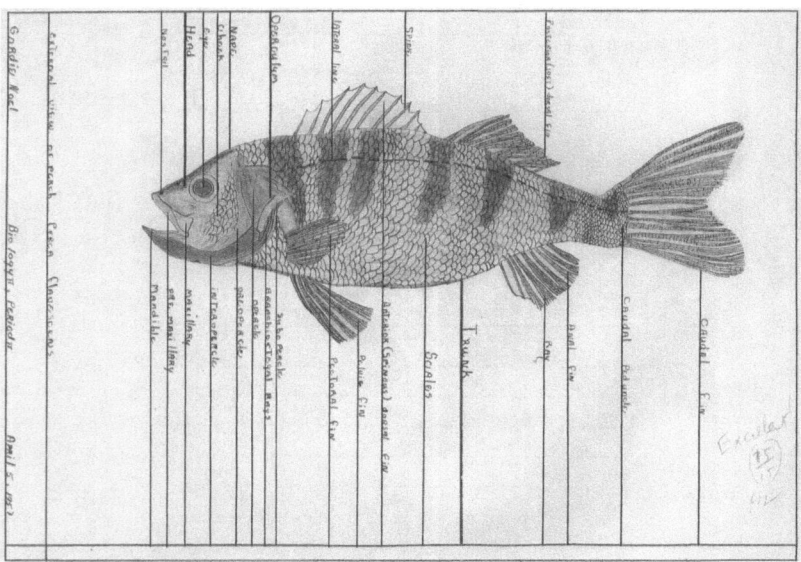

My weekly Biology drawing—This one is a perch

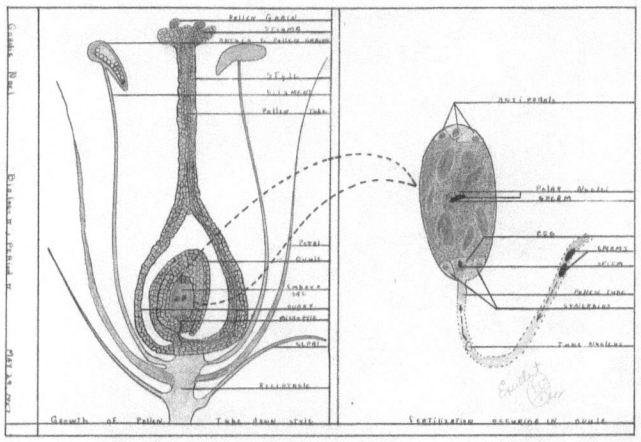

Biology drawing: growth of pollen tube down style, and fertilization in ovule

INSTRUCTOR'S COMMENT: An excellent student but MUST learn to control his tongue.
21 Jan. '57

The best biology student I've ever had.

Sophomore Biology report card from Mr. Hossack

Christmas day at the Beverly Avenue house, about 1957, with Mom and my dog Jet.

Rollie sitting on the trunk of my 1950 Chevy Turtleback on the North Fork of the Flathead River before heading up to Logging Lake in Glacier Park, August, 1957

From the National Youth Leadership Conference at Camp Cheley, in Estes Park, Colorado, 1958. I am in the front row at the far right

Picking up a charitable contribution at Angelo's Men's shop for Key Club, 1958

My bedroom wastebasket and guide to college selection

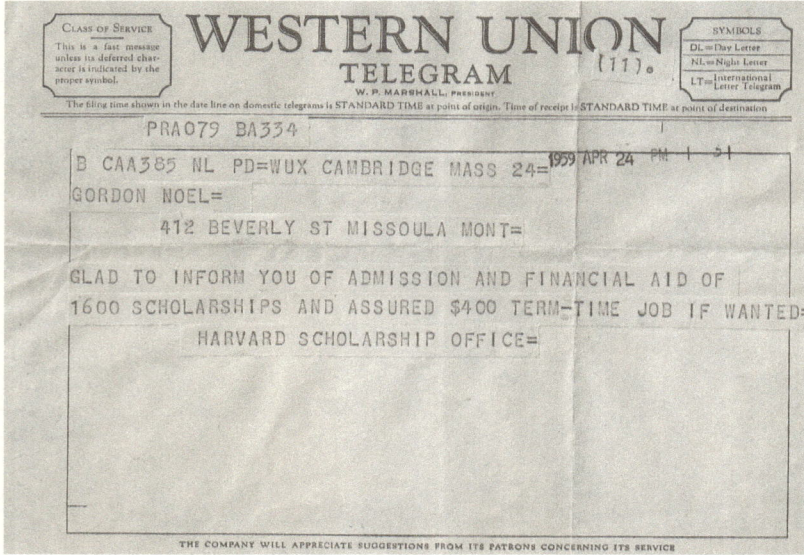

Telegram from Harvard

High school graduation photo, 1959

CHAPTER
TWENTY-SIX

POSTSCRIPT

AFTER I LEFT Missoula for college I rarely saw Dad. I visited him once or twice in the summer when I came home for my summer job fighting forest fires and stopped by his house for a few hours at Christmastime. He didn't write letters or send care packages to Boston, and I didn't write to him.

The first summer back I had dinner with him and Marjorie. After dinner Dad and I sat in his living room. He showed off his new stereo console and played a classical recording—Vaughn Williams' "Variations on a Theme by Thomas Tallis". I was impressed. "This stereo's sound is exactly what the conductor would hear," he told me. The music was useful to fill the silence: he didn't ask questions about my courses or roommates or Boston, and I didn't feel like there was much that he would find interesting, so I volunteered nothing. Still, I hadn't known that Dad liked classical music and I felt an unexpected flicker of communion with him.

It didn't last: as I got up to leave he said: "You talk differently, you don't sound like a Montanan any more. You sound just like John F. Kennedy." I took it as a compliment, but he meant it as disrespect for Kennedy and Democrats and Harvard and the whole world of the East Coast to which I had defected.

A few years later he met my college girlfriend when she came to Montana for a few weeks. He informed me that she looked fat. After spending a summer working at a Newfoundland orphanage eating three starchy meals a day, Margaret had become a little plump since the last time I saw her, but I was angry that he dumped his unsolicited opinion in order to belittle me and to inflate his self-regard.

My last summer in Missoula, just before starting medical school, I ate dinner with him and Marjorie. Columbia University had awarded me a full scholarship for tuition and fees, and I had made enough money that summer fighting fires to pay the $1000 for room and board and the $200 I needed to fly east, but money would be tight. I asked him if he could help me pay the $400 I needed for a microscope. I had graduated with honors from Harvard and had been accepted and given a scholarship at a very competitive medical school, but he chose that moment to inform me that I would make a terrible doctor because I had "no bedside manner." I thought he was wrong, of course. While he clearly wasn't thrilled about paying for the microscope, he did it, but there was never a single word of praise or encouragement.

Dad decided to come to Boston for my Harvard graduation. We spent a few days site-seeing in Boston and on the north coast. He wanted to eat a lobster. They came in three sizes; his stomach was small after an operation for ulcer disease and he got a "small"; I ordered a large lobster stuffed with the meat of a small lobster. That may have been one of the rare times I did something that impressed him.

Mom was annoyed that he flew to Boston for my graduation, which she couldn't afford to do. After that she made sure—in her

POSTSCRIPT

words "damned sure"—that he wasn't invited to my wedding a few years later.

After Margaret and I were married and began having children he was decent to us: he let us stay in his cabin on Flathead Lake for a few weeks each summer until he died, and when he married Alex, his third wife, he brought her to New York City to meet Margaret and me and our daughters, sleeping uncomfortably on a hide-a-bed sofa in our living room. That was the first time since I was seven that I slept in the same house with Dad, and one of the last times I saw him. He was a few years younger than sixty but already thin and short of breath and tremulous. He died a few years later.

If Dad had a heart of gold, I never discovered it. He was opinionated, often disparaging, almost never warm or supportive. Beyond giving me a chance to learn how to fly fish, he didn't teach me much. He was never my hero, sometimes he was an embarrassment to me, but mostly he was just missing in my life.

When I was a high school sophomore my brother Sammie began college at the University. At some point he joined a fraternity, but when he dropped out of college and moved back home Dad wanted him to pay rent since he wasn't going to college and was working, as a messenger at Dad's bank. Outraged, Sammie left home.

My experience of Sammie's relationship with Dad was like the Montana August thunder storms that blew up over the mountains a hundred miles away: I heard the thunder, I imagined that there were damaging lightening strikes and fires, but the storm was far away and didn't affect me. Sammie occasionally made bitter comments about Dad, but growing up he never confided in me how much he hated Dad.

After he and his high school girlfriend Pam married they moved to Seattle, where he worked in a large commercial bank. His two

PART THREE

sons were born there, but eventually he moved back to Montana and managed a series of bank chains that were consolidating.

Some summers we shared time at the Flathead Lake cabin, but we were never close and our values couldn't have been more incongruent. In the 1980's he expressed amazement when, after broadcasting his distaste for the Democratic candidate, Fritz Mondale, Margaret told him we were voting against Ronald Reagan and for Mondale.

"You are voting for a Democrat?"

"Yes."

"But Gordon is a doctor. Why is he voting for a Democrat?"

I pretty much opposed everything that Reagan and all the previous Republican candidates for any office you could mention represented. Sammie had never bothered to find out anything about my values. He had similar presumptions about how terrible it would be to live near New York City and Washington DC. He and Pam stopped by on their way back to Montana from a trip to the Caribbean. I drove them from National Airport to our home in Montgomery County and he kept asking where the slums and railroad yards were; he couldn't believe that Washington, DC had lush trees and yards and flower gardens or that only fifteen minutes from the center of Washington we and our neighbors had neither high fences nor locked gates.

While he and Pam were warm hosts and welcomed our visits to their homes and did most of the work of keeping up the Flathead cabin after Dad died, Sammie and I never talked about our personal lives or the basis of our beliefs. Our interests converged solely around Mom and our love for Flathead Lake.

Dad had passed the Noel family addiction gene to Sammie. He drank much more than anyone I had stayed friends with. When we were together I kept my mouth shut, but I was uncomfortable with the drinking and it further distanced me from him.

POSTSCRIPT

Although he was successful at managing several failing banks back to solvency, eventually the jobs in Montana ran out and he and Pam returned to Washington state. We lived only about ninety minutes away, but our visits were a year or two apart. When he was sixty-two, his drinking got him fired from his bank and a few days later, with very little put away for retirement and no prospects of a job, in despair, he took his pistol into his garage and put a bullet in his brain.

Not long before his suicide I had bought back Grandpa and Grandma's house at Flathead Lake so that our far-flung daughters would have a place to bring their families for vacation without having to fit into the tight schedule and limited space at Dad's cabin. I had been asking Sammie, who wanted to retire at the Lake, to buy me out. While saying that he wanted to, he kept putting it off. He was too proud to tell me what his circumstances were: that he couldn't afford to buy me out.

I never learned if he sensed my poorly disguised righteousness because of his drinking and his political and social beliefs, or if he resented me for the very different ways our lives had played out.

As distant as we were, his death left a hole in my life, and I still regret that he never realized his dream of retiring to Flathead Lake. He and Pam had kept up a summer place where Dad's four children could have some connection with each other, a place where our children could know their cousins. After Sammie died the cabin had to be sold; it was the last tie from our Montana childhoods that had kept Dad's family together and it faded away.

Johnny Butler invited Miss Fowler to our thirtieth high school reunion banquet. I had no idea that Johnny or anyone else had been fond of her. Johnny introduced her at the beginning of the banquet. Surprised, I stood up, trying to spot her in the room, but I couldn't see her. For the whole dinner I felt anxious, as though I was going

PART THREE

to have to tell an already disapproving person that I had again done something terribly, embarrassingly wrong.

Immediately after dinner I found her at a table at the back of the room. Now she had short hair and was wearing glasses, but her clothes were more modern versions of what she wore in high school—a straight dark skirt and a white blouse with a string of small pearls. She wore no makeup and had the first fine wrinkles of middle age. I doubt I would have recognized her had I not been looking for her.

"Miss Fowler, I don't know if you remember me. I'm Gordon Noel... Gordie Noel."

"Yes Gordie, of course I remember you. We were all so proud of you."

"You... you were?"

"Yes of course we were. You went east to college—didn't you go to Harvard?—and you studied English literature—I was so pleased—and you became a doctor, I think even a professor."

I was totally taken aback: Miss Fowler had been pleased with me?

"Miss Fowler, do you remember what happened in your English class? What I did?"

"No Gordie, I don't. What did you do? Please tell me."

"Miss Fowler, I have thought about this, and about you, nearly every day of my life. I copied a story and gave it to you. Or I rewrote it, an Orson Welles' radio play about a lighthouse keeper. After I turned it in you heard the story on the radio. You wanted me thrown out of school but ended up giving me an F for the quarter. You don't remember?"

"No I totally forgot about that." She paused for a few moments. "I was so foolish then. I had just finished college. I expected way too much of that class, as though you were college students, not high school sophomores. Everyone in that class was plagiarizing. Nearly every student was going to the high school library and copying their book reports from the *New York Review of Books*, and turning in obscure poems they found in old magazines or collections."

"I had no idea, Miss Fowler. I thought I was the only one."

"No, no. I am so sorry. I am glad everything has come out alright for you."

"Miss Fowler, you changed my life, you and Mr. Hossack and Mr. Low, and I have never stopped thinking about it. Well, it's a surprise to see you, and so nice."

She smiled. I wanted to just sit with her and bask in her now forgiving presence. But we didn't have anything more to say to each other, and I walked back to my table, disappointed that I hadn't asked if I could see her the next day.

By the time I had graduated from high school she had moved away from Missoula. I don't know how she knew that I had become an English major. Perhaps she and Mr. Low stayed in touch after she left.

I was awake a long time that night. She had been 22, only six years older than I was when she changed my A+ for "The Lighthouse Keeper" to E. From the morning I walked alone to school to meet her before classes until my thirtieth reunion I had known that my life changed course because she had listened to the radio one night. The shame I felt then had gradually evolved into gratitude. For more than thirty years I had wanted to see her again and in some way tell her what had become of me. I wish that I had had the presence of mind to ask to see her again so that I could hear about her life since my fateful encounter with her.

I have asked, but none of my high school friends knows what happened to her.

Once we left high school the teachers who we had sworn we would see when we came back to town faded in importance. Our first summer

PART THREE

back Ted Smith and I went to see Dan Low at his home overlooking farm fields near Fort Missoula. The house was small and tidy, with wooden walls and book-crammed shelves in the living room and a small study in a corner of the house where he could read or write while watching pheasants and grouse court and ducks swoop low on their way to the sloughs along the Bitterroot River. He was cordial and courteous to us. He offered us small glasses of tomato juice, but as always he was reserved and slightly nervous. He did not ask much about our first years at Oberlin or Harvard, and I suppose we took for granted that we knew what his year was like, having had him as our English and French and homeroom teacher for four years. I had wanted him to be excited to see us, and pleased and proud, but he didn't seem to be. After that, I didn't go back to see him.

Now I understand that no matter how much a teacher means to a student, it is rarely a relationship that can evolve into an adult friendship: the students move on and their teachers can't go with them.

That same summer Ted and I made a long, rocky drive to a mountain west of Missoula where Gus Hossack was spending the summer on a lookout tower. Gus had piles of books scattered around the various corners of his tower. He showed us how the fire-locater worked and pointed out the glass-footed stools, beds, and kitchen table: towers sometimes took direct lightning hits and the insulators kept the lookouts safe, although a direct hit was incredibly loud and rattled most people's nerves.

Mr. Hossack had suddenly appeared at MCHS in the fall of 1956, his first teaching job in the US. Before starting at MCHS he had just returned from a Fulbright Scholarship teaching mathematics, physics, and sciences at the Adelaide, Australia, boys' high school, after a stint in the Navy, undergraduate studies at two colleges, and getting a master's degree in administration and counseling at the University of Maine. A year after I left for college, and after his summer on the lookout tower, he became director of guidance for the Billings, Montana public schools. By 1966 he had gotten a PhD in Education at the University of Wyoming. After that he headed counseling programs in a half dozen other cities in Montana and then taught at Lewis and Clark College in Portland, Oregon. Gus was a free spirit and one of the two best teachers I had at MCHS. He was by both character and training well positioned to put his arm around my shoulders, praise me for scholarship, advise me to clean up my act, and provide me with opportunities to become involved in high school beyond the classroom. In retrospect his decision to take us to the St. Louis National Student Council Convention in spite of being told that we were too late fit what I later learned about his life's pattern: he was restless, intuitive, willing to take a risk, and a gifted learner.

He also wasn't beyond stretching the truth a little. When he wrote on my report card that I was the best biology student he had ever had, there had not been many to compare me with—a few during his year in Adelaide, and my MCHS classmates. Until then I mostly had heard what I was doing wrong. Gus lit a fire under me by telling me what I was doing right and suggesting that my future was limited only by my imagination and my ability to take responsibility for my life.

Roland Trenouth and I saw each other during the summers while we were in college. He took the fearsome Columbia pre-med curriculum and then spent a year after college applying for medical school. He was a medical student, medicine resident, and cardiology fellow at the Universities of Colorado, Wisconsin, and Oregon. After his internship he went off to Vietnam as a general medical officer and was badly injured in a helicopter crash. When he settled into practicing cardiology in Bellingham, Washington he was immediately beloved as a physician, community leader, and friend. We see each

PART THREE

other now at long intervals and laugh about many of the stories that I have retold in these pages.

Ted Smith started college at Oberlin. I hitchhiked the Massachusetts, New York, Pennsylvania, and Ohio Turnpikes to see him during our freshman-year spring break. After that we spent one summer fighting fires together on the Nine Mile Hotshot crew, and then he memorized the eye chart, lied about being able to see perfectly, and spent the next few summers as a smokejumper. I wasn't bold enough to even consider that possibility since I assumed everyone knew I needed glasses. He got a PhD in international affairs, worked overseas for the Ford Foundation, and then spent the years before retirement as the president of an environmental organization. Tragically, he died when he fell from a high mountain trail hiking in his own backyard, the Mission Mountains near Flathead Lake.

Sandy Bouchard's Air Force training kept him away from Missoula during our college summers and I have rarely seen him outside of a few of our class reunions. He finished a career as an Air Force pilot, and although he moved to Portland before I did, I have only seen him once.

Layne ended our romance after her freshman year: the long distance relationship was hard for her to sustain and while I thought I was prepared to not date anyone else for four years, she wanted to enjoy her college's social life. I went back to Harvard sad, but then had my best academic year—seven A's and one B.

The B was in a classic philosophy course in which everything I read put me to sleep: no plot, no narrative arc, very little sex, and endless questions most of which I decided had been sufficiently pondered two thousand years ago. I thought that course would lead me to a clear understanding of the meaning of life now that Layne wasn't there to focus on. Instead it led me to the Brattle Theater where, rather than reading Plato and Aristotle, I watched foreign films, mostly French

POSTSCRIPT

and Bergman, got over my broken heart, and realized that everyone else seemed as confused about life as I was.

I can't tell the story of leaving Mom on the Northern Pacific depot platform as a tribute to my empathy or generosity. I have always known that among many acts of selfishness in my life, this was one of the worst. It was selfish not because I was choosing to go away to college rather than staying at the University of Montana—about half of our high school's graduation class left Missoula for college every year—but because in the days before I left I didn't make the effort to show simple affection or gratitude. I didn't hide from her how excited I was to leave. It was not an isolated act: in the four years I was in college there were milder repetitions every summer when I left. After the first few days in Missoula I was impatient to go "back East."

There is a natural yearning that children have for autonomy. The stronger the intimacy between a child and his or her parents, perhaps the more likely it is that the child will break those bonds violently: keeping a parent at arms-length may be emotionally easier than comforting them.

Mom and I never fought. She avoided confrontation, and I was clearly not interested in living with someone who was angry with me. To an astonishing degree I rarely acknowledged anger with anyone and it was a decade before I finally dug deeply enough to turn up resentment I had suppressed at growing up without the affection and support of a father who, even if it had been possible to admire him, Mom would have blocked. Her fury was entirely appropriate and the world around me—her friends and Grandpa and Grandpa and even the parents of some of my friends—let me know that I should be thankful for what my mother did for me every day and not complain. And so I never did.

PART THREE

In time I realized that Mom was the hero in my life—but it was entirely an intellectual construct. I was never able to treat her with the humor and tenderness that I gave to other people and that I imagine she felt was her due. I might have gotten over that if I had asked her to explain to me why our family broke apart, what her life was like while raising me alone, what she felt when I left and then became both geographically and emotionally remote. But there was no model for talking about feelings in Grandpa and Grandma's house or in my life with Mom, and I think perhaps that was not uncommon in the transplanted Northern European culture of Montana, where people looked forward and tried as much as possible to bury the past, to turn their backs on what had driven them from their homelands and what had gone wrong along the way.

I encountered this when, in 1965, Grandma came back from a trip to Eastern Europe where she had visited her few remaining relatives. Almost everyone she had known growing up in Lithuania had been killed or fled. I took her to a Greenwich Village performance of the Euripides' play *The Trojan Women*. Afterwards I asked her how she liked the play. Her answer was short and categorical: "When you have grown up with brutality all around you and then have lived through two world wars in which almost everyone you knew as a child was killed, you don't need to see a play to know about the suffering of women in wartime."

Mom never remarried. She had a lot of friends in Missoula, and she often hosted or went out with the young men and women students who worked with her at the University. If she had suitors she never talked about them. She kept up her end of our family as well as she could with limited income: she was good about sending cards at holidays, remembering birthdays, sending Christmas presents, finding clippings in the local newspapers or magazines that related to where we were living in the East or that brought me up to date with familiar parts of Montana. Every few years she came east to see

POSTSCRIPT

us, and we visited with her for a few days on each of our summer vacation trips to Flathead Lake. She and Margaret got along well, and the kids liked and admired her.

In 1985 she was found to have leukemia. A year of chemotherapy lengthened her life but at the price of growing anemia, weakness, and fatigue. In the summer of 1986 she decided to discontinue treatment and transfusions. Our family was about to depart for a month trip to England, France, and Africa. I flew back to Missoula to see her. When I asked if she could keep up treatment for another month so that I could be with her in her final days, she said she didn't know. While we were in Africa I learned that she had refused transfusions and died a gentle death. I took her decision not to keep herself alive for me as both just and an appropriate rebuke.

I grieved far more than I had expected I would, especially since I didn't grieve at all when Dad died. It lasted for two years. Much of the sparkle and joy in my life diminished; I looked at life as though seeing it refracted through a jar of dirty water. Finally, I wrote two letters—one a list of what I felt had been difficult about growing up in a broken family that I had never been able to talk to her about, and the other a thank you note to her for faithfully spending 18 years raising me and launching me into a wonderful life, thanks that I had never sufficiently expressed. I buried them at her grave in the Missoula cemetery, next to Grandma and Grandpa. And with that, the lingering disappointments and sorrows of my childhood went quietly to rest, twenty-seven years after I left her alone on the Northern Pacific depot platform where Dad was silently watching me leave, out of her sight.

Before she died Mom wrote her own obituary and left it on the desk in my old room, with a note of instructions clipped to it.

"Do not mention that I was married to Bob Noel."

ACKNOWLEDGMENTS

MY DAUGHTER, THE novelist Katharine Noel, has been my beacon, teacher, and companion at every stage of this project and has provided incisive feedback on structure and character development with incredible gentleness and grace. My daughter Margaret provided expert artistic advice about the cover design. I am deeply grateful to my smart, generous friends Rachel Gribby and Christine Hunter who read early drafts of this memoir and whose helpful comments and encouragement were invaluable. In preparing the University of Montana Press edition, I benefited from the close reading and insightful suggestions of Professors Ashby Kinch, Phil Condon, and Kathy Kuipers.

Thanks to Arlene Noel Worthington, Colleen Higgins, Dick and Linda Ainsworth, Steve Smith, Jerry Agen, and Roland Trenouth who helped me recall details from more than six decades ago.

My amazing daughter Jennifer Noel, Elizabeth Allen, Tom and Barbara Cooney, Sarah Dunham, Jake Harvey, Solhee Jung, Eric Puchner, Kelly Redfield, the late Ted Smith, Larry Strausbaugh and Kenny Wachtel and countless medical students, residents, and running partners have listened to my Montana stories and in vastly different ways have been companions and muses, sharing their love and knowledge of Montana, literature, art, music and film.

I learned the fundamentals of literature and writing in the excellent public schools of Missoula, Montana in the 1950's, and at

Harvard in the early 1960's; although I gave up my notion of becoming a teacher of literature, they were the foundation for my love of stories and good writing that has sustained me during a life in medicine. In high school I was lucky to have many teachers who went far beyond what they needed to do to nurture and support my classmates and me. My life would be different now if it were not for the guidance and encouragement of Dan Low and Gus Hossack. In her enthusiasm for excellence and achievement, Ann Fowler challenged me beyond what I believed I could legitimately achieve, and in the event changed the trajectory of my life.

ABOUT THE AUTHOR

GORDON NOEL GREW up in Missoula, Montana and spent his childhood summers at Flathead Lake. While in college he spent five summers in Montana fighting fires for the U.S. Forest Service and then spent the next thirty-three years living on the East Coast, but he never stopped returning to Montana. In 1992 he was recruited to the Oregon Health and Sciences University and returned to the West, and in 1998 he bought back his grandparents' home on Flathead Lake, where much of this memoir was written. He is Emeritus Professor of Medicine at Oregon Health and Sciences University. He was previously on the faculties of the Columbia University College of Physicians and Surgeons in New York City, the Uniformed Services University of the Health Sciences in Bethesda, MD, and the Dartmouth University School of Medicine in Hanover, NH.

www.ingramcontent.com/pod-product-compliance
Lightning Source LLC
Chambersburg PA
CBHW030429010526
44118CB00011B/564